Private Law, Digital Assets, and Infrastructure

P. T. Babie · Mark Giancaspro
Editors

Private Law, Digital Assets, and Infrastructure

Springer

Editors
P. T. Babie
Adelaide Law School
The University of Adelaide
Adelaide, SA, Australia

Mark Giancaspro
Adelaide Law School
The University of Adelaide
Adelaide, SA, Australia

ISBN 978-981-96-7120-5 ISBN 978-981-96-7121-2 (eBook)
https://doi.org/10.1007/978-981-96-7121-2

This Springer imprint is published by the registered company Springer Nature Singapore Pte Ltd.
The registered company address is: 152 Beach Road, #21-01/04 Gateway East, Singapore 189721, Singapore

To the Memory
of
Juliet M. Moringiello
1962–2025
Teacher, Scholar, Colleague, Friend

Contents

Digital Assets and Fraud

Introduction: The Brave New World of Private Law and Digital Assets

Mark Giancaspro and P. T. Babie

1 A Brave New World: Private Law and Digital Assets

'Private law', Ernest Weinrib wrote, 'is a pervasive phenomenon of our social life, a silent but ubiquitous participant in our most common transactions'.[1] Indeed, private law regulates a range of ordinary interactions between people, including the use and ownership of property, the formation of contractual agreements, and the undertaking of work.[2] It is also concerned with one's right not to be injured by the acts or omissions of others without just cause, and with their rights as a consumer within the market. Private law, as the term suggests, is therefore concerned with the legal rights and wrongs arising out of relationships and disputes between individuals.[3]

Yet, as a body of law, private law has often been accused of ineptness in adapting to rapidly evolving social conditions, and of failing adequately to serve the needs of the society it governs.[4] This book leaves that debate to others. Instead, here we explore the ways in which various, unique technological developments in recent years have profoundly impacted private law and are poised to continue doing so in the near future. Many such developments have occurred within the context of digital assets and distributed ledger technology. This, in turn, has challenged governments and

[1] Ernest J Weinrib, *The Idea of Private Law* (Oxford University Press, 2012, 1).

[2] See John Gardner, *From Personal Life to Private Law* (Oxford University Press, 2018).

[3] William Lucy, *Philosophy of Private Law* (Oxford University Press, 2007, 22–5).

[4] See for example, Alan Watson, *Society and Legal Change* (Scottish Academic Press, 1977).

The title to this chapter borrows from Aldous Huxley's dystopian novel, *Brave New World* (Chatto & Windus, 1932).

M. Giancaspro · P. T. Babie (✉)
Adelaide Law School, The University of Adelaide, Adelaide, SA, Australia
e-mail: paul.babie@adelaide.edu.au

M. Giancaspro
e-mail: mark.giancaspro@adelaide.edu.au

P. Babie and M. Giancaspro (eds.), *Private Law, Digital Assets, and Infrastructure*,
https://doi.org/10.1007/978-981-96-7121-2_1

courts the world over to contemplate appropriate regulatory responses and to answer novel, pressing, and nuanced legal questions. Such a seismic shift in the status quo warrants—indeed, compels—discussion among legal experts. In many ways, this book, borrowing from Alduous Huxley, maps the terrain of what we might call the brave new world of private law as it struggles to respond to the challenges presented by digital assets.

Since the pseudonymous programmer (or programmers) Satoshi Nakomoto created the Bitcoin open-source software and released the famed white paper entitled 'Bitcoin: A Peer-to-Peer Electronic Cash System' in 2008,[5] distributed ledger technology and the digital assets that harness it, notably cryptocurrency, have exploded in use and popularity. The emergence of the blockchain infrastructure underlying the operation and transfer of digital assets such as cryptocurrencies, non-fungible tokens, and digital securities has popularised the notion of decentralised exchange. The control of, and decision-making authority within, these decentralised exchanges is distributed across a network of miners (participants), as opposed to being centralised in a single institution, such as a bank intermediating a transfer between a vendor and a purchaser.

At the same time, we see the emergence of smart contracts—computerised transaction protocols which autonomously execute the terms of a contract on behalf of their human parties. These contracts fundamentally challenge established principles of contract law through automation of their enforcement and, in some circumstances, their formation, functions traditionally performed by natural persons. All of which calls into question the roles of the orthodox contractual elements of agreement, legal intent, consideration, certainty, capacity, and legality, as well as the doctrines of interpretation, mistake, and remedies. Doubts remain as to whether smart contracts are compatible with the common law rules governing contractual exchange, and whether existing statutes designed to accommodate electronic transactions are equipped to govern them. Reconciling the more rigid structures and principles of contract law with the fluid and complex nature of smart contracts has already proven immensely problematic.

Proponents argue that all of these technologies will revolutionise financial markets in particular by democratising, and improving the cost and efficiency of the exchange of digital currencies and assets and doing away with traditional intermediaries such as financial institutions, thereby enabling greater security, transparency, and autonomy for users. Detractors cite the uncertainty deriving from the present lack of regulation of digital assets and the disputed functions and values of those assets as cause for concern and hesitation.

Some of the promising issues canvassed in this volume include the corporate benefits of 'live' smart contracting, and the opportunity before us to modernise aspects of private law to integrate digital asset technologies and leverage their various benefits for society and the market. Fostering innovation in a world confronted by a growing range of challenges, while safeguarding the rights and interests of all stakeholders,

---

[5] A collection of works attributed to Satoshi Nakomoto is available at <https://satoshi.nakamotoinstitute.org/>.

is crucial, and private law plays a significant role in this context. Among the more concerning issues arising out of the digital asset space are criminal activity and environmental impacts associated with cryptocurrency use, both of which deservedly receive increasing exposure. The technical and legal implications of the integration of machine learning (a subset of artificial intelligence) with blockchain technology are also largely unknown, though there is promise that this integration could benefit a range of applications across critical industries. The operational issues arising out of smart contract use must also not be ignored. Compounding the difficulty of digital asset regulation, of course, is the struggle to conclusively identify the proprietary status, practical uses, and legal value of such assets.

For all of these reasons, and building on these diverse perspectives, the collection of essays in this volume explores a range of issues currently emerging in this dynamic and exciting space of private law and digital assets. It is a topographical map of this brave new world into which private law finds itself thrust, not entirely prepared for the task of navigating a way through.

2 Plan of the Book

The book contains ten chapters, divided into four parts. Part I deals with the broader question of private law as it attempts to respond to digital assets. Parts II and III deal with specific issues that arise in the interplay between this new technology and the doctrinal categories of contract and fraud, respectively. Part IV deals with perhaps the most important issue in this field: the impact that AI and digital assets have on the environment. Each chapter makes a novel and cutting edge contribution to the ever expanding body of scholarship in this exciting field.

Part I of the book, which contains four chapters, sets the scene. In our own chapter, 'Private Law is both the Question and the Answer: Property, Contract, and Enduring Questions About the Legal Treatment of Digital Assets', we examine the way in which private law is attempting to respond to the challenges presented by digital assets. We argue that as governments and legal systems attempt to address the adoption of new technologies of any kind, digital objects included, the development of law often lags behind technological advances, playing a catch-up game, responding to change once it has happened and, far too often, once it is too late for the law to manage challenges that emerge. It is important, we suggest, that a legal system consider those challenges before they occur, and that it be ready to respond to them with innovative solutions. We identify just one aspect of necessary legal change, which we call the private law question: How, when forced to answer, will the private law respond to the changes being wrought by the emergence of digital assets and so ensure that it progresses logically and efficiently? The remaining chapters in the book represent attempts to answer that question.

Not everyone, though, agrees that lag leads only to detrimental outcomes in this field. True, the speed of digital innovation means consumers are relentlessly subject to offers to engage with innovative new products that once would only have been available to the tech elite, including smart contracts. Yet the legal narrative around these developments is fragmented. Jeannie Paterson, in 'Innovation and Regulation: Consumer Protection, Crypto Assets, Smart Contracts and Algorithmic Contracting', argues that while private law is often presented as struggling with the speed of change, it may be possible that the hype and concern may dissipate as technological development stabilises and the next generation of consumers necessarily become more technically literate. Thus, with some exceptions, and contrary to suggestions that the law is too slow to respond to changes in digital technology, the current combination of private law and statutory consumer protection regimes dealing with developments in blockchain and crypto may be more than sufficient.

Similarly, in 'Decentralising AI: Can Blockchain Technology Solve Data Privacy Challenges in Machine Learning?', Devlin Greatbatch Murphy, Alex Lundie, Raymond Sun, and Susannah Wilkinson argue that blockchain is often portrayed as a solution looking for a problem and suggest that Machine Learning (ML) might be that problem. A subset of AI, ML covers machines which process and identify patterns in data to make predictions. ML powers an increasing number of applications involving data and predictive analytics, across many industries; generally, it relies on a single system or server to receive data and perform all computational tasks required to train the ML model. This centralised approach to training of a ML model (or 'ML training'), raises significant data security and privacy concerns. And, in an attempt to resolve these challenges, alternate forms of ML, namely federated learning and distributed learning, are being considered. It seems clear, though, that data security and privacy challenges persist, and new challenges relating to 'trust' arise between trainers and the central server. To meet this challenge, blockchain technology may offer a solution to these critical privacy issues. It is possible that the technical and legal implications of this blockchain-ML integration may offer a solution to the privacy challenges in ML training.

In the final chapter of this part, 'Controlling Intangibles: The United States Approach to Digital Assets in Commerce', Juliet Moringiello discusses the new Article 12 of the Uniform Commercial Code, the American law that, when enacted by the states, governs a variety of commercial transactions. The chapter explains the uniform law drafting process in the United States, and the considerations that led to the drafting of Article 12, which provides a framework for the transfer of a category of digital assets called 'controllable electronic records'. It concludes by outlining the key elements of Article 12, including the definition of control as the electronic analogue to possession and the take free rules that make controllable electronic records negotiable.

Part II of the book, which contains two chapters, turns to issues surrounding the law of contract. In 'Why Should Contracts be Smart?' Eliza Mik tackles the practical implications of making contracts smart. To many, any questions about the desirability of expressing contracts in code may seem like unnecessary academic nit-picking by someone who 'clearly does not understand the unstoppable potential of the crypto economy'. Code is, after all, supposed to remedy commercial uncertainty and guarantee performance. Code is, if one follows the dominant crypto-narrative, the solution to most of the world's problems! The simple question about the reason why contracts should be made smart may, however, lie at the very core of the misunderstandings surrounding smart contracts. Both lawyers and crypto-enthusiasts often overlook the important distinction between the source of contractual obligations and the expression of such obligations, not to mention the distinction between the *tools* used to perform an obligation and the contract itself. They also seem to assume that the manner of expressing a contract can guarantee its performance. In reality, Mik concludes, the fact that an obligation or a contractual term are expressed in code can hardly be regarded as beneficial. Once a contract is expressed in code, the risk of breach is effectively replaced with the risk of programming errors, incorrect compilation, or the unexpected execution of code.

Natasha Blycha, James Myint, and Lachlan McCalman, in 'Stealing Fire from The Gods: The Creation of Digital Assets and New Markets Derived from Legal Agreements – A Qualitative and Quantitative Exploration of Contract Value' examine the positive benefits that may follow the use of Smart Legal Contracts or Live Contracts, arguing that these contracts may become valuable assets following their digitisation and automation. To demonstrate that, they introduce a foundational empirical function of the Value Co-Efficient (V_s) to quantitatively assess Smart Legal Contract dimensions of value, cost, and risk. The V_s is contrasted with the traditional analogue Contract Value Co-Efficient (V_T). Real-world examples, such as a $100 m invoicing factoring agreement and a twenty-year mining operation, are used to demonstrate the value that traditional contracting leaves on the table compared to Live Contracting. The 'enlivening' and assetisation of contracts, if hosted securely with adequate legal guardrails, will be crucial to modern corporate governance. In an intriguing conclusion, and one which challenges our assumptions of lag, they conclude that directors and executives who do not maximise shareholder value through use of Live Contracting as it becomes commercially available may, in fact, be in breach of duties owed to those shareholders.

Part III of the book entitled Digital Assets and Fraud, contains three chapters. Kelvin Low and Jason Allen consider the role that property may play when applied to ideational objects. In the 'Third Thing or Sixth Sense? I See Ideational Objects?', Low examines whether the English law of personal property stands poised to make a dramatic shift to recognise an 'unbounded' category of third things (or *tertium quid*). The implications of such a shift, Low argues, will reverberate well beyond the realm of cryptoassets. However, since the push for this category was very much driven by the United Kingdom Law Commission's desire to accommodate cryptoassets within English law, this chapter critically analyses the Law Commission's proposal in relation to cryptoassets.

Jason Allen's 'Through the Looking Glass: We All See Ideational Objects Here' explores the property law treatment of both cryptoassets and other digital artefacts that are not clearly rights to anything or against anyone. Arguing that such artefacts are well described as 'ideational objects', Allen draws together insights from private law theory and social ontology to explore how we should think about complex objects with a social and a technical dimension and how the law of property can accommodate ideational objects as possible objects of rights (including the right of ownership) and dealing, and the challenges and implications this poses for the traditional doctrines and concepts of property law. Engaging directly with Kelvin Low's chapter, Allen defends the United Kingdom Law Commission's suggested 'third category' of personal property and introduces a new conceptual framework drawn from Christian von Bar's 'things as objects of property rights'.

What happens, though, when these new technologies are used for improper purposes, whether as part of the law of contract or of property? Aaron Lane, in 'Private Law Remedies for Cryptocurrency Fraud', analyses available legal mechanisms used to combat fraud and scams involving cryptocurrency, drawing on both practical legal experience and the new comparative economics. Although illicit transactions account for a small portion of total cryptocurrency transaction volumes, when that does occur, individuals can incur significant private losses and face unique enforcement challenges. While the prevalent legal approach to addressing cryptocurrency-based fraud is though public enforcement mechanisms, Lane argues that in some circumstances private law and civil litigation mechanisms can offer a more efficient mechanism for addressing cryptocurrency-based fraud with tools to identify perpetrators, tailored legal claims, and secure assets. Lane concludes with recommendations designed to enhance these available private law remedies.

Part IV turns to an issue which cannot be overlooked as we enter this brave new world: the environment. In a searching chapter that should give us pause—'The Future of Crypto-Asset Mining: The Inflation Reduction Act and The Need for Uniform Federal Regulation'—Liz Guinan demonstrates how, as crypto-asset mining gains traction, its environmental footprint intensifies, demanding our attention as part of a legal response. Drawing upon the US experience, Guinan's analysis shows that, at best, we find regulatory uncertainty which cannot manage an energy consumption akin to 10.9 million households and emissions paralleling seven million conventional vehicles. Guinan scrutinises the fragmented state-led responses inherent in a federal system, highlighting New York state's rigorous stance juxtaposed with Wyoming's relaxed regulatory regime. Guinan argues for a holistic federal regulatory mechanism, underscoring the potential role of the US *Inflation Reduction Act* and prior federal interventions. Guinan concludes that a unified federal blueprint is necessary to balance economic benefits with environmental stewardship. This same model is one which must be applied not only within states, but internationally as well.

* * *

On 27 February 2025, while this book was being compiled for the publisher, we received the very sad news that Professor Juliet M Moringiello had passed away. We came to know Juliet well through this project, and we were deeply saddened to learn of her passing. Juliet was a wonderful teacher, scholar, colleague, and friend. Working with Juliet's family, with Dean andré douglas pond cummings of Widener University Commonwealth Law School, and with Springer, we obtained permission to publish Juliet's outstanding chapter in this collection notwithstanding the fact that she had not yet seen the final edited and proof versions. We undertook to complete those steps for Juliet; we very much hope that our work would have pleased Juliet. We also decided that this entire volume should be dedicated to Juliet's memory. On behalf of each of the contributors, we hope that this will stand as a fitting tribute to her enormous contributions to scholarship and to the global scholarly community.

A book of this complexity requires the input of many people—here we thank those who have been central to bringing this project to a conclusion. Sincere thanks go, first, to Lucie Bartonek, who was the Springer Commissioning Editor who encouraged us to undertake this project; and as we brought it to a conclusion, Mamun Mishra took on that role. Thanks so much to both of you. Deep gratitude, too, to the editorial team at Springer, led by Saranya Kalidoss. And thanks to our research assistant, Michail Ivanov, for his outstanding research assistance and editorial precision, both of which were invaluable in finalising the manuscript.

Private Law and Digital Assets

Private Law Is Both the Question and the Answer: Property, Contract, and Enduring Questions About the Legal Treatment of Digital Assets

P. T. Babie and Mark Giancaspro

Abstract As governments and legal systems attempt to address the adoption of new technologies of any kind, digital objects included, the development of law is often overlooked. More often than not, law plays a catch-up game, responding to change once it has happened and, far too often, once it is too late for the law to manage challenges that may emerge. It is important, then, that a legal system consider, to the extent possible, challenges posed by new technologies before they occur, and that it be ready to respond to them with innovative solutions. Here we identify just one aspect of necessary legal change, what we call the private law question. How, when forced to answer, will the private law respond to the changes being wrought by the emergence of digital assets and so ensure that it progresses logically and efficiently? The private law question is easily demonstrated by reference to two major classifications of private law: property and contract. The former asks when the law will recognise and enforce rights and entitlements concerning novel digital assets. The latter asks how the law of contract, which facilitates legal exchanges and imposes a mandatory minimum threshold of 'legal sufficiency', sees value in digital assets. In suggesting how these questions might be answered, this chapter contains three Parts. The first two summarise the core responses to both the property question and the contract question. The third draws two conclusions that follow from the analysis: (i) that what we see revealed in the emphasis, both in law and scholarship, on the property question is a legal form of the Matthew Effect—that the focus on one question necessarily impoverishes the development of answers to other important questions about the legal response to digital assets. And, (ii), we suggest that the answer to this legal Matthew Effect is to see the questions that we might ask—property, contract, and so forth—not as discrete questions, but as components of a larger, more holistic approach to law which, we argue, is contained within the concept of private law.

P. T. Babie (✉) · M. Giancaspro
Adelaide Law School, The University of Adelaide, Adelaide, SA, Australia
e-mail: paul.babie@adelaide.edu.au

M. Giancaspro
e-mail: mark.giancaspro@adelaide.edu.au

P. Babie and M. Giancaspro (eds.), *Private Law, Digital Assets, and Infrastructure*,
https://doi.org/10.1007/978-981-96-7121-2_2

1 Introduction

'As technology advances and humans spend increasing amounts of time online, our relationships with digital assets will become ever more important' (Law Commission UK 2023: para [1.2]). So begins the UK Law Commission's Final Report into Digital Assets; a work exploring the application of private law principles, notably those of property law, to digital assets. The report ultimately concludes that certain types of digital asset can be things to which personal property rights relate and recommends that a third category of personal property be recognised at law alongside choses in possession and choses in action: 'digital objects'.

As governments and legal systems attempt to address the adoption of new technologies of any kind, digital objects included, the development of law is often overlooked. More often than not, law plays a catch-up game, responding to change once it has happened and, far too often, once it is too late for the law to manage challenges that may emerge. Long known about, this is the lag problem in law (Beutel 1953). As Frederick K Beutel wrote over half a century ago:

> It is a generally recognized fact that law and legal procedures lag far behind any type of social change. This is true even in matters of change in social custom, religion, and habits of the people. But it seems to be far more marked when one approaches the problem of picking up scientific developments and transposing them to be used as tools in legal and governmental procedures. (Beutel 1953: 1)

Those words could have been written today. It is important, then, that a legal system consider, to the extent possible, challenges posed by new technologies before they occur, and that it be ready to respond to them with innovative solutions. Here we identify just one aspect of necessary legal change, what we call the private law question. How, when forced to answer, will the private law respond to the changes being wrought by the emergence of digital assets and so ensure that it progresses logically and efficiently? John Gardner says that 'private law…is an exotic category as far as many lawyers trained in the common law tradition are concerned. It has a faintly Napoleonic flavour. It suggests a more hermetic departmentalization of the law than the common law is capable of sustaining' (Gardner 2018: 14). Here, we mean it, broadly, to define those cognate bodies of law generally known as contract, tort, property, unjust enrichment, and equity (Gardner 2018: 14).

Answering this question was the task confronting the Law Commission. The private law question is easily demonstrated by reference to two major classifications of private law: property and contract. The former asks when the law will recognise and enforce rights and entitlements concerning novel digital assets. The latter asks how the law of contract, which facilitates legal exchanges and imposes a mandatory minimum threshold of 'legal sufficiency', sees value in digital assets. Yet, what one finds is that the property question has monopolised the discourse in this space, to the near complete exclusion of the contract question. We see in this tendency a form of the 'Matthew Effect', so named for the Biblical parable speaking to the general principle that advantage tends to beget further advantage.

This chapter contains three sections. The first two summarise the core responses to both the property question and the contract question. In the third section we draw two conclusions that follow from our analysis of these private law questions: (i) that what we see revealed in the emphasis, both in law and scholarship, on the property question is a legal form of the Matthew Effect—that the focus on one question necessarily impoverishes the development of answers to other important questions about the legal response to digital assets. And, (ii), we suggest that the answer to this legal Matthew Effect is to see the questions that we might ask—property, contract, and so forth—not as discrete questions, but as components of a larger, more holistic approach to law which, we argue, is contained within the concept of private law. It is imperative that a legal system account for all relevant perspectives as part of the process of facilitating changes to law that will keep pace with changes in technology. We argue that the concept of private law is capacious enough to accomplish that objective.

2 The Property Question

Property plays many roles in contemporary life. Joseph William Singer and Jack M Beerman write that:

> property rights are various. A wide variety of property interests have been created by private arrangement and recognized by government.... [T]he definition of property rights depends on a host of instrumental and value judgments and cannot be derived simply by a logical process that appears to be value neutral and nondiscretionary.... [P]roperty rights are socially and politically constructed by both private action and government policies. (Singer and Beermann 1993: 228)

Property exists as a dynamic social construct which, at any one moment in time, is 'a cultural creation and a legal conclusion' (C Edwin Baker 1986: 744). But before we get to that legal conclusion, Felix Cohen adds that property is always, first, 'a *relationship among human beings* such that the so-called owner can exclude others from certain activities or permit others to engage in those activities and in either case secure the assistance of the law in carrying out [that] decision' (Cohen 1954: 373 (emphasis added)). Property, then, is power—power to decide how to use a resource, whatever it is, and power to decide who in addition to the holder of property can make use of that resource. That power emerges from relationships structured by law: '[p]roperty concerns legal relations among people regarding control and disposition of valued resources. Note well: Property concerns relations *among people*, not relations between people and things' (Singer 2017: 2 (citations omitted) (emphasis in the original)). We typically call the collection of these rights a 'bundle of rights', the rights constituted by relations *between people* concerning control of things and power over others (Penner 1996).

The difficulty, of course, is deciding when property exists in a given resource. That decision carries awesome implications, for with it comes the power to control the resource, and to control others as concerns that use. Typically, the need to decide whether property exists arises when a human person (individual) or a legal person (such as a corporation) seeks to protect a relationship in respect of a thing—which can be tangible (such as land or chattels) or intangible (such as intellectual property, shares in a corporation, or money)—against the predations of others. When that happens, a person who feels that such a relationship is threatened by others seeks legal redress in support of the claim against interference. A court or a legislature is thus faced with what we might call 'the property question', the need to resolve a novel dispute concerning the thing in question (Ziff 2018: 59–61). Any given answer, though, is not fixed, for just as property serves many different social functions, those can change over time, for '[p]roperty is not a static concept, but rather is in a constant state of flux. This fluidity is apparent when disputes over new forms of property erupt' (Ziff 2018: 59).

The property question has largely been settled for some parts of our world. Consider land. Over 1,000 years have passed since feudalism and the twin pillars of tenure and estates first began to provide a set of answers to disputes over possession and ownership of land, worked out in the freehold estates, supplemented over time by incorporeal hereditaments, the leasehold estate, and equitable refinements; all of which was crystallised in the contemporary *numerus clausus* of estates and interests in land.[1]

But there are a great many things, largely personal and intangible, about which the property question has either not been asked and answered, or about which whatever answer might currently exist there remains a good deal of contingency.[2] Thus, it is by no means clear whether and why property might exist in cases of (Ziff 2018: 62–66): cultural appropriation[3]; university degrees[4]; government-issued licences to fish[5]; domain names[6]; one's personality or celebrity[7]; patents over such things as mice[8]; genetically modified plant cells[9]; isolated human genes[10] or other genetic

[1] The classic treatment of the *numerus clausus* is Rudden 1987.

[2] Parts of the following list (with case citations) are drawn from Ziff 2018: 59–60, 28–298, 308–311.

[3] And see Ziff and Rao 1997; Brown 2004.

[4] See *Graham v Graham*, 574 P2d 75 (1978).

[5] See *Saulnier v Royal Bank of Canada* [2008] 3 SCR 166.

[6] See *Tucows.Com Co. v Lojas Renner S.A.*, 2011 ONCA 548.

[7] See *Athans v Canadian Adventure Camps Ltd.* (1977) 17 OR (2d) 425.

[8] See *Harvard College v Canada (Commissioner of Patents)* [2002] 4 SCR 45.

[9] See *Monsanto Inc. v Schmeiser* [2004] 1 SCR 902.

[10] See *Association for Molecular Pathology v Myriad Genetics*, 569 US 576 (2013); *D'Arcy v Myriad Genetics Inc* (2015) 258 CLR 334.

material[11]; human pre-embryos[12]; cells extracted from a spleen[13]; the right of next-of-kin to a human brain in paraffin[14]; the distinctive sound of a singer's voice[15]; an entertainment spectacle[16]; and 'know how'.[17] Digital objects are the latest novel resource or thing about which the property question arises.

In answering the property question, courts typically adopt one of two methodologies. The first Bruce Ziff calls the 'attributes approach'; the focus of 'the enquiry hinges on whether the right being asserted looks like property: one searches for a strong family resemblance' (Ziff 2018: 60–61 (footnotes omitted)). Here a court looks for some external indicator that property in fact exists in a given case, rather than understanding that it is the court's answer to the property question, in that very case, that determines whether there is property in respect of the thing in question. Judges look at the thing in question and its relationship to the parties in order to determine whether the thing, the relationship, or both, reveal the existence of property. An example of this approach as applied to cryptocurrency is found in the New Zealand case of *Ruscoe and Moore*. There it was suggested that the *Ainsworth* indicia to determining the existence of property could be used in relation to cryptocurrency. But in deciding the case, Gendall J demonstrated that a more nuanced approach was possible—that there is something deeper, something more profound, about finding property in a novel thing or relationship, and that attributes alone cannot identify that deeper profundity.

This raises the second methodology employed by judges. If property is about relationship then what matters in any given case is whether the relevant relationship exists, at that point in time, in respect of the thing or relationship in question. Only then can a court or a legislature conclude that property is present. Ziff calls this approach 'functional'—it involves '[l]ook[ing]…at the policy factors at play. It takes account of how property, as a tool of social life, should be used. This approach recognizes that property is not an acontextual entity that demands conceptual purity, but a purposive concept, to be used to meet social needs' (Ziff 2018: 61).

Having answered the question in any given case, though, does not settle the matter for all time. Thinking that it does is to fail to understand that property is not a static, but a fluid concept, one that can, and often does change as circumstances change. That is true not only in respect of the way in which the concept is applied to novel disputes but also in the way it might have been applied in the past to given things or relationships. In other words, an answer given at any one point in time cannot be determinative of what property is, or of how it might apply to any given circumstance,

[11] On the ownership of human sperm, for instance, see *Re Leith Dorene Patteson*, [2016] QSC 104; *Chapman v South Eastern Sydney Local Health District*, [2018] NSWSC 1231; *Re Cresswell*, [2018] QSC 142.

[12] See *Davis v Davis*, 842 SW2d 588 (1992).

[13] See *Moore v The Regents of the University of California*, 793 P 2d 479 (1990).

[14] See *Dobson v North Tyneside Health Authority* [1997] 1 WLR 596.

[15] See *Midler v Ford Motor Co.*, 849 F2d 460 (1988).

[16] See *Victoria Park Racing & Recreation Grounds Ltd v Taylor* (1937) 58 CLR 479.

[17] See *Roth v R*, 2007 FCA 38.

even one that seemed to have been settled at some point in the past. This is a subtle point, but one that Gendall J understood in deciding *Ruscoe and Moore*. In that case, Gendall J understood that property is a dynamic and integral tool in social life, and that it must be recognised by law—by the courts and by legislatures—in order to meet those social needs.[18]

But while the courts have already spent a good deal of time addressing the property question as it applies to digital objects, finding that cryptocurrency does, in fact, constitute property,[19] the same cannot be said for its private law sibling, the contract question.

3 The Contract Question

Contract law regulates the legal obligations voluntarily assumed through the agreement of parties. Within limits, such as the general requirement of legality, the parties can impose upon one another any terms they see fit, including what they choose to exchange with one another by way of consideration (*Prime Sight Ltd v Lavarello* 2014: 450 [47] (Lord Toulson)). One of the common law's few restraints upon this freedom is that the parties must proffer to one another only those promises or things possessing sufficient legal value. The consideration need not, however, be adequate,[20] the rule famously branded the 'peppercorn principle' (*Chappell & Co Ltd v Nestlé Co Ltd* 1960: 114). One can trade a peppercorn for a Spanish villa, a diamond ring, or a Maserati. The price does not have to be proportionate but merely recognised at law. The threshold, clearly, is low, so low that some judges have doubted whether any consideration can truly fail for want of sufficiency (*Blue v Ashley* 2017: para [58] (Leggatt J)).

Respectfully, this is a clear overstatement given the law has on countless instances, primarily in the renegotiation context, determined that the alleged consideration put forward by the promisor has failed. Where consideration lacks any detectable value, as in *Placer Development Ltd v Commonwealth* (1969) 121 CLR 353 where the Commonwealth enjoyed an unfettered prerogative to make any payments to its contractor under the agreement between the parties, it is invalid. Admittedly, this evaluative exercise becomes more difficult with novel forms of consideration the likes of which the common law has not previously encountered. Digital assets are a topical example. Broadly defined, digital assets are assets represented digitally or electronically (Law Commission UK 2023: ix) and include such things as digital files and records, email accounts, domain names, crypto-tokens, and non-fungible tokens ('NFTs'). Of the many established and emerging digital assets, cryptocurrency is by far the most controversial. Most media reports in respect of cryptocurrency, certainly

[18] This finds support in Anning 2015: sec.1.1.4.

[19] For a recent review of the caselaw, see Huang et al. 2023; Sarel 2021.

[20] See, eg, *Haigh v Brooks* (1839) 10 Ad. & E. 309, 320; 113 ER 119; *Westlake v Adams* (1858) 5 C.B. (N.S.) 248; 141 ER 99; *Attrill v Dresdner Kleinwort Ltd* [2012] EWHC 1189.

of late, relate to criminal charges and convictions against its traders.[21] The legal fraternity, on the other hand, has concerned itself primarily with the property question examined in Sect. 2, above. Regrettably, one of the most fundamental questions—the contract question—has received no attention. This section directly responds to this question in the context of cryptocurrency, the most prominent and contentious of all digital assets and the one which poses the greatest conceptual challenges to answering the contract question.

Synthesising an informed answer requires a perfunctory understanding of cryptocurrency. Put simply, cryptocurrency is 'a medium of exchange that functions like money (in that it can be exchanged for goods and services) but, unlike traditional currency, is untethered to, and independent from, national borders, central banks, sovereigns, or fiats' (Maese et al. 2016: 468). Cryptocurrencies operate and are traded within a vast, distributed ledger system: the blockchain.[22] They are not currently legal tender anywhere in the world. Cryptocurrencies are denominated virtually in 'tokens' or 'coins', with Bitcoin being the most well-known. But how does one obtain cryptocurrency? This involves utilising an exchange, either centralised (privately owned and administered) or decentralised (collectively administered by the exchange members) (Johnson 2021). The buyer can pay fiat currency or other cryptocurrency to obtain the desired type and quantity of cryptocurrency. These transactions are cryptographically processed, and the parties are identified pseudonymously by an alphanumeric code linking to their respective digital 'wallets', as opposed to traditional financial purchases which involve the vendor being connected to the purchaser's personal and financial information via a trusted intermediary.

Hundreds of millions of cryptocurrency transactions occur each day (Blockchain.com 2024), each contributing to the crypto market's total capitalisation estimated at approximately USD $2.58 trillion (CoinMarketCap 2024). Media reports tell tales of those who invested early and have since discovered fortune (Weiss 2021). At play here are two critical assumptions. First, the various crypto assets being exchanged have the values assigned to them by their users. Second, the transactions through which these assets are exchanged are entirely lawful and are supported, rather than invalidated, by the legal principles governing these agreements. Through the lens of contract law, these assumptions are inherently linked, and proof that the second is incorrect inevitably negates the first. Let us then evaluate these assumptions. First, we note that cryptocurrency is being traded through market exchanges, meaning they are the subject of contract law. The traditional English law of contract is the foundation for all common law systems, and we consider the position under Anglo-Australian contract law. 'The basic requirements of a contract are that: (i) the parties have reached an agreement, which (ii) is intended to be legally binding, (iii) is supported by consideration, and (iv) is sufficiently certain and complete to be

[21] A recent, high-profile example is the conviction of FTX cryptocurrency exchange founder Sam Bankman-Fried, who was sentenced to 25 years in prison and ordered to forfeit USD $11 billion in assets following proven charges of securities and commodities fraud, conspiracy, and money laundering. See Robins-Early 2024.

[22] For a detailed explanation of the basic infrastructure of blockchain, see Pal 2021: chap.1.

enforceable' (*Blue v Ashley* 2017: para [49] (Leggatt J)). In the interests of scope, and because it is at the heart of the 'contract question', we focus solely on the consideration requirement, noting that the other requirements would likely be satisfied in most crypto transactions (Giancaspro 2022).

Contracts must be founded on sufficient legal consideration. This means whatever is exchanged by the parties must have value 'in the eye of the law' (Thomas v Thomas 1842: 333–334).[23] In Currie v Misa 1875: 162, Lush J described a valuable consideration, in the sense of law, as consisting in 'some right, interest, profit, or benefit accruing to the one party, or some forbearance, detriment, loss, or responsibility, given, suffered, or undertaken by the other' (Currie v Misa 1875: 162). Put differently, there must be a benefit to the promisor or a detriment to the promisee, and the subject matter of the agreement must form part of a bargained-for exchange.[24] Unfortunately, the common law courts have for centuries been unhelpful in elucidating how one determines whether a particular 'thing', be it a benefit or detriment, holds sufficient legal value to support a simple contract. What they have made clear, however, is that the subjective values attributed to consideration are irrelevant.[25] The legal value of consideration is determined objectively. In practical terms, this means that the values that digital asset users subjectively attribute to those assets is inconsequential to the question of whether they actually hold such value (or, indeed, a different value). Just because a Bitcoin owner says that coin is worth USD $70,000, as it is currently 'valued' on the market (CoinDesk 2024),[26] this does not mean it is actually worth that much. In any event, purported economic value is not equivalent to legal sufficiency under contract law.[27]

Cryptocurrency is not fiat currency. If it were, then its value as a legal and trusted medium of exchange would be vested by executive authority from the relevant government (Singhal 2018: 155). It would be measured by reference to international exchange rates. Without this authority, the value of cryptocurrency is defined merely through consensus of its users (Matharu 2019; Zhang 2023) and that value may not be commensurate with true *legal* value. If that legal value is not *sufficient* as required, the contract facilitating its exchange fails. The parties might be entirely satisfied with their arrangement, which is fine, but the arrangement would have no legal effect. This is the essence of the contract question. If the question were asked alongside the property question, it would likely have significant consequences for parties who litigate over their rights in respect of cryptocurrency and other digital assets. The problem with a unit of cryptocurrency is that it is essentially a token said

---

[23] The traditional measure for such value is the test propounded by Lush J in Currie v Misa (1875) LR 10 Ex 153.

[24] *Dunlop Pneumatic Tyre Co Ltd v Selfridge and Co Ltd* 1915: 855; *Australian Woollen Mills Pty Ltd v Commonwealth* 1954: 456–457.

[25] *Eastwood v Kenyon* 1840.

[26] That said, like most other cryptocurrencies, Bitcoin is extremely volatile. The price fluctuates so wildly that by the time this chapter reaches print 1 Bitcoin could be worth a fortune or practically worthless.

[27] For cases substantiating this point, see *Hamer v Sidway*, 124 NY 538 (1891); *Jamieson v Renwick* (1891) 17 VLR 124; *Chappell & Co Ltd v Nestlé Co Ltd* [1960] AC 87.

to carry value. In much the same way as a casino chip, the token indicates that the holder has paid another party for the token and that it carries the values those parties assign to it.[28] That the token can be redeemed with the issuer or another willing buyer does not in itself establish the token as an item of legal value. Just because something is *called* a currency and is *used by factions of society* as a currency, it does not *make it* a currency. Similarly, just because a crypto owner believes their token has legal value, it does not mean it does. If this was all that was required to generate legal value, then the consideration doctrine would lose relevance.

The UK Law Commission's Final Report into Digital Assets is one of the most substantial works examining the place of digital assets in private law. It exhaustively considers the property question but regrettably ignores the contract question.

4 Two Conclusions

We come, then, to two conclusions. The first is to state the problem—what we see is an example of the Matthew Effect in action. The second conclusion suggests that in private law we find the solution to the problem created by the over-emphasis on the property question.

4.1 The Problem: Matthew Effect in Action

We have canvassed both the property question and the contract question in the context of digital assets. We also suggested that the property question has monopolised the discourse in this space, so much so that the contract question has been almost entirely overlooked. This is odd given the equivalent legal importance of both questions. We posit that this tendency is a manifestation of the Matthew Effect,[29] deriving from a parable in *Matthew* 13:12, where Jesus is speaking to a crowd of Israelites about the kingdom of Heaven. Jesus states: 'for whosoever hath, to him shall be given, and he shall have more abundance: but whosoever hath not, from him shall be taken away even that he hath'.[30] The message is that those who believe and who yearn to discover the truth of Christ's love will be rewarded for doing so, while those that do the opposite will naturally fail to learn and therefore be deprived of enlightenment. In a broader sense, the parable has been interpreted as standing for the general principle that an

[28] For a case explaining the value of casino chips and similar tokens, see *Lipkin Gorman (a firm) v Karpnale* [1991] 2 AC 548.

[29] The term was first coined by sociologist Robert K Merton as a means of explaining discrepancies in recognition received by eminent scientists and unknown researchers for similar work: Perc 2014.

[30] A similar sentiment is expressed in *Matthew* 25:29 though in a slightly different context (use of allocated commodities for greater gain).

initial advantage begets further advantage, and disadvantage further disadvantage.[31] This principle operates among individuals and groups across a variety of social institutions throughout time.

So why has the Matthew Effect manifested itself in respect of the property and contract questions? More specifically, why has the property question received greater and greater attention from scholars, regulators, and the courts compared to the contract question? We suggest several potential reasons. First, it is arguable that the property question was logically the first to arise. It was necessary to first understand what digital assets are, in the eyes of the law, before the question of how those assets are lawfully transferred could be considered. Second, the parties to disputes involving digital assets, particularly cryptocurrencies, will invariably agree that those assets hold the values they assign to them. The contract question is fundamentally concerned with the inherent legal value of consideration (in this case, digital assets). If the parties impugned such value through legal proceedings, they would be undermining their own bargains and be counterintuitively arguing that they have traded and/or argue for title to something which is legally worthless. The natural consequence is that the contract question seldom arises, or at least arises less commonly than the property question.

Third, and flowing from the second suggested reason, most disputes in the digital asset space—at least, in respect of cryptocurrency—have gravitated to the proprietary status of such assets, and how this status impacts their custody and ownership. As mentioned earlier, the common law courts have hitherto generally accepted that cryptocurrency constitutes property.[32] Other cases have reached the same conclusion while also determining that cryptocurrency can be the subject of a proprietary injunction (*AA v Persons Unknown, Re Bitcoin* 2019) or a trust (*Ruscoe and Moore v Cryptopia Ltd (in liq)* 2020). Not even the most recent cases involving cryptocurrency consider the contract question though all consider the property question.[33] Importantly, we should not immediately assume that just because something is property it holds legal value. Property can lack value. A small pebble in your shoe is a chattel as it is a tangible, physical item—but it is worthless, even if you personally consider it to be worth a million dollars. Similarly, narcotics are chattels and are clearly valuable

[31] For a thorough analysis of the Matthew Effect as a general phenomenon in social science, see Rigney 2010.

[32] This was the finding in one of the first cases addressing the property question in *B2C2 Ltd v Quoine Pte Ltd* [2019] SGHC(I) 03.

[33] See, e.g., *Fetch.AI Lrd v Persons Unknown Category A* [2021] EWHC 2254; *Danisz v Persons Unknown and Huobi Global Ltd* [2022] EWHC 280; *ByBit Fintech Ltd v Ho Kai Xin* [2023] SGHC 199; *Re Gatecoin Limited* [2023] HKCFI 91. Of course, this can in part be explained by how the pleadings are drafted and the fundamental issues being contested by the parties and open to decision from the courts. Nonetheless, the contract question must surely arise organically in light of its symbiotic relationship with the property question?

to the dealers and users that trade in them, but this is *street value* not *legal value*.[34] Subjective appraisals of worth are of no consequence to contract law.

4.2 The Solution: Private Law

Why does it matter that we account for the full range of doctrinal categories of law encompassed by the private law question? In this chapter, we have examined only two of those categories: property and contract. But in doing so, we immediately see the importance of understanding the interplay of the diverse categories of private law. To take one example, in order for a trust of cryptocurrency to exist, the cryptocurrency itself must be property. There is a wider reason. Property has implications for the operation of contract; or, put another way, there is an interplay between property and contract. Two forms of that interplay are clearly recognisable. First, the finding that cryptocurrency is property bears consequences for the availability of remedies available for breach of contract, such as specific performance,[35] and for whether a trust of cryptocurrency can exist (*Ruscoe and Moore v Cryptopia Ltd (in liq)* 2020).

The existence of interplay between property and contract is merely symptomatic of wider interplay throughout the law; the truth is that one cannot really understand property without understanding contract, tort, unjust enrichment, and equity (Leeming 2013).[36] It simply does not make sense to speak of property in a vacuum that omits these other dimensions of law. This is too often forgotten today: at one time, not so very long ago, it would have been anathema to attempt to treat law as a set of loosely related doctrinal categories—contract, tort, property, unjust enrichment, equity (with all of its intricacies and idiosyncrasies). Instead, it was seen, by writers like Sir William Blackstone (Blackstone 1979), as an integrated whole, understandable only when all of its parts were viewed at once. This was not easy to do, of course, but it was the way that common lawyers understood their craft. Some still understand that truth; Mark Leeming writes:

> The legal system is more complicated than it may appear. That complexity matters. In it lies the capacity for development coupled with continuity which is the greatest feature of common law legal systems. The complexity comes about in large measure because different attitudes and approaches at common law and in equity necessarily interact with statutes, new and old. Statutes are constantly informed by, and modify, judge-made law, statutes tend to accrete a body of judge-made law upon themselves, and statutes have chaotic consequences throughout the legal system. (Leeming 2023: 299 (footnote omitted))

It was not until the rise of the treatise, largely in the nineteenth and twentieth centuries, that the law begins to be disaggregated in separate, doctrinal categories

---

[34] Selling narcotics without authority to do so (and such authority is limited to a narrow selection of cases, such as analysis or research) amounts to trafficking under controlled substances legislation. See, e.g., *Drugs, Poisons and Controlled Substances Act 1981* (Vic) Pt V.

[35] Compare Paterson 20 February 2020.

[36] See also Leeming 2023.

(Simpson 1981; Hedley 1999). But this development, and its attempt to define categories of law by their differentiation from other categories denies the truth about law, at least in the common law tradition—that it is chaotic. Joachim Dietrich writes:

> The law is a chaotic jumble of (surviving) common law rules and piecemeal, inconsistent and unsystematic statutory incursions, whether we like it or not. … We could of course ignore the legislation and carry on with our taxonomy regardless, but to what end? Given the piecemeal nature of statutory intervention, those parts of the common law remaining are even less likely to be capable of systematic ordering, one would imagine. (Dietrich 2006: 573)

The reality is that interplay happens across the totality of law (Leeming 2013: 1010–1011). What, then, can we do? The answer, or the solution to the problem created by disaggregation—this legal Matthew Effect—is found in private law itself, or, more accurately, in the potential contained in using 'private law' as a concept to describe or define the totality of those categories of law not otherwise thought of as public law. This begins where we started: in the definition of private law. Remember what John Gardner said about private law: it is Napoleonic, or hermetic departmentalization. What Gardner means is that it is civilian in origin. Indeed, it is—the private law-public law division is well established in the civilian tradition, and can be traced to its very sources. Barry Nicholas writes that:

> The Romans themselves made a distinction between public law and private law. The former was concerned with the functioning of the state, and included in particular constitutional law and criminal law; the latter was concerned with relations between individuals. It was the private law to which the Roman lawyers devoted their main interest, and it was the private law which gave to the second life of Roman law its great importance. (Nicholas 1962: 2)

It is this second life to which Gardner refers when he says that private law is 'Napoleonic'—he means the adoption, from the twelfth century on, of the ancient Roman law, as compiled in the sixth-century *corpus iuris civilis* of Justinian, and culminating in 1804 with the *Code civil des Français*, or *Civil Code of the French*, or simply, the *Napoleonic Code*, named for its progenitor, Napoleon Bonaparte, which both replaced the fragmented pre-Revolutionary laws of France and influenced civil law codes across the world. Thus, in France today, it can be said that 'it is common to distinguish between two separate fields of law: one of private law, the other of public law…. Taken in its broad meaning, private law regulates the relationship of citizens as between themselves. However, within the area of public law falls: (i) constitutional law…, and (ii) administrative law' (Steiner 2018: 247). And, 'even in England, where… "the appreciation of the distinction in substantive law between what is private and what is public law had itself been a latecomer to the English legal system"…, there is today a wide recognition of this distinctive separation….'.[37]

How do we mean then to use the concept of the private law at least to attempt to resolve the legal Matthew Effect which seems to bedevil the treatment of digital assets? Gardner again provides a clue to what is meant today by the concept of private law. He says that:

[37] Steiner 2018: 247 (quoting *O'Reilly v Mackman* [1982] 3 WLR 1096, 1102 (Lord Diplock)).

> the big themes of private law…are also among the big themes of life. And how we should think about them in connection with private law is none other than the same way in which we should think about them in the connection with everything else to which they are relevant—for example, when we reflect on how to bring up our children, on how to put our friendships back on an even keel, on how to respond to our failures, on how to relate to people who have disappointed us, on how to make a fresh start, and so on. (Gardner 2018: 10)

In other words, life is deeply interrelated, interconnected—there is interplay between all aspects of our life. And if private law is about the mediation and regulation of relationships of citizens between themselves, then that means the whole of life, and that means the whole of law. One part of law, just as one part of life, cannot be segregated, hived-off, disaggregated from the rest.

And so, if we are to overcome the legal Matthew Effect in relation to digital objects, then we must see law as a totality, as a whole, as interconnected, interrelated, and as one of interplay between its diverse components. The concept of private law, as responding broadly to the regulation of relationships between citizens, as the civilian tradition understands it, and as responding to the totality of life, as Gardner applies it, provides the potential for a solution to the problem posed by digital objects. Only when we see law in this way will we be able fully to understand, and fully to respond to, the challenges—legal and social—posed by digital objects.

References

AA v Persons Unknown, Re Bitcoin [2019] EWHC 3556

Anning P (2015) *The Law of Bitcoin*, S Hoegner (ed), iUniverse, Bloomington

*Association for Molecular Pathology v Myriad Gene*tics, 569 US 576 (2013)

Athans v Canadian Adventure Camps Ltd. (1977) 17 OR (2d) 425

Attrill v Dresdner Kleinwort Ltd [2012] EWHC 1189

Australian Woollen Mills Pty Ltd v Commonwealth (1954) 92 CLR 424

Beutel FK (1953) The lag between scientific discoveries and legal procedures. Nebraska Law Review 33:1

Blackstone SW (1979) Commentaries on the Laws of England (1765–1769), Vol 1–4. The University of Chicago Press

Blockchain.com (2024) Total Number of Transactions, https://www.blockchain.com/explorer/charts/n-transactions-total. Accessed 10 April 2024

Blue v Ashley [2017] EWHC 1928

Brown MF (2004) Who owns native culture?, 1st edn. Harvard University Press, Cambridge, Mass

ByBit Fintech Ltd v Ho Kai Xin [2023] SGHC 199

Edwin Baker C (1986) Property and its relation to constitutionally protected liberty. Univ Pa Law Rev 134:741

Chapman v South Eastern Sydney Local Health District [2018] NSWSC 1231

Chappell & Co Ltd v Nestlé Co Ltd [1960] AC 87

Cohen FS (1954) Dialogue on private property. Rutgers Law Review 9:357

CoinDesk (2024) Bitcoin Price Index and Live Chart, https://www.coindesk.com/price/bitcoin. Accessed 10 April 2024

CoinMarketCap (2024) Today's Cryptocurrency Prices by Market Cap, https://coinmarketcap.com/. Accessed 10 April 2024

Currie v Misa (1875) LR 10 Ex 153

D'Arcy v Myriad Genetics Inc (2015) 258 CLR 334
Danisz v Persons Unknown and Huobi Global Ltd [2022] EWHC 280
Davis v Davis, 842 SW2d 588 (1992)
Dietrich J (2006) What is "lawyering"? The challenge of taxonomy. Cambridge Law Journal 65:549
Dobson v North Tyneside Health Authority [1997] 1 WLR 596
Dunlop Pneumatic Tyre Co Ltd v Selfridge and Co Ltd [1915] AC 847
Eastwood v Kenyon (1840) 113 ER 482
Fetch.AI Lrd v Persons Unknown Category A [2021] EWHC 2254
Gardner J (2018) From personal life to private law. Oxford University Press, Oxford
Giancaspro M (2022) 'Cryptocurrency and the consideration conundrum: Does Crypto have legal value under contract law?. J Bank Financ—Law Pract 33(1): 3
Graham v Graham, 574 P2d 75 (1978)
Haigh v Brooks (1839) 10 Ad. & E. 309, 320; 113 ER 119
Hamer v Sidway, 124 NY 538 (1891)
Harvard College v Canada (Commissioner of Patents) [2002] 4 SCR 45
Hedley S (1999) How has the common law survived the 20th century?: "Gouverner, C'est Choisir." North Irel Leg 50:283
Huang RH, Deng H, Chan AFL (2023) The legal nature of cryptocurrency as property: Accounting and taxation implications. Comput Law Secur Rev 51:105860. https://doi.org/10.1016/j.clsr.2023.105860
Jamieson v Renwick (1891) 17 VLR 124
Johnson KN (2021) Decentralized finance: Regulating cryptocurrency exchanges. William and Mary Law Review 62(6):1911
Law Commission UK (2023) Digital assets: Final report
Leeming M (2013) Theories and principles underlying the development of the common law—the statutory elephant in the room. UNSW Law Journal 36(3):1002
Leeming M (2023) Common law, equity and statute: A Complex entangled system. Federation Press
Lipkin Gorman (a firm) v Karpnale [1991] 2 AC 548
Maese VA, Avery AW, Naftalis BA, Wink SP, Valdez YD (2016) Cryptocurrency: A Primer. The Banking Law Journal 133(8):468
Matharu A (2019) Understanding cryptocurrencies: The money of the future, 1st edn. Business Expert Press, New York
Midler v Ford Motor Co., 849 F2d 460 (1988)
Monsanto Inc. v Schmeiser [2004] 1 SCR 902
Moore v The Regents of the University of California, 793 P 2d 479 (1990)
Nicholas B (1962) An introduction to the roman law. Oxford University Press
Pal A (2021) Cryptomania: An Essential Guide to Cryptocurrency. Notion Press
Paterson J (20 February 2020) Smart Contracts, AI Informed Automation and Specific Performance: Considering the Reflexive Potential of Equity. Equity and Trusts in the Digital Economy Conference. University of Queensland, Brisbane, QLD
Penner JE (1996) The "bundle of rights" picture of property. UCLA Law Rev 43(3):711
Perc M (2014) The Matthew effect in empirical data. J R Soc Interface 11(98):20140378. https://doi.org/10.1098/rsif.2014.0378
Placer Development Ltd v Commonwealth [1969] 121 CLR 353
Prime Sight Ltd v Lavarello [2014] AC 436
Re Cresswell, [2018] QSC 142
Re Gatecoin Limited [2023] HKCFI
Re Leith Dorene Patteson [2016] QSC 104
Rigney D (2010) The Matthew effect: How advantage begets further advantage. Columbia University Press, New York

Robins-Early N (2024) He knew it was wrong': Sam Bankman-Fried sentenced to 25 years in prison over FTX fraud. *The Guardian*, https://www.theguardian.com/business/2024/mar/28/sam-bankman-fried-sentenced-prison-ftx-fraud. Accessed 13 November 2024

Roth v R [2007] FCA 38

Rudden BH (1987) Economic theory v. property law: The numerus clausus problem. In Bell J Eekelaar J (eds) Oxford Essays in Jurisprudence, Third Series, Clarendon Press

Ruscoe and Moore v Cryptopia Ltd (in liq) [2020] NZLR 809

Sarel R (2021) Property rights in cryptocurrencies: a law and economics perspective. NCJL & Tech. 22:389

Saulnier v Royal Bank of Canada [2008] 3 SCR 166

Simpson AWB (1981) The rise and fall of the legal treatise: Legal principles and the forms of legal literature. The University of Chicago Law Review 48(3):632

Singer JW (2017) Property, 5th edn. Wolters Kluwer, Alphen aan den Rijn, Netherlands

Singer JW, Beermann JM (1993) The social origins of property. Can J Law Jurisprud 4:217

Singhal B (2018) Beginning blockchain: a beginner's guide to building blockchain solutions. Apress L. P, Berkeley, CA

Steiner E (2018) French law: a Comparative Approach, 2nd edn. Oxford University Press, Oxford, United Kingdom

Thomas v Thomas (1842) 114 ER 330

Tucows.Com Co. v Lojas Renner S.A., 2011 ONCA 548

Victoria Park Racing & Recreation Grounds Ltd v Taylor (1937) 58 CLR 479

Weiss S (2021) Meet the Bitcoin Investors Who Got Insanely Rich Off Crypto. *New York Post*, https://nypost.com/2021/01/13/meet-the-bitcoin-investors-who-got-insanely-rich-off-crypto/

Westlake v Adams (1858) 5 C.B. (N.S.) 248; 141 ER 99

Zhang ZJ (2023) Cryptopricing: whence comes the value for cryptocurrencies and NFTs? Int J Res Mark 40:22

Ziff BH (2018) Principles of Property Law, 7th edn. Carswell

Ziff BH, Rao PV (eds) (1997) Borrowed power: essays on cultural appropriation. Rutgers University Press, New Brunswick, N.J

Innovation and Regulation: Consumer Protection, Crypto-Assets, Smart Contracts, and Algorithmic Contracting

Jeannie Marie Paterson

1 Introduction

Rapid technological change means that ordinary consumers have opportunities to engage with digital products that once would have only been available to specialists. These newly accessible products include the subject matter of this book: crypto-assets and smart contracts. There is still debate about the extent to which these products present valuable opportunities for ordinary consumers that outweigh the associated risks. Moreover, the relative novelty and complexity of both crypto-assets and smart contracts mean that the relevant legal and regulatory interventions are still being developed (Mik 2022b). These decisions are influenced by long-standing debates about the relationship between legal regulation and incentives for innovation.[1]

From the outset, the promotion of crypto-assets and smart contracts has been premised on something close to an ideological opposition to traditional markets and general law norms in regulating financial transactions. The combination of products has been accompanied by an aspiration to encouraging peer-to-peer transactions, avoiding intermediaries, and transcending the legal rules that would otherwise be applicable (Blockchain Council 2023). Nevertheless, this chapter suggests that the framing of a choice between innovation *or* legal regulation is unhelpful in considering the interests of consumers. The benefits of innovation in the forms of crypto-assets and smart contracts for ordinary consumers are far from certain without regulation and, in any event, the products are already subject to cognate legal/regulatory regimes.

For most consumers, the promised potential of crypto-assets and smart contracts has not been realised. Rather, the growth in intermediaries providing financial and

[1] See e.g., discussion in (Larsen 2023).

J. M. Paterson (✉)
University of Melbourne, Melbourne, VIC, Australia
e-mail: jeanniep@unimelb.edu.au

P. Babie and M. Giancaspro (eds.), *Private Law, Digital Assets, and Infrastructure*,
https://doi.org/10.1007/978-981-96-7121-2_3

investment services involving crypto-assets has tended to confirm consumers' vulnerability to losses arising from high-risk but misunderstood investments, mismanagement, or fraud.[2] As a result, the case for regulating crypto-assets has become increasingly compelling. In many jurisdictions, and certainly in the UK, EU, and Australia, there is a move to clarify the application of existing financial legislation and even develop new regimes to respond to the risks of crypto-asset investment for consumers.

Regulators have paid less attention to smart contracts. The operationalised reality of the smart contract seems to be a legal contract with some performance obligations largely irrevocably automated through the combination of computer code and distributed ledger technology. Yet despite the promise of groundbreaking transformation, such techniques change very little of the reality of business-to-consumer transactions, and indeed, most smart contract use cases concern highly specialised commercial transactions. This more realistic characterisation of smart contracts brings them firmly within the domain of the law of contract and, with that, the imperative of being subject to consumer protection regimes.

The smart contract concept is sometimes merged with the idea of 'algorithmic contracts' (Scholz 2020). Algorithmic contracts use artificial intelligence to automate significant elements of the contracting process, including contract drafting, pricing, formation, management, and enforcement. It seems likely that the more significant changes to be wrought by new technologies on contract law are likely to come not from smart contracts but from the use of algorithmic contracts. Contract automation has been developing for sometime, and the use of increasingly sophisticated large language models produces more nuanced and context-specific automation. AI further makes possible the emergence of contracting agents deployed to represent the interests of each party in this process (European Law Institute 2023: 28). Again, however, the impact of these developments on consumers should not be exaggerated. For consumers, the impact of algorithmic contracts may be a continuation of current trends, whereby a contract is presented as a completed product rather than a relationship (Radin 2012; Leff 1970). Moreover, not only may algorithmic contracting amplify the 'take it or leave it' character of many business-to-consumer transactions, it may change the impact of law as a regulatory mechanism applying to those transactions.

Automation, whether by a smart contract on the blockchain or informed by artificial intelligence in algorithmic contracts, embeds an interpretation of what the law requires (or is likely to enforce) from the perspective of the business utilising the technology. For a consumer, 'code as law' is likely to mean the law of the supplier of goods or services. It may be possible to protect consumers by using this technology to contain the pursuit of the kind of unconstrained business self-interest that leads to poor outcomes for them. However, without public regulation and enforcement, even purportedly consumer-protecting technology may prove to be empty rhetoric.

Section 2 explores the purported tension between innovation and regulation in the context of new technology. Section 3 considers this tension in the domain of crypto-assets. Section 4 considers the related domain of smart contracts. Section 5

---

[2] See e.g., summary of risks from the (Canadian Securities Administrators 2024).

considers the disruptive and regulatory potential of algorithmic contracting. Section 6 discusses the changes these technologies signal for consumers. Section 7 concludes.

2 Innovation, Regulation, and Consumer Protection

In the world of new technology—crypto-assets, distributed ledger technology, smart contracts, and AI—the law, or regulation, is often pitted against innovation and even creativity. Lawrence Lessig, for example, complained, 'Overregulation stifles creativity. It smothers innovation … It wastes the extraordinary opportunity for a democratic creativity that digital technology enables' (Lessig 2005: 151). Lessig is criticising *over*-regulation, which leaves scope for some level of acceptable regulation. However, it seems that for Lessig, legal regulation becomes overreaching quite quickly. Lessig is, of course, a proponent of the idea of smart contract embodying 'code as law' and moving regulation beyond the law into the very architecture of (innovative) technology (Lessig 2000).[3] Sonia Katyal observes that Lessig's single quote encapsulates:

> the union of three presumptive ideals in digital technology—first, the idea that regulation would stifle innovation; second, implicitly, that digital technology ruled by norms, rather than law, was preferable; and third, that digital technology enabled a democratisation of creativity. (Katyal 2021: 864)

This is a convenient and compelling position for those developing technology. Certainly, it influences government approaches so that initiatives to regulate technology are commonly justified by reference to support for innovation. Thus, for example, in the context of artificial intelligence, the (previous) UK government emphasised a proportionate, cohesive, and adaptive approach to regulation in pursuit of a 'pro-innovation framework' (United Kingdom Government Department for Science 2024). As this statement suggests, good regulatory design can support innovation, whereas the alternatives of overly complex, uncertain, or incoherent schemes certainly impede that objective (World Economic Forum 2023).[4] Nonetheless, public regulation may—and in some instances must—prioritise objectives other than an innovation agenda.

Focusing on consumer protection imperatives in contractual settings shows that innovation's benefits are not always widely spread. Innovation often masks the continuation of practices that disadvantage consumers, demonstrating the point that targeted, proportionate regulation is not a trade-off with innovation but necessary to protect consumers' interests. In contracting, automation represents a form of private regulation that determines the norms and standards of the market in question.[5]

[3] See also (Yeung 2019): Discussing the different approaches ranging from blockchain as hostile evasion, efficient alignment, and alleviating transitional friction.

[4] Discussing principles for coordinated coherent crypto-asset regulation in a global context. Also, (PwC Global 2022).

[5] On rule of law concerns with private law making via contract, see (Slawson 1971).

This increases power for private firms operating on a largely unobservable basis. Only public regulation holds any real pretence of mediating against asymmetries of bargaining power and information to preserve consumer interests and doing this in a publicly accountable manner. There are many examples of this tension between the rhetoric of innovation subsequently being used to distract attention from the reality of a need for public regulation. However, in keeping with the themes of this collection, this trend is well demonstrated when considering the domain of crypto-assets, smart contracts, and algorithmic contracting.

3 Crypto-Assets

Crypto-assets are a store of value that can be transferred or exchanged digitally (Government of the United Kingdom 2024), such as crypto coins and non-fungible tokens.[6] Transfers of crypto-asset are typically executed by smart contracts operating on or above[7] a distributed ledger platform (Lim et al. 2016; King & Wood Mallesons 2016b). Distributed ledger technology is effectively a database that stores a record of transactions in a way that is (relatively) decentralised, transparent, and secure (King & Wood Mallesons 2016b; Zhu et al. 2017; Bratanova et al. 2019: 14). The ledger is distributed because the records are stored across many computers, or 'nodes' (Green and Sanitt 2020). The most widely discussed implementation of a distributed ledger is blockchain (Green and Sanitt 2020). In blockchains, the database is organised as a chain of blocks. A block contains a set of transactions, which are encrypted and verified according to the internal requirements of the blockchain (Weldon and Epstein 2019: 848). The block is linked to the blockchain through a cryptographic hash, which has a unique value created by an algorithm following a validation process (Weldon and Epstein 2019: 848).

Agreement on the validation process is determined by a consensus mechanism (Bratanova et al. 2019: 13). In a permissionless blockchain, transactions are validated through 'miners' using an algorithm to perform a complex mathematical equation. In a permissioned blockchain, which is more common in complex financial and commercial transactions, the transaction is validated according to a protocol agreed upon between its members or imposed by the administrators (Bratanova et al. 2019: 13; Low and Mik 2020: 140). Transactions that are validated and entered on a block cannot be altered or deleted (at least not without significant difficulty) because proof of the computation that verified the information is distributed across multiple nodes (Low and Mik 2020: 137; Zetzsche et al. 2018: 1370–1373). Any alternations to a

---

[6] On crypto-asset as property, see (UK Jurisdiction Taskforce, Lawtech Delivery Panel 2019; Law Commission UK 2023; *Tulip Trading Ltd v Bitcoin Association for BSV* 2023; Cf Stevens 2023). The issue was considered but not decided in (*Australian Securities and Investments Commission v Web3 Ventures Pty Ltd* 2024).

[7] See generally (King and Wood Mallesons 2016a): 'A smart contract can be executed "above" the blockchain (where the software program runs outside the blockchain and feeds information to the blockchain) or "on" the blockchain (where the software program is coded into blocks)'.

block can be identified by comparing the hash in the subsequent block (Weldon and Epstein 2019: 849). The information on the block can be viewed generally (permissionless ledger) or by all participants who have permission to do so (permissioned ledger) (Weldon and Epstein 2019: 850).

The promise of crypto-assets, particularly under a permissionless ledger, is in offering decentralised, anonymous, and secure transactions between peers (Government of the United Kingdom 2024). For consumers, this ideal presents as an opportunity to exercise a profound agency in contracting not available in other contexts. In practice that aspiration is typically not realised, with much crypto investing coming closer to the mediated transactions seen in traditional financial markets. Consumers and other investors may invest directly in crypto-assets through decentralised digital wallet exchanges. However, most consumers rely on intermediary services, which provide more accessible and novel ways of crypto-asset investing. Crypto intermediary services include facilitating trades between crypto tokens and fiat money, creating crypto tokens representing conventional financial instruments (King & Wood Mallesons 2023), and providing digital wallet (Maurushat and Halpin 2022: 240), custodian (Sandor 2022), and lending (Duggan 2022) services. Intermediary crypto-asset services have introduced a new level of risk for consumers.

Crypto-assets themselves carry considerable risk, arising from their conceptual complexity, legal uncertainty, and market instability (Joseph Longo 16 October 2023). These risks might be considered a worthwhile trade-off for investors, but this requires them to be well understood. Moreover, the risks of crypto investing include involvement in illegal activity. As explained by the Board of the International Organization of Securities Commissions, the stability of the crypto market is tainted by 'financial crime, fraud, money laundering and other illegal crypto-asset market practices' (The Board of the International Organization of Securities Commissions 2023: 11).

The novelty and complexity of crypto-assets and the multitude of services offered by various intermediaries have raised concerns that consumers may find it difficult to assess the value of the 'assets', the efficacy of the role played by various intermediary services and the products or services that are legitimate 'as opposed to those that are fraudulent or highly speculative to be predatory' (Maurushat and Halpin 2022: 258–259). The Board of the International Organization of Securities Commissions goes further to justify more sustained regulatory attention being given to crypto-asset intermediaries, arguing that:

> those with the largest market share and highest trading volumes, have demonstrated a consistent lack of willingness to comply with applicable regulatory frameworks that seek to achieve investor protection and market integrity outcomes, and in many cases structured their operations in a way to evade such frameworks. (The Board of the International Organization of Securities Commissions 2023: 12)

Indeed, the collapse of FTX, leaving many investors out of pocket, has highlighted the need for robust regulation of intermediaries (Cohen and Godoy 2023; Hanrahan 2022).

These kinds of concerns have led governments in many jurisdictions to seek tighter financial regulation of crypto-asset-based products or services (King & Wood

Mallesons 2023: 5), primarily by bringing them within the remit of financial regulation (King & Wood Mallesons 2023: 5).[8] Thus, in Australia, the financial services regulator, the Australian Securities and Investments Commission, has reiterated its regulatory jurisdiction where a crypto-asset is promoted or sold in Australia and the offer is in substance a financial product or service (ASIC 2021). The Australian Government has signalled more definitive regulatory measures to ensure crypto-asset financial services are subject to existing Australian financial services laws (Commonwealth of Australia 2023). These kinds of measures propel crypto-asset intermediaries into the realm of statutory financial services regulation, accompanied by robust protections for investors and demands for probity, skill, and good governance from service providers (Government of the United Kingdom 2024).

It is increasingly recognised that consumers, or less sophisticated investors, warrant stronger protections in their dealings with crypto-assets and crypto intermediaries (World Economic Forum 2023: 13, 14, 18). In the UK, the Financial Conduct Authority regulates digital asset offerings that resemble investment products. Marketing for financial investment products is required to be fair, clear, and not misleading, and all firms are subject to these general obligations (2023a: para. 2.33). The Financial Conduct Authority considers crypto-assets to be high-risk investments, stating that consumers 'should be prepared to lose all the money they invest' (Financial Conduct Authority 2023b). Consequently, in 2023, the Financial Conduct Authority introduced extended guidance for firms promoting crypto-assets to retail consumers, including requiring: 'clear risk warnings, banning incentives to invest, positive frictions, client categorisation requirements and appropriateness assessments' (2023a).[9]

Complying with these rules may increase costs for firms offering crypto-asset investment services. The Financial Conduct Authority has justified the measures as consistent with the regulatory obligations on firms promoting functionally similar, high-risk investments, as well as to maintain trust in the market. It explains that the approach aims 'to support long-term economic growth in the UK by reducing the instances of loss of trust in financial services caused by customers not fully understanding the risk when purchasing crypto-assets' (Financial Conduct Authority 2023a: para. 1.5). Similarly, the Board of the International Organization of Securities Commissions has recommended more uniform regulation of crypto-asset investment and financial products as 'pivotal to help ensure that any useful innovation can occur without the risk of regulatory arbitrage and lessening standards of investor protection and market integrity' (The Board of the International Organization of Securities Commissions 2023: 11).

The EU has gone further in crypto-asset regulation. Crypto-assets that are financial products are already regulated under financial services regimes such as MiFid II. The

[8] See also (The Board of the International Organization of Securities Commissions 2023: 1): calling for more consistency and cooperation in the regulation of crypto-assets across jurisdictions.

[9] See also (2023a: para. 2.25) explaining that, 'qualifying crypto-assets' are 'any cryptographically secured digital representation of value or contractual rights that are transferable and fungible. They do not include crypto-assets which meet the definition of electronic money or an existing controlled investment'.

Markets in Crypto-Assets Regulation (European Union 2023)[10] aims to provide a legal framework for crypto-assets not covered by existing EU legislation on financial services (Berger and Kalokyris 2023). The regulation enhances consumer protection and market oversight through transparency and disclosure requirements for firms issuing and trading crypto-assets. It also authorises and supervises various crypto-asset service providers (Hallak 2023).

In all of these contexts, regulation is framed as complementing innovation in the crypto-asset market. Nonetheless, the balance has moved from minimal regulation justified by a pro-innovation stance, towards stronger regulatory oversight ensuring more robust consumer protection. What then of the impact of smart contracts on consumer interests?

4 Smart Contracts

Smart contracts have been surrounded by notoriety because of their link to crypto-currencies (Tapscott and Tapscott 2019), and the assertion sometimes made that they render legal enforcement redundant.[11] The purported attractions of smart contracts have attracted attention in commercial (Guilliean Pacheco 2023), regulatory (ASIC 2017) and law reform (UK Jurisdiction Taskforce, Lawtech Delivery Panel 2019) sectors. The essential aspiration of smart contracts is twofold, encompassing 'self-execution' and 'self-enforcement', or perhaps more accurately 'automation' and 'immutability' (Woebbeking 2019: 107–108). Smart contracts consist of instructions for completing aspects of contract performance expressed in computer code (Cieplak and Leefatt 2017) and an assurance that the records of those transactions are transparent and immutable (Poncibó and Dimatteo 2018: 806) through distributed ledger technology (Mik 2017: 276–277).

One of the purported attractions of smart contracts is that automation through computer code increases the efficiency, accuracy, and reliability of the performance obligations in question (King & Wood Mallesons 2016a; Green and Sanitt 2020). Performance automation can reduce the time and cost of completing difficult but routine tasks, as well as increase the transparency and certainty of compliant performance.[12] Farrell et al. explain:

> Efficiency is improved because of the automation of contractual actions, which reduces the need for human involvement and, as a result, the potential for human error. Speed is improved as actions can occur in real-time as information is collected and verified. Performance is improved as the terms are unambiguous and results predictable and auditable. (Farrell et al. 2018)

---

[10] The majority of which came into force in Dec 2024.

[11] See discussion in (De Filippi and Wright 2018). For a critical discussion of this view in (Mark Verstraete 2020: 746; Zou 2020).

[12] See also (Radin 2012): smart contracts also have 'potential to use easily verifiable elements to create incentives to reduce hold-up and other contractual difficulties'.

For example, complex payment calculations that are based on a fluctuating standard, such as CPI or LIBOR, might be made more quickly and accurately through a smart contract than could be done by a human (Lim et al. 2016).

The coupling of automated performance through computer programs with distributed ledger technology also reduces the need for institutional intermediaries to verify a transaction, by providing a secure and transparent record of compliant contract performance (Gans 2019: 1). Consistently, the fields where the potential use of smart contracts have been given most attention (Eaton and Blycha 2017)[13] are those involving payment obligations where real time transaction verification is important. For example, smart contracts have been proposed and utilised in capital and derivative markets (Clements 2018), trade finance (International Swaps and Derivatives Association 2019; SETL 2024 (providing financial services infrastructure, asset management and payment systems); Castillo 2020), shipping (Herd 2019), supply chain (Deloitte n.d.) and in responding to concerns about food security.[14]

The apparent immutability (Low and Mik 2020)[15] of obligations expressed in code and recorded on a distributed ledger platform has led smart contracts to be described as 'self-enforcing' (ISDA and Linklaters 2017) and as an automated 'self-help' mechanism for contracting parties (Poncibó and Dimatteo 2018: 807; Papantoniou 2020). The smart contract concept had its origins in Nick Szabo's 1996 description of 'a set of promises, specified in digital form, including protocols within which the parties perform on these promises' (Szabo 1996). This premise led to assertions of a new kind of contracting which would render redundant traditional reliance on the law for ensuring the security of promises. Under this vision, the smart contract code would ensure performance of the transaction, leading to strong associations between early iterations of smart contracts and the concept of 'code as law' (Lessig 2000; Yeung 2019).[16] As has now been well recognised, this early conception of smart contracts was misconceived (Low and Mik 2020). Whatever the aspiration, smart contracts cannot be perfectly immutable or self-enforcing. This limitation arises because it is simply not possible to code the complexity of a contractual agreement nor insulate contract performance from real-world events.

Smart contract code merely represents a set of instructions about reaching an outcome determined by identified inputs (Lim et al. 2016; ISDA and Linklaters 2017). Instructions expressed in computer code to enable the performance of particular promises are not of themselves a contract (ISDA and Linklaters 2017; ISDA and King & Wood Mallesons 2018). For the coded instructions to be binding in law, they must have some link with a legal contract. For a legally binding contract, there must be a set of terms and conditions that the parties have agreed to in a manner that

[13] DLT commonly known as blockchain technology is driving a new wave of innovation and productivity in the mining industry (Herbert Smith Freehills 2023; Australian National Blockchain 2019 Note: the website is no longer accessible – this is an archived version; Bratanova et al. 2019).

[14] In response to the risks of food fraud: see, e.g., (Smith 2018; Woollacott 2019; IBM 2024).

[15] Commenting that '"Immutability", it turns out, is a surprisingly mutable concept'.

[16] Discussing the different approaches ranging from blockchain as hostile evasion, efficient alignment, and alleviating transitional friction.

satisfies the legal requirements for a valid contract and which are sufficiently certain to be enforced. It is possible that legal status might be given to coded performance instructions through an agreement to incorporate such instructions into the contract or an agreement to embody certain obligations in code. It is also possible that a set of performance instructions embodied in code might be treated as evidence of a prior agreement between the parties to undertake those obligations (Lipton and Levi 2018). However, there are real-world limitations in striving for this fully coded contract goal.

Not all of the terms commonly found in commercial contracts will be capable of being expressed in code to enable automated performance (Lim et al. 2016; Mik 2017: 294) meaning in all but the most straightforward transactions, smart contract code will be necessarily incomplete (Hadfield-Menell and Hadfield 27 January 2019). The kinds of terms that are most conducive to being expressed in code are those that can be reduced to logic statements. This is because coding for automated performance will work best where the obligations in question are deterministic (Green 2018: 237; ISDA and Linklaters 2017; Lim et al. 2016). As already observed, one of the prime use cases for smart contract technology is in qualifying and processing payments obligations requiring complex calculations (Zhu et al. 2017: 5–6; Cieplak and Leefatt 2017: 417–418; ISDA and Linklaters 2017: 10). These kinds of transactions can be expressed in a linear form, such as: if X event occurs, then calculate *Y and transfer $*Y from A to B. Other possibilities are the transfer of assets in return for payment, which again can be expressed as: if $Y is paid to A, then transfer X to B. These sort of instructions affect performance but do not cover the range of rights and obligations typically addressed in a functional contract.

Contracts for more than immediate exchanges are typically incomplete. Contracting parties cannot foresee and draft responses to every contingency that may affect performance *of* their agreement (MacNeil 2020: 112–120). For this reason, contracting parties commonly rely on a variety of contractual devices that provide flexibility in ongoing performance and allow the parties an element of discretion over how the contact is to be performed (Sklaroff 2017). This is the function of terms that rely on open-textured standards or some element of judgement, such as requirements of 'satisfactory' or 'merchantable quality', 'reasonableness', or 'good faith' (Lim et al. 2016; ISDA and Linklaters 2017: 11). The decisions required to give content to these kinds of terms go beyond the simple 'if–then' statements that can be expressed in code.

This reality of the limitations of drafting complete contracts, means that smart contracts for the immediate time being will be expressed as a combination of natural language and computer code (Farrell et al. 2018). Thus, while the smart contract terminology continues to be used in a variety of ways (Government of the United Kingdom 2024), 'smart legal contract' (UK Jurisdiction Taskforce, Lawtech Delivery Panel 2019: 31 [136])[17] is now often used to refer to a legally enforceable natural language contract which has discrete aspects of performance embodied in computer

[17] 'We do not think it is a good reason for treating smart contracts as being different in principle from conventional contracts'.

code within a distributed ledger (Lim et al. 2016; King & Wood Mallesons 2016a, b). In other words, as described by Farrell et al., for a smart legal contract a '"digital" strand has to be blended with an "analogue" strand' (King & Wood Mallesons 2016b). Or as described by Cheng et al., 'there should be a dumb contract between the parties, in the form of a "legal wrapper" which sets out terms of the contract which are not deterministic and not suitable for execution through the smart contract' (Lim et al. 2016; King & Wood Mallesons 2016b). The natural language contract is required to compensate for the vagaries of code and to encompass the discretionary and open-textured provisions that allow all but the most immediate contracts to respond to the contingencies that inevitably affect performance.

The self-executing capacity of smart contracts is also limited by the need for an external trigger for the performance obligations facilitated by code (Lim et al. 2016; King & Wood Mallesons 2016b). As we have seen, the blockchains and other distributed ledgers to which smart contracts are linked are primarily databases. They may record and transfer crypto-assets but they do not of themselves contain or move real assets. This happens in the real world. Accordingly, the performance of a smart contract will in most cases be dependent on events external to the distributed ledger on which it operates (Low and Mik 2020: 146). The performance trigger for a smart contract may be built into the smart contract program, such as where the instruction is simply to direct the payment of money on a particular date. In many cases, the trigger for automated performance will relate to a contingent event, such as a change in interest rates, a floor in the market, the transfer of an asset, or the loading of goods on a ship. In some instances, these processes may be digitised so as to allow the automatic transfer of the relevant information to the smart contract program. In other instances, they will rely on the actions of the parties or their agents. For example, in a supply chain transaction, there will necessarily be human involvement in inspecting, loading, and unloading goods (Deloitte n.d.).

The occurrence of these contingent events will need to be verified before the automated execution of performance obligations triggered by these occurrences, such as payment or the release of title documents. Verification may be provided by one of the parties, a third party, or a computer program sometimes known as an 'oracle', that provides the smart contract code with instructions that the conditions precedent to automated performance have been satisfied (Zhu et al. 2017: 33; Lipton and Levi 2018; Collao and Winship 2019: 749). Regardless of the mechanism, it is apparent that there will usually be numerous points in a transaction where the self-contained ecosystem of a smart contract will be reliant on the verification of external, or 'off chain', events.

This necessity for discretionary or open-ended contract terms expressed in natural language, and the inevitability of performance being dependent on external triggers, means smart contracts cannot be entirely self-executing (Zetzsche et al. 2018). Additionally, even coded performance obligations may be disrupted by disagreement between the parties. Parties may find the code does not execute as expected, they may have different views about what is required by the natural language elements of their transaction or one of them may hold up the input needed to trigger the automated performance. Thus, even assuming the legal validity of the contract, performance flexability and effective use of oracles, the automated performance obligations will not be fully guaranteed, and contractual disputes may still arise (Poncibó and Dimatteo 2018: 807; Lim et al. 2016). The weak links in smart contract execution remain language, humans, and unforeseen events (Gans 2019: 2).

There are technical and contractual responses to these uncertainties. To allow for the possibility that the contract may not work as expected or be disrupted by external events, legal commentators often advise parties to build into the very architecture of their smart contract 'a method for relieving the contract from the constraints of [the blockchain] technology' that renders it otherwise immutable (Farrell et al. 2018: 5; ISDA and King & Wood Mallesons 2018: 17–18). Thus, Cheng Lim argues that smart contracts should contain a fail-safe override mechanism (Lim et al. 2016). This fail-safe might, for example, involve a mechanism for reversing a transfer of assets, amending the smart contract code or utilising 'off ramps' that allow parties to exit the automated process of performance where circumstances change or the law demands (Farrell et al. 2018: 6). Somewhat similarly, Schmitz and Rule suggest that smart contract code should be designed to include resort to redress systems, primarily online dispute resolution, which may have particular compatibility with the aspirations of smart contracts (Schmitz and Rule 2019: 112). Such a mechanism might, for example, 'freeze' performance should a dispute arise and upload information to an online dispute resolution platform (Schmitz and Rule 2019: 116).[18] For these technical 'override' mechanisms to work as intended there needs to be a way of triggering their intervention. This will necessarily sit in the natural language contract. Notably, this response firmly places the smart contract code as an adjunct to the natural language contract, as opposed to being a contractual element of equal status. This in turn undermines the promise of the smart contact to ensure the immutability of transacting, as the code automating performance remains contingent on human decisions to allow them to continue to run as programmed (Low and Mik 2020: 143).

What do these insights into the pre-eminence of the written contract over code in a smart (legal) contract mean for contracting consumers? Primarily, it means that consumers need to be aware of the gap between the promise and the hype. The fragility of smart contracts certainly raises risks for those who believe them to be immutable and infallible. However, other than in relation to crypto-assets, there are currently very few applications of smart contracts embedded in or likely to affect consumer transactions. Additionally, these insights confirm that, to the extent smart contracts are legal contracts, they are subject to the law of contract and consumer protection regimes. Code on a blockchain may, in a practical sense, be beyond the reach of courts. However, the features already described—the need for a natural language contract to which the smart contract automated performance obligations apply and the need for interventions to trigger performance by an oracle—provide multiple touch points for the law to intervene to correct or dictate the parties' contemplated performance arrangements (Green 2018). In this field, 'the existing body of law can

[18] Discussing the provider 'Sagewise'.

be meaningfully adapted to deal with the situation at hand' (*Quoine Pte Ltd v B2C2 Ltd* 2020: para. 79). Perhaps the more significant changes to be wrought by new technologies on consumer contracts is likely to come, not from smart contracts, but from another, albeit related, source.

5 Algorithmic Contracts

While the idea of smart contracts has attracted considerable attention, arguably the most impactful developments on consumer contracts are occurring in regard to what are sometimes termed 'algorithmic' contracts (Scholz 2020: 128). Scholz describes algorithmic contracts as 'contracts in which one or more parties use an algorithm to determine whether to be bound or how to be bound' (Scholz 2020: 134). This possibility effectively envisages AI as a dynamic contracting tool, adjusting contract price/risk combinations according to preset parameters. It is possible to envisage even more nuanced and personalised operations. Scholz envisages the possibility of 'a computer program [that] customises terms in a contract based on real-time availability of the product or buyer characteristics' (Scholz 2020: 141). Here the AI agent represented by the algorithmic contract might be reviewing terms to identify those most suitable for a transaction including, in consumer contexts, by taking into account their objectives, budget and tolerance for risk.

These possibilities may seem far-fetched. However, advances in machine learning, natural language processing, foundational models, and generative AI have already significantly transformed contracting practices (Sears 2019; Robaldo et al. 2019). The possiblities of algorithmic contracting with next generation agentic AI go well beyond the AI tools for predicting the outcome of certain kinds of litigation (Thompson 2019) or recidivism for the purposes of sentencing (Eckhouse 2017) that have received the most attention in the media. Contracting parties and their lawyers are already making use of digital technologies based on expert systems and predictive modelling to assist with contract preparation, review, management, aspects of performance, and dispute resolution (Thomson Reuters 2023). Increasingly, algorithms may inform contract offer and acceptances (Mik 2022b), with discrete uses already evidenced in high-frequency trading and in online differential pricing (Scholz 2020). In other contexts, dispute resolution is at least partially managed through automated systems (Tan 2019; Cortes 2011; Rabinovich-Einy 2006; Thiessen and McMahon Jr 1999). Online platforms such as Amazon (2024), eBay (2024), PayPal (2024), and Alibaba (2024) provide their own, online-automated dispute resolution systems for common kinds of low-value dispute.

The next stage in this trend of AI automated elements of contract practice may be highly personalised contracts in otherwise 'off the shelf' or standard form transacting contexts. It is possible to envisage contracts being produced to adapt to the circumstances of individual transactions by generating new content for any given prompt scenario based on a large body of training data. Predictive analysis using machine learning already allows differential pricing in contracts, with prices tailored to the characteristics of different cohorts. With the addition of generative AI, algorithmic contracts may be producing different terms across cohorts or refining the price/ risk trade-off in a more fine-grained way than currently exists for non-negotiated transactions.

The overall impact of algorithmic contracting on consumers is difficult to assess. Algorithmic contracts may reduce the cost to consumers, particularly in low-value transactions. Currently, consumers typically do not closely review the terms of the contracts they enter into, beyond the salient features such as price, delivery, and payment requirements. Thus, consumers may benefit from a better fit of prices and terms to their circumstances. However, this benefit is not inevitable, and is dependent on who controls the technology. Additionally there is a risk that algorithmic contracts may amplify existing problematic trends, such as discriminatory treatment in certain markets (Bednarz and Manwaring 2021: 455) and predatory pricing in others (Paterson et al. 2021). Personalisation in contracts and other kinds of automated decision-making may also impede the oversight of regulators and consumer advocates by making systemic trends harder to identify (Willis 2020). This is why transparency in the design, deployment, and performance of such systems is central to demands for responsible AI, both as a matter of ethical practice and, increasingly, legal regulation (Paterson 2023). Additionally, it is possible that the innovation associated with algorithmic contracting will shift both the role of relationship in contracting and the public character of regulation.

6 Algorithmic Contracts, AI Agents and Contractual Relationships

Smart and algorithmic contracting may have an effect on our understanding of the interpersonal relationships that are sometimes said to underlie the real, as opposed to the paper, deal of the contract (Mik 2022a: 100). The insights of relational contract theories have been to highlight the role of extra-legal values in successful contractual relationships. In many kinds of transactions, the parties use legal contracts as a framework for their transaction but manage the day-to-day interactions with a considerable degree of trust, cooperation, and flexibility that is not captured in the terms of the documented contractual obligations (Levy 2017; Wheeler 2017). The use of distributed ledger technology is sometimes said to remove the need for trust between the parties to a smart contract (Green and Sanitt 2020). It has been propounded as a 'trustless' transaction (Green 2018: 236). Under this vision, parties do not need to rely on reciprocal trusting realtionships to ensure the successful performance of their contract. Rather they can trust in the certainty of performance ensured by automation on a secure system,which is transparent and searchable (Green 2018: 236).[19]

These aspirations are also apparent in algorithmic contracts, which, through automating contract formation, preparation, and oversight, reduce the need for human

[19] Citing (Dewey and Amuial 2015).

oversight and interaction in these processes. Automation, therefore, changes the character of the 'classical' contractual relationship, replacing it with a technological process. Trust in contracting traditionally refers to trust in a contracting partner backed up by the instrument of the state in lending its power to enforce contracts. Trust comes from a relationship. As aspects of contracting are automated, trust in the contractual relationship, with a shared degree of interest and cooperation, becomes trust in a technological process. It might be questioned if this even remains a form of trust.

Philippa Ryan describes smart contracts on a blockchain as creating new concepts of automated or artificial trust (Ryan 2019: chap.13). Sally Wheeler ponders whether trust in people and relationships will be transformed into trust in technology, a form of trust without communicative social relations (Wheeler 2017: 608). DeMatteo and Poncibo predict new kinds of trust placed on coders and oracles to give integrity to the transaction (Poncibó and Dimatteo 2018: 822). Commenting on the rise of automation in contracting, Brownsword predicts a move towards what he characterises as 'technological management' (Brownsword 2019: 23; Cf Gans 2019: 2). These descriptions capture the idea that as contracting parties rely on innovative new technologies to support contract performance, this technology does more than merely automate aspects of the contract lifecycle. Technological processes replace the rules that make up the law, even in so far as they purport to apply the law. Moreover, they also replace the more human-centred mechanisms that hold contracts together, such as relationship, reputation, or even taking a hard line in negotiations or renegotiation.

In business-to-consumer contracts the effect of this change should not be exaggerated. For consumers, the element of relationship has long gone from most kinds of contracts; a forced trust in automated processes is already the reality. There is not a lot of nuance, human intervention, or relationship in most business-to-consumer contracts. Standard-form contracts are common. Effectively, such transactions are already automated since they are formed online and managed by employees with little discretion to depart from the terms imposed. A number of commentators have observed that standard-form contracts no longer come close to resembling the paradigm of consensual exchange as understood by classical contract theory (Radin 2012; Leff 1970). Consumers do not make contracts; they are offered contracts as products or artefacts of the market (Radin 2012; Leff 1970).

None of this changes with algorithmic contracts. Certainly, unlike traditional standard-form contracts, algorithmic contracts may be personalised to the contemplated transaction. There may be variations of price and terms according to the identified relevant attributes of the contracting consumer. However, like a standard-form contract, business-to-consumer algorithmic contracts will largely be presented rather than negotiated. Greater levels of automation across the contract life cycle further distance humans from the contract. Indeed, the human consumer may largely be removed from the process as smart objects or agentic AI chatbots initiate contractual transactions on behalf of the consumer, such as already seen in smart printers and fridges restocking items running low (Mik 2020). Despite an element of personalisation, therefore, the growth in investment in legal automation, whether by smart or algorithmic contracts, might be seen as a further continuation of the trend of commodifying consumer standard-form contracts. Indeed, this process may be seen as an *uber*-commodification of contract, which amplifies the reality of contract as a product, not a relationship and increases the distance between consumer-facing standard-form contracts and the textbook model of the negotiated, relationship-driven contract. It is also very far from the original vision of the smart contract as decentralised peer-to-peer transacting.[20]

It is possible that AI will enable new intermediary services that help rebalance the information asymmetries in business-to-consumer transactions. For example, the same tools used by firms for contract drafting and review might be developed for consumers to identify and avoid unfair terms or misleading representations, effectively complementing the work of regulators. The European Law Institute has considered the possibility of algorithmic agents, via agentic AI, that review contract prices and terms on behalf of the consumers that deploy them (European Law Institute 2023: 18; Busch et al., 2025). Regardless, however, these kinds of intermediary services will influence the balance between regulation and innovation.

The use of technology to select, assess, and conclude consumer contracts represents Brownsword's concept of technological management. In this context, technological managerialism represents a form of privatised regulation (Katyal 2021). The choices made by those designing the technology will determine how consumers understand and respond to their contractual rights, and how those legal rights are interpreted in the context of particular contracts. In other words, the technology will frame the scope and content of the contract experienced by consumers. This would suggest that even the emergence of AI agents to review and conclude contracts for consumers is not akin to the work of public regulators. Public regulators inevitably represent a different balance of values and interests in overseeing consumer contracts, the capacity to monitor market trends, and a commitment to safeguarding the interests of consumers experiencing vulnerability. Thus, regulatory oversight of algorithmic agents will be a necessary response to this kind of innovation, notwithstanding its apparently beneficial aspiration to support the decision-making agency of contracting parties.

7 Conclusion

Crypto-assets continue to evolve even without widespread acceptance of their worth and with increasing levels of regulation. The trajectory of their associated technology, smart contracts, is difficult to predict, especially given the real limitations on the promise of immutable, self-executing performance. However, for many, the ambition to comprehensive automation in contracting that characterises smart contracts

[20] The trend is not uniform. Notably, digital technology has facilitated other kinds of contractual relationships. Facebook marketplace and eBay have made peer-to-peer transactions involving the sale of second-hand goods on a scale possible.

remains 'on-trend'. In this regard, the more significant impact on contracting practice is likely to come from the use of AI-informed automation, or algorithmic contracts, influencing in particular the way in which contracts are made and managed. The outcome of such developments may be a kind of hyper-commodification of the contract, in which relational values are significantly reduced. However, for consumers, this chapter has suggested that the impacts of these trends are less significant than might at first appear. This is because most consumer contracts are already far from the relational paradigm and, for the majority of cases, highly standardised. Contract automation may introduce greater personalisation but not necessarily more bargaining power for consumers. Consumers' experience of contracting will be determined by the interests of those who deploy the technology. Even the introduction of AI agents acting for contracting consumers may not change this one-sided relationship. It has accordingly been suggested that despite the apparent attractions of smart and algorithmic contracts, the public regulatory regime for consumer protection should not cede its ground to the technological management implicit in these forms of innovation.

References

Alibaba Public Jury (2024) Alibaba Public Jury (大众评审), http://pan.taobao.com/. Accessed 21 Nov 2024

Amazon (2024) Buyer Dispute Program, Amazon, https://pay.amazon.com/help/201751580. Accessed 21 Nov 2024

ASIC (2017) Evaluating Distributed Ledger Technology (Information Sheet No 219), ASIC, https://asic.gov.au/regulatory-resources/digital-transformation/evaluating-distributed-ledger-technology/. Accessed 21 Nov 2024.

ASIC (2021) Crypto-assets (Information Sheet No 225), ASIC, https://asic.gov.au/regulatory-resources/digital-transformation/crypto-assets/. Accessed 21 Nov 2024

Australian National Blockchain (2019) Australian National Blockchain, Australian National Blockchain, https://web.archive.org/web/20190305125725/https://www.australiannationalblockchain.com/. Accessed 21 Nov 2024

Australian Securities and Investments Commission v Web3 Ventures Pty Ltd [2024] FCA 64

Bednarz Z, Manwaring K (2021) Keeping the (Good) faith: implications of emerging technologies for consumer insurance contracts. Sydney Law Review 43(4):455–487

Berger PE and Kalokyris N (2023) MiCA & TFR: the two new pillars of the EU crypto-assets regulatory framework, DLA Piper, https://www.dlapiper.com/en-au/insights/publications/2023/06/mica-tfr-the-two-new-pillars-of-the-eu-cryptoassets-regulatory-framework. Accessed 21 Nov 2024

Blockchain Council (2023) What are Peer-to-Peer Transactions?, Blockchain Council, https://www.blockchain-council.org/blockchain/what-are-peer-to-peer-transactions/. Accessed 21 Nov 2024

Bratanova A, Devaraj D, Horton J, Naughtin C, Kloester B, Trinh K, Weber I and Dawson D (2019) Blockchain 2030: A Look at the Future of Blockchain in Australia, CSIRO, http://rgdoi.net/10.13140/RG.2.2.22133.42720. Accessed 21 Nov 2024

Brownsword R (2019) Regulatory fitness: fintech, funny money, and smart contracts. European Business Organization Law Review 20(1):5–27. https://doi.org/10.1007/s40804-019-00134-2

Busch C, Sørensen MJ, de las Heras Ballell TR, Twigg-Flesner C (2025) Towards the next generation of consumer law: the ELI guiding principles and model rules on digital assistants for consumer contracts. Journal European Consumer and Market Law 14(3):89–91

Canadian Securities Administrators (2024) Recognizing Crypto Risks, Canadian Securities Administrators, https://www.securities-administrators.ca/investor-tools/crypto-assets/recognizing-crypto-risks/. Accessed 21 Nov 2024

Castillo M del (2020) Citi, Goldman Sachs Conduct First Blockchain Equity Swap On Ethereum-Inspired Platform, Forbes, https://www.forbes.com/sites/michaeldelcastillo/2020/02/06/citi-goldman-sachs-conduct-first-blockchain-equity-swap-on-ethereum-inspired-platform/. Accessed 21 Nov 2024

Cieplak J, Leefatt S (2017) "Smart contracts": a smart way to automate performance. Georgetown Law Technology Review 1:414

Clements R (2018) Evaluating the costs and benefits of a smart contract blockchain framework for credit default swaps. William & Mary Business Law Review 10:369

Cohen L and Godoy J (2023) Sam Bankman-Fried convicted of multi-billion dollar FTX fraud, Reuters, https://www.reuters.com/legal/ftx-founder-sam-bankman-fried-thought-rules-did-not-apply-him-prosecutor-says-2023-11-02/. Accessed 21 Nov 2024

Collao VV, Winship V (2019) The new ICO intermediaries. Italian Law Journal 5:731

Commonwealth of Australia (2023) Regulating Digital Asset Platforms. Commonwealth of Australia, https://treasury.gov.au/sites/default/files/2023-10/c2023-427004-proposal-paper-finalised.pdf.

Cortes P (2011) Online Dispute Resolution for Consumers in the European Union. Routledge, Abingdon, Oxon New York, N.Y, https://doi.org/10.4324/9780203847756

De Filippi P, Wright A (2018) Blockchain and the law: the rule of code. Harvard University Press, Cambridge, MA London

Deloitte (n.d.) How Blockchain Can Reshape Trade Finance, Deloitte, https://www2.deloitte.com/content/dam/Deloitte/global/Documents/grid/trade-finance-placemat.pdf

Dewey J and Amuial S (2015) What is a Smart Contract, Bloomberg Law, https://web.archive.org/web/20220123225508/https://news.bloomberglaw.com/business-and-practice/what-is-a-smart-contract/

Duggan W (2022) Crypto Lending: Earn Money From Your Crypto Holdings, Forbes Advisor, https://www.forbes.com/advisor/investing/cryptocurrency/crypto-lending/. Accessed 21 Nov 2024

Eaton E and Blycha N (2017) Distributed Ledger Technology (DLT): DLT commonly known as blockchain technology is driving a new wave of innovation and productivity in the mining industry, Herbert Smith Freehills, https://www.herbertsmithfreehills.com/insights/2017-08/distributed-ledger-technology-dlt-dlt-commonly-known-as-blockchain-technology-is. Accessed 21 Nov 2024

eBay (2024) Resolution Centre, eBay, https://resolutioncentre.ebay.com.au/. Accessed 21 Nov 2024

Eckhouse L (2017) Big data may be reinforcing racial bias in the criminal justice system, Washington Post, https://www.washingtonpost.com/opinions/big-data-may-be-reinforcing-racial-bias-in-the-criminal-justice-system/2017/02/10/d63de518-ee3a-11e6-9973-c5efb7ccfb0d_story.html. Accessed 21 Nov 2024

European Law Institute (2023) EU Consumer Law and Automated Decision Making.

European Union (2023) Regulation (EU) 2023/1114 of the European Parliament and of the Council of 31 May 2023 on markets in crypto-assets, and amending Regulations (EU) No 1093/2010 and (EU) No 1095/2010 and Directives 2013/36/EU and (EU) 2019/1937, European Union, https://eur-lex.europa.eu/eli/reg/2023/1114/oj

Farrell S, Machin H, Hinchliffe R (2018) Lost and found in smart contract translation considerations in transitioning to automation in legal architecture. Journal of International Banking Law Regulation 33:24

Financial Conduct Authority (2023a) Finalised Non handbook Guidance on Cryptoasset Financial Promotions

Financial Conduct Authority (2023b) Guidance for crypto firms to help them comply with marketing rules, Financial Conduct Authority, https://www.fca.org.uk/news/news-stories/guidance-crypto-firms-help-them-comply-marketing-rules. Accessed 21 Nov 2024

Gans J (2019) The Fine Print in Smart Contracts. National Bureau of Economic Research, Cambridge, MA. https://doi.org/10.3386/w25443

Government of the United Kingdom (2024) Economic Crime and Corporate Transparency Act 2023: Factsheets, GOV.UK, https://www.gov.uk/government/publications/economic-crime-and-corporate-transparency-act-2023-factsheets. Accessed 21 Nov 2024

Green S (2018) Smart Contracts: Interpretation and Rectification. Lloyd's Maritime and Commercial Law Quarterly 2018:234–251

Green S and Sanitt A (2020) Smart Contracts. In: Davies PS Raczynska M (eds) Contents of Commercial Contracts: Terms Affecting Freedoms, Hart studies in private law, Hart, Oxford

Guilliean Pacheco (2023) 10 examples of smart contracts on blockchain, Search CIO, https://www.techtarget.com/searchcio/feature/Examples-of-smart-contracts-on-blockchain, accessed 21 Nov 2024

Hadfield-Menell D and Hadfield GK (27 January 2019) Incomplete Contracting and AI Alignment. In: Proceedings of the 2019 AAAI/ACM Conference on AI, Ethics, and Society, AIES '19: AAAI/ACM Conference on AI, Ethics, and Society, ACM, Honolulu HI USA, https://doi.org/10.1145/3306618.3314250

Hallak I (2023) Markets in crypto-assets (MiCA). European Parliamentary Research Service, https://www.europarl.europa.eu/RegData/etudes/BRIE/2022/739221/EPRS_BRI(2022)739221_EN.pdf

Hanrahan P (2022) How FTX Australia was able to claim it was 'ASIC-licenced'. The Conversation, http://theconversation.com/how-ftx-australia-was-able-to-claim-it-was-asic-licenced-196361. Accessed 21 Nov 2024.

Herbert Smith Freehills (2023) Blockchain and Digital Assets, Herbert Smith Freehills, https://web.archive.org/web/20230324032316/https://www.herbertsmithfreehills.com/our-expertise/services/blockchain-and-digital-assets. Accessed 21 Nov 2024

Herd JM (2019) Blocks of lading. QUT Law Review 18(2):306. https://doi.org/10.5204/qutlr.v18i2.755

IBM (2024) IBM Supply Chain Intelligence Suite—Food Trust, IBM, https://www.ibm.com/products/supply-chain-intelligence-suite/food-trust. Accessed 21 Nov 2024

International Swaps and Derivatives Association (2019) Digital Asset and ISDA Introduce Tool to Help Drive Adoption of ISDA CDM, ISDA, https://www.isda.org/2019/04/09/digital-asset-and-isda-introduce-tool-to-help-drive-adoption-of-isda-cdm. Accessed 21 Nov 2024

ISDA and King & Wood Mallesons (2018) Smart Derivatives Contracts: From Concept to Construction

ISDA and Linklaters (2017) Smart Contracts and Distributed Ledger—A Legal Perspective

Joseph Longo (16 October 2023) Crypto-assets: The case for strong regulation and enforcement. Australian Financial Review (AFR) Cryptocurrency Summit.

Katyal SK (2021) Lex reformatica: five principles of policy reform for the technological age. Berkeley Tech Law Journal 36:861

King & Wood Mallesons (2016a) 10 points... on financial market smart contracts, King & Wood Mallesons, https://www.kwm.com/content/dam/kwm/media/library/Files/Knowledge/Insights/au/2016/06/30/smart-contracts-briefsheet-10-things.pdf

King & Wood Mallesons (2016b) How to use humans to make "smart contracts" truly smart, King & Wood Mallesons, https://www.kwm.com/content/kwm/au/en/insights/latest-thinking/smart-contracts-open-source-model-dna-digital-analogue-human.html. Accessed 21 Nov 2024

King & Wood Mallesons (2023) Not by the same token—Treasury releases its Token Mapping consultation, King & Wood Mallesons, https://www.kwm.com/content/kwm/au/en/insights/latest-thinking/not-by-the-same-token-treasury-releases-its-token-mapping-consultation.html. Accessed 21 Nov 2024

Larsen S (2023) Embracing Collaboration Over Isolation: Navigating The Shift In Global Cryptocurrency Regulations, Forbes, https://www.forbes.com/sites/digital-assets/2023/10/08/embracing-collaboration-over-isolation-navigating-the-shift-in-global-cryptocurrency-regulations/. Accessed 21 Nov 2024

Law Commission UK (2023) Digital Assets: Final Report

Leff AA (1970) Contract as thing. Am Univ Law Rev 19:131

Lessig L (2000) Code: and other laws of cyberspace. Basic Books, New York

Lessig L (2005) Free culture: how big media uses technology and the law to lock down culture and control creativity. Penguin Books, New York, NY, Reprint

Levy KEC (2017) Book-Smart Not Street-Smart: Blockchain-Based Smart Contracts and the Social Workings of Law. Engaging Science, Technology, and Society 3:1–15. https://doi.org/10.17351/ests2017.107

Lim C, Saw T and Sargeant C (2016) Smart Contracts: Bridging the Gap Between Expectation and Reality, Oxford Business Law Blog, https://blogs.law.ox.ac.uk/business-law-blog/blog/2016/07/smart-contracts-bridging-gap-between-expectation-and-reality

Lipton A and Levi S (2018) An Introduction to Smart Contracts and Their Potential and Inherent Limitations. The Harvard Law School Forum on Corporate Governance, https://corpgov.law.harvard.edu/2018/05/26/an-introduction-to-smart-contracts-and-their-potential-and-inherent-limitations/. Accessed 21 Nov 2024

Low KFK, Mik E (2020) Pause the blockchain legal revolution. International and Comparative Law Quarterly 69(1):135–175. https://doi.org/10.1017/S0020589319000502

MacNeil I (2020) Company Law Rules: An Assessment from the Perspective of Incomplete Contract Theory' (2001). J Corp Law Stud 1(1):107

Maurushat A and Halpin D (2022) Investigation of Cryptocurrency Enabled and Dependent Crimes. In Goldbarsht D, De Koker L (eds) Financial Technology and the Law, Law, Governance and Technology Series, Springer International Publishing, Cham, https://doi.org/10.1007/978-3-030-88036-1_10

Mik E (2017) Smart contracts: terminology, technical limitations and real world complexity. Law Innov Technol 9(2):269–300. https://doi.org/10.1080/17579961.2017.1378468

Mik E (2020) The disappearing computer: consent and disclosure in the world of smart objects. European Journal of Consumer Law 3:567. https://doi.org/10.2139/ssrn.3732677

Mik E (2022a) Smart Contracts: Tales of Trust and Certainty. Technology and Regulation, 100–112, https://doi.org/10.26116/TECHREG.2022.010

Mik E (2022b) Much Ado about Artificial Intelligence or: the Automation of Contract Formation. International Journal of Law and Information Technology 30(4):484–506. https://doi.org/10.1093/ijlit/eaad004

Papantoniou AA (2020) Smart Contracts in the New Era of Contract Law. Digital Law Journal 1(4):8–24. https://doi.org/10.38044/2686-9136-2020-1-4-8-24

Paterson J (2023) Misleading AI: Regulatory Strategies for Algorithmic Transparency in Technologies Augmenting Consumer Decision-Making. Loyola Consumer Law Review 34(Symposium): 558

Paterson J, Bush G, Miller T (2021) Transparency to contest differential pricing. Journal for the Australian and New Zealand Societies for Computers and the Law 13:93

PayPal (2024) Manage Customer Concerns, Disputes & Chargebacks, PayPal, https://www.paypal.com/au/webapps/mpp/customer-concerns. Accessed 21 Nov 2024

Poncibó C, Dimatteo LA (2018) Quandary of smart contracts and remedies: the role of contract law and self-help remedies. European Review of Private Law 26(6):805–824. https://doi.org/10.54648/ERPL2018056

PwC Global (2022) Crypto Regulation Report 2023

Quoine Pte Ltd v B2C2 Ltd [2020] 2 SLR 20

Rabinovich-Einy O (2006) Technology's impact: the quest for a new paradigm for accountability in mediation. Harvard Negotiation Law Review 11:253

Radin MJ (2012) Boilerplate: The Fine Print, Vanishing Rights, and the Rule of Law, 1st edn. Princeton University Press, Princeton

Robaldo L, Villata S, Wyner A and Grabmair M (2019) Introduction for Artificial Intelligence and Law: Special Issue ? Natural Language Processing for Legal Texts? Artificial Intelligence and Law 27(2):113–115, https://doi.org/10.1007/s10506-019-09251-2

Ryan P (2019) Trust and Distrust in Digital Economies. Routledge, Abingdon, Oxon ; New York, NY

Sandor K (2022) What Is Crypto Custody? CoinDesk, https://www.coindesk.com/learn/what-is-crypto-custody/. Accessed 21 Nov 2024

Schmitz A and Rule C (2019) Online dispute resolution for smart contracts. Online Journal of Dispute Resolution 103

Scholz LH (2020) Algorithms and Contract Law. In W Barfield (ed) The Cambridge Handbook of the Law of Algorithms, Cambridge Law Handbooks, Cambridge University Press.

Sears M (2019) AI Challenges And Why Legal Is A Great Place To Kick-Start Great NLP, Forbes, https://www.forbes.com/sites/marksears1/2019/05/14/ai-challenges-and-why-legal-is-a-great-place-to-kick-start-great-nlp/. Accessed 21 Nov 2024

SETL (2024) SETL—Powering digital finance, SETL, https://setl.io/. Accessed 21 Nov 2024

Sklaroff JM (2017) Smart contracts and the cost of inflexibility. Univ Pa Law Rev 166:263

Slawson WD (1971) Standard form contracts and democratic control of lawmaking power. Harv Law Rev 84:529–566

Smith M (2018) Blackmores on board as Alibaba tests blockchain in Australian fake food clampdown, Australian Financial Review, https://www.afr.com/companies/retail/blackmores-on-board-as-alibaba-tests-blockchain-in-australian-fake-food-clampdown-20180426-h0zawl. Accessed 21 Nov 2024

Stevens R (2023) Crypto is not property. Law Quarterly Review 139:615. https://doi.org/10.2139/ssrn.4416200

Szabo N (1996) Smart contracts: building blocks for digital markets, phonetic Sciences, Amsterdam, https://www.fon.hum.uva.nl/rob/Courses/InformationInSpeech/CDROM/Literature/LOTwinterschool2006/szabo.best.vwh.net/smart_contracts_2.html. Accessed 21 Nov 2024

Tan V (2019) Online dispute resolution for small civil claims in victoria: a new paradigm in civil justice. Deakin Law Review 24:101–138. https://doi.org/10.21153/dlr2019vol24no1art873

Tapscott D and Tapscott A (2019) Blockchain revolution: how the technology behind Bitcoin and other cryptocurrencies is changing the world. Penguin Business, UK.

The Board of the International Organization of Securities Commissions (2023) Policy Recommendations for Crypto and Digital Asset Markets

Thiessen EM, McMahon JP Jr (1999) Beyond win-win in cyberspace. Journal on Dispute Resolution 15:643

Thompson B (2019) Big data: legal firms play 'Moneyball'. Financial Times, https://www.ft.com/content/ca351ff6-1a4e-11e9-9e64-d150b3105d21. Accessed 21 Nov 2024

Thomson Reuters (2023) Tech & the Law 2023 Report: Perceptions and Priorities, Thomson Reuters Legal Insight, https://insight.thomsonreuters.com.au/legal/resources/resource/tech-and-the-law-2023. Accessed 21 Nov 2024

Tulip Trading Ltd v Bitcoin Association for BSV [2023] 4 WLR 16

UK Jurisdiction Taskforce, Lawtech Delivery Panel (2019) Legal Statement on Cryptoassets and Smart Contracts

United Kingdom Government Department for Science (2024) A pro-innovation approach to AI regulation: government response, GOV.UK, https://www.gov.uk/government/consultations/ai-regulation-a-pro-innovation-approach-policy-proposals/outcome/a-pro-innovation-approach-to-ai-regulation-government-response. Accessed 21 Nov 2024

Verstraete M (2020) The stakes of smart contracts. Loyola University Chicago Law Journal 50:743

Weldon MN and Epstein R (2019) Beyond Bitcoin: Leveraging Blockchain to Benefit Business and Society. Trans Tenn J Bus L 20:837

Wheeler S (2017) Modelling the contracts of the future. Griffith Law Review 26(4):593–614. https://doi.org/10.1080/10383441.2017.1552547
Willis LE (2020) Deception by design. Harvard Journal of Law & Technology 34:115
Woebbeking MK (2019) The impact of smart contracts on traditional concepts of contract law. J Intellect Prop Inf Technol E-Commer L 10:105
Woollacott E (2019) How do you know where your olive oil really comes from? BBC, https://www.bbc.com/news/business-47553054. Accessed 21 Nov 2024
World Economic Forum (2023) Pathways to the regulation of crypto-asset: a global approach
Yeung K (2019) Regulation by blockchain: the emerging battle for supremacy between the code of law and code as law. The Modern Law Review 82(2):207–239. https://doi.org/10.1111/1468-2230.12399
Zetzsche DA, Buckley RP and Arner DW (2018) The Distributed Liability of Distributed Ledgers: Legal Risks of Blockchain. U Ill L Rev 1361, https://doi.org/10.2139/ssrn.3018214.
Zhu J, Xu S, Weber I, Tran AB, Rimba P, Ponomarev A, Falamaki S, Chen S and Staples M (2017) Risks and opportunities for systems using blockchain and smart contracts, CSIRO, https://publications.csiro.au/publications/publication/PIcsiro:EP175103. Accessed 21 Nov 2024
Zou M (2020) Code, and other laws of blockchain†. Oxf J Leg Stud 40(3):645–665. https://doi.org/10.1093/ojls/gqaa018

Decentralising AI: Can Blockchain Technology Solve Data Privacy Challenges in Machine Learning?

Devlin Greatbatch Murphy, Alex Lundie, Raymond Sun, and Susannah Wilkinson

Abstract Blockchain has been charged as a solution looking for a problem. Could machine learning be that problem? Machine learning ("ML") is a subset of Artificial Intelligence ("AI") that covers machines which process and identify patterns in data to make predictions. Machine learning powers an increasing number of applications involving data and predictive analytics, across many industries including healthcare and finance. Generally, machine learning relies on a single system or server to receive data and perform all computational tasks required to train the ML model. This centralised approach to training of a ML model (or "ML training"), raises significant data security and privacy concerns. In an attempt to resolve these challenges, alternate forms of machine learning, namely federated learning and distributed learning, are being considered. These alternative approaches divide the training responsibilities, and reduce data flows and communication, amongst cooperative participants. However, extensive literature identifies that data security and privacy challenges persist, and new challenges relating to "trust" arise between trainers and the central server. In the context of federated learning, these trust challenges are manifested in ensuring active and honest participation in the ML training. Without proper incentives, encouraging participation in the federated system and providing guarantees to the quality of the siloed ML training is difficult to ensure, particularly where ML models are trained by separate and distinct entities (as compared to different computers or devices controlled by the same entity). Blockchain technology, which enables enhanced security, particularly through the immutability and traceability of data, may offer a solution to these critical privacy issues. Significantly, a blockchain-enabled solution may also leverage smart contracts, the consensus mechanism and crypto assets to offer opportunities to provide economic and non-economic incentives for ML trainers. Ultimately, this chapter analyses the technical and legal implications of this blockchain-ML integration, in particular its efficacy as a solution to the privacy challenges in ML training.

D. G. Murphy · A. Lundie · R. Sun · S. Wilkinson (✉)
Herbert Smith Freehills Kramer, Sydney, Australia
e-mail: Susannah.Wilkinson@hsf.com

P. Babie and M. Giancaspro (eds.), *Private Law, Digital Assets, and Infrastructure*,
https://doi.org/10.1007/978-981-96-7121-2_4

1 Introduction

Distributed ledger technology (including blockchain) ("DLT") and AI are developing technologies offering revolutionary capabilities for a variety of applications.

AI is widely considered to be the "general purpose technology" of this era due to its tremendous ability to automate manual tasks and processes, generate predictions or insights from data, and generate content. From automating vehicles to generating art based on text prompts, AI (particular machine learning) is a highly versatile technology that can work with different complementary technologies to change the ways things are done across every industry and sector (including healthcare, transport, infrastructure, finance, etc.).

Blockchains offer advanced and comparatively secure information technology infrastructure that decentralises control (removing dependency on centralised authority and intermediaries), and enables heightened communicative and financial capabilities through efficient, cost-effective transactions, supported by smart contracts.

However, adoption of these emerging technologies requires careful consideration in relation to potential harms, and compliance with existing technology neutral laws aimed to regulate such harms.

This chapter highlights key data security challenges inherent in traditional machine learning (see Sect. 2) and explores whether federated machine learning ("FML", defined in Sect. 4.1) can address some of these challenges and it considers the benefits of FML and residual issues that limit its uptake. These limitations include two challenges, namely residual data security issues (see Sect. 4.3.1 and 4.3.2), and the trust problem that arises in collaborative network-based systems (see Sect. 4.3.3). The chapter goes on to consider whether blockchain integrated solutions for AI machine learning models, coined "blockchain-enabled federated learning" ("BEFL") can provide practical mitigations to solve some or all of these challenges to accelerate wide-scale adoption of machine learning applications.

BEFL promotes data security by collecting and processing data locally on devices, to train a collective ML model, and is underpinned by secure and transparent record keeping using a distributed ledger. This combination promotes secure and efficient data and model sharing (Goh et al. 2023: 3). This is achieved through verification by the blockchain consensus algorithm, decentralised data storage and privacy tools enabled by using a distributed ledger. BEFL removes reliance on the central, master server, thereby also reducing many of the data security challenges in traditional ML (Goh et al. 2023: 3). Accordingly, BEFL may present significant opportunity for organisations seeking to collaborate in developing an ML model, such as a consortium of hospitals training a diagnostic tool, or corporations seeking to deploy external ML models whilst protecting proprietary interest and confidentiality of their data.

2 Centralised Machine Learning

Machine learning ("ML") is a subset (or implementation) of AI that produces an output based on a set of patterns or rules that it has detected (or "learned") by seeing lots of examples (a process called "training" or "learning"). Data is therefore at the core of any ML system. The quality and quantity of the data directly influence the system's performance and accuracy. Without data, the system would have no basis for learning and improving.

The traditional approach to ML is known as "centralised machine learning" ("centralised ML") where all data is gathered into one place (e.g. data is aggregated in a single system or server) for processing and model training. The lifecycle of a centralised ML system typically involves five key steps:

1. **Data Collection**: All data, which could be from various sources like user data, sensor data, or log files, is collected and sent to a central database.
2. **Data Processing**: The collected data is pre-processed into the appropriate format and cleaned of any missing values, outliers or errors.
3. **Model Training**: The cleaned dataset is fed into an algorithm (or a "model") which is designed to identify patterns within the data and continuously adjusts its parameters based on those patterns. The idea is that each piece of data gives the model a better idea of how its parameters should be configured. Once trained, the model is capable of making predictions or identifications for never-seen data
4. **Model Deployment**: If the model's performance is satisfactory, it is deployed to produce an output. Depending on the context in which the model is deployed, the output could take the form of a prediction (e.g. predicting the future stock price based on historical examples), a classification (e.g. identifying objects in an image), or a piece of content (e.g. AI generated art or text).
5. **Monitoring and Updating**: The model's performance is continually monitored, and the model is updated or retrained as necessary with new data.

3 Data-Related Legal Issues of Centralised Machine Learning

An essential aspect of ML is to train the model on large datasets. However, if the dataset contains any personal information ("PI"), confidential information or commercially sensitive data, such data would be subject to legal and regulatory obligations, including:

- **Confidentiality Obligations** which require that confidential information (which could include commercially sensitive information and trade secrets) is not disclosed to third parties without authorisation; and

- **Data Protection and Privacy Laws**. In Australia, the key data protection and privacy law at the federal level is the *Privacy Act 1988* (Cth) ("Privacy Act"), which includes a set of binding principles known as the Australian Privacy Principles ("APP"). A distinction between "privacy" and "data protection" is that the former focuses on personally identifiable information being collected, stored, used and/or disclosed on an authorised or legitimate basis, whilst the latter ensures PI is handled securely to minimise risk of unauthorised disclosure of, or access to, the PI (whether locally or across borders). For clarity, concepts of data security and cybersecurity relate to data protection, whilst concepts of consent, licence and authorisation relate to privacy.

For the purposes of this chapter:

- confidential **information** and PI will be collectively referred to as '**sensitive data**'; and
- confidentiality, privacy and data protection issues will be collectively referred to as '**data-related issues**'.

Centralised ML models pose the following data-related issues.

3.1 Privacy

The fact that centralised ML involves the transfer of PI from the individual to the centralised server triggers issues around consent and notification. The Privacy Act includes requirements for organisations to notify, and in some cases, procure the consent from individuals to handle their PI. Therefore, an obvious risk with the centralised ML process arises when an organisation has handled, or has been handling, PI without adequately notifying, or obtaining any necessary consents from, the relevant individuals, potentially in breach of the Privacy Act.

The same issue applies in the scenario where the PI is transferred from a data custodian (who collected the PI from individuals) to the centralised server. In this case, the custodian must have obtained the rights to *collect* that PI in the first place, as well as *disclose* that PI to the centralised server (whom in turn would need to procure authorisation from the custodian to use that PI for the purposes of training the ML model).

Generally, the more sensitive the personal information is, the higher the standard of notification and consent that is required (i.e. more explicit and unequivocal). This is particularly relevant in the context of facial recognition technology, which is a type of AI application that can detect, authenticate, identify or monitor faces. Facial recognition technology is trained on facial images and biometric templates, which under the Privacy Act is considered "sensitive information" that generally requires express consent of the individual as well as higher protections compared to other types of PI.

However, the procurement of consent is only one half of the equation. Equally important is the scope of that consent, which is dictated by the terms upon which consent was provided. The mere fact that an individual had previously consented to their collection and use of their PI by an organisation for a specific purpose does not automatically mean the organisation is authorised to use the same personal information for other unrelated, undisclosed purposes. This is known as 'function creep'.

3.2 Confidentiality

The issue of confidentiality is similar to that of privacy. But whereas privacy is regulated under the Privacy Act, confidentiality is typically governed in the contractual terms between the *discloser* and *recipient* of the confidential information, the scope of which is defined by the parties themselves based on the context of the transaction. However, where a contract is not present, confidentiality may also arise in common law or equity. In fact, confidentiality may be seen as the supplementary form of protection for PI, or the alternative form of protection for non-PI.

Regardless of the source of obligation, the issue of confidentiality typically turns on whether the discloser has rights to disclose the confidential information to the recipient, and whether the recipient has rights to use that confidential information (whether based on the recipient's consent, in specific circumstances or by law). Similar to the discussion on privacy, issues of function creep also apply here, and there is a fundamental question as to whether the discloser can use confidential information to train a ML model.

3.3 Data Protection

Centralised ML is heavily reliant on the central server. A centralised storage could be vulnerable to data breaches, either as a result of poor data governance (e.g. data is inadvertently leaked by staff), or adversarial cyber-attacks. In other words, a centralised storage represents a single point of vulnerability, which if compromised or corrupted, could render the whole centralised ML system inoperable.

4 Federated Machine Learning

4.1 Background and Rationale

In 2016, in response to privacy challenges experienced with centralised ML, Google Research pioneered an approach to ML called federated machine learning ("FML") which enables multiple parties to collaboratively train a model without sharing their data, under supervision of a central server (McMahan et al. 20 April 2017). As participants can train AI models without anyone seeing or interacting with their data, this unlocks access to new sources of information to feed new AI applications (Martineau 2022), and a possible means to mitigate some data security risks.

It is worth noting at the time of writing, FML remains an early but evolving research area. Academic papers propose proofs-of-concepts, and some industry leaders (e.g. IBM and Nvidia) have explored different implementations (IBM 2024; Wen et al. 2019).[1] Literature demonstrates there remain obstacles to mainstream adoption, such as the amount of data required for accurate training and managing datasets with significant diversity (Aledhari et al. 2020: 140700). However, its potential merits analysis for the purposes of this chapter.

4.2 How FML Works and Its Associated Benefits

FML allows multiple participants to collaboratively train a single ML model algorithm (Martineau 2022). In short, each participant (also known as "**trainer**") is provided with a copy of the ML model (from the central server), and trains their model on their own device (also known as a "**node**") and on their own data, before sending back their trained model (but not the data) to the central server, which will then combine that model with other models into one "**global model**". This process repeats for multiple rounds until the global model achieves a certain performance threshold.

Therefore, the key difference between centralised ML and FML lies in the data collection and processing steps. In FML, these steps occur at the trainer level (as opposed to within a centralised server). Each trainer maintains a private database, that is not visible by other trainers or the central server.

A comparison between centralised ML and FML is shown in Fig. 1 (Shen et al. 2022: 2).

[1] See e.g. (Jochems et al. 2016).

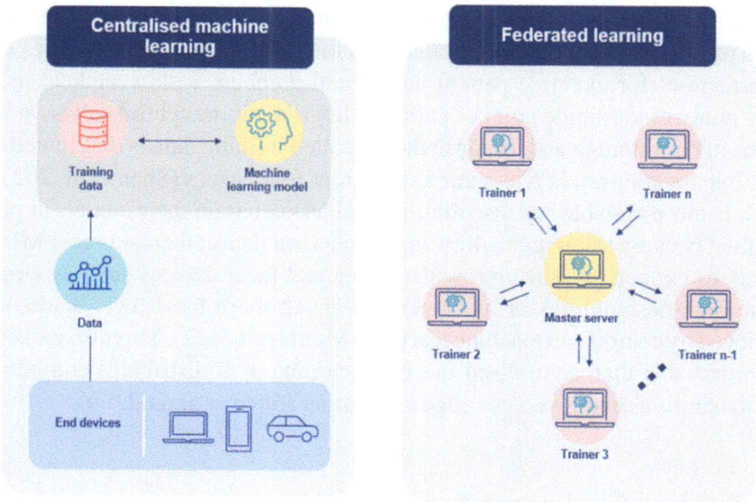

Fig. 1 Comparison of centralised machine learning and federal learning

FML is therefore a distributed approach to ML.[2] This technical design difference of FML offers the following advantages:

- There is no transfer of training data from the trainer to the central server, which bypasses the privacy and confidentiality disclosure issues previously noted for centralised ML. The data stays within the trainer's node which the trainer retains control over. This is perhaps the key advantage of FML because it enables organisations to harness ML opportunities without having to disclose sensitive data.
- Only the models are transferred between trainers and central server. Models are generally less vulnerable assets than raw data, because by design, models comprise of weights and parameters which are not comprehensible to the human. Models also require the right support tools and software application to be of utility. So even if the model was improperly obtained by a bad actor (such as during the transfer from trainer to central server), it is unlikely that the model itself would provide much value to the perpetrator (though see later point about inferred training data).
- Data protection is also improved as FML decentralises responsibility for both data collection, storage and control, as well as aspects of model training. Because data stays within each trainer node rather than on the central server, the central server effectively relinquishes responsibility for primary data storage and governance, and data control to the nodes (Shen et al. 2022: 2). FML seeks to resolve some

[2] In simple terms, distributed learning is appropriate for ML training based on homogenous datasets (i.e. where the size of the dataset and reliability of the source are consistent i.e. datacentres), whereas federated learning lends itself to heterogeneous datasets from different sources with varying degrees of reliability (i.e. smart phones). For further commentary on the differences between federated learning and distributed learning see (Liu et al. 2022).

of the data security challenges by limiting shared data to the weights and parameters (or metadata) and not the actual data that may identify sensitive or personal information (for example patient names and numbers within medical records). This removes the single point of vulnerability risk for the central server, at least in terms of data storage and, because the federated training data is distributed across multiple locations, it is a less attractive target for hackers (Shen et al. 2022: 6).
- FML is more scalable because multiple trainers can train their models in parallel. Further, because trainers can draw upon their own data at their source, FML offers a way to extract value from raw data streamed from devices such as wearables or sensors on buildings or machines at a much more local level than could be achieved by centralised machine learning (Martineau 2022). This also makes FML more scalable than centralised machine learning as it distributes computational responsibilities and leverages edge computing (Shen et al. 2022: 6).

4.3 Residual Challenges Faced by FML

Whilst FML offers promising ways to mitigate key data-related issues, it is not yet a panacea. Due to the distributed design of the FML process, the following challenges remain.

4.3.1 Data Security

Whilst distribution of data across multiple devices reduces the single point of failure risk identified above, some data security vulnerabilities now exist at both the trainer level and the central server. Each source remains vulnerable to traditional and unique cyber-attacks as well as malicious trainers or "(un)intentional misuse" of the network (Zerka et al. 2020). Poisoning attacks, where adversaries inject malicious data in local model training, are detrimental to the global model's accuracy (Li et al. 2020). Other attacks and malicious activity can lead to data breaches particularly where raw data is extracted and information is retrieved or inferred from the models submitted to the aggregator (Song et al. 30 October 2017). These network attacks generally target both trainers and the central server. Communication channels between trainers and the central servers are also a key point of vulnerability. The more rounds of information exchanged in learning task, the easier it is to infer information (Martineau 2022). Examples of this include:

- inference attacks (such as membership inference attacks) which involve attackers compromising trainer data privacy by revealing data used in the global model update
- generative adversarial network attacks, where malicious attacks pose as honest trainers and induce trainers to reveal sensitive data, man-in-the-middle attacks, which impede communication from the trainer to the server (Hasan 2023; Zhang et al. October 2021; Mahmood and Jusas 2022; Qammar et al. 2023: 3959); and

- distributed denial of service attacks ("DDoS"), which can shut down the federated network and prevent the operation of machine learning algorithm.

Furthermore, despite the restricted form of data communicated (not shared in plaintext form), data leakage can still occur in transfers. It is technically possible to infer plaintext data by analysing model weights or parameters provided by the trainers to the global model (Nasr et al. May 2019; Song et al. 30 October 2017). This enables an actor to effectively eavesdrop on communications between trainers and the aggregating, master server, enabling model reconstruction of the submitted local model (Melis et al. 19 May 2019).

4.3.2 Heavy Reliance on Communication

Another challenge of FML is the communication frequency and load between trainers and the central server. In most FML frameworks, there are numerous rounds of communication between trainers and the central server, because greater accuracy in the global model is achieved through larger quantities of training iterations. However, this creates issues for managing computational efficiency and the resources required to maintain a FML system, as well as vulnerabilities for cyber-attacks that threaten the communication channels between network participants. There is ongoing research into reducing the number of communication rounds in a learning task to minimise these risks (Hasan et al. 2022).

4.3.3 Federated Learning Introduces Trust Problems

In this context, trust refers to a "relationship between two or more parties, where one party voluntary decides, under a condition of uncertainty, to rely on another for the achievement of a particular task" (Hasan et al. 2022; Gambetta 1988). In FML systems, trust is required in both the central servers and the trainers. On the one end, the central server must be trustworthy and reliable in distributing, receiving and aggregating models (Ma et al. 2020). On the other end, the FML system relies on trainers to honestly and actively participate in the network responsibly, adhere to agreed protocols and not misuse data. Otherwise, a trainer who violates agreed protocols of the FML network could trigger privacy leakage, expose vulnerabilities to cyber-attack, or introduce bias and inaccuracy in the AI model's outputs, amongst other issues.

However, achieving and maintaining trust in FML can be challenging for two reasons. First, FML relies on trainers to voluntarily participate in the network and contribute resources in good faith. However, by design, the FML process does not offer any inherent incentive for trainers to commit time, data and energy to the process. FML deployers would likely need to build in a commercial incentive into the FML process to attract trainer participation. Second, absent commercially agreed terms to incentivise cooperation, there are no inherent incentives to encourage trainer compliance with protocol nor penalties to deter trainers from non-compliant or malicious practices.

Is there a solution to these data security, communication and trust challenges in FML? This is an area where blockchain could come in to bolster and fill in the gaps of FML—in other words, "blockchain-enabled federated learning" ("BEFL").

5 Can Blockchain-Enabled Federated Learning Solve These Challenges?

Blockchain, as a form of DLT, refers to technology that allows simultaneous secure access, validation, recording and sharing of data in an immutable manner across a decentralised network. In other words, it is essentially a "write-once read-only" database (or "ledger") that is identical and accessible to every participant in the network, and updates in real-time whenever a new entry is recorded onto the ledger. In a blockchain, each participant holds its own identical record of the ledger. Whenever a transaction or event happens, the transaction or event goes through an approval process (known as a consensus mechanism) for it to be recorded on the blockchain. The consensus mechanism differs between different blockchain platforms. Once "approved", the data of that transaction or event (such as a timestamp, description, and metadata) is added as an immutable "block" onto a "chain" of historic transactions, hence the name "blockchain" (Wilkinson 2022).

Blockchain technology seeks in part to alleviate the degradation of trust in traditional intermediated systems. However, the need for trust is not eliminated entirely because a blockchain-based system involves a large variety of actors, including miners, service providers (for example wallets or exchanges) or developers. Effective blockchain governance maximises the trust and confidence in a blockchain system. Some literature in this area has tried to address trust issues been participants without blockchain technology (Luo et al. July 2023), including without economic incentives (Kong et al. 2022). However, as blockchain capabilities and research improve, BEFL is increasingly being explored as a potential solution. Rewards can be both economic, for example crypto asset tokens from consensus, or non-economic, such as recording and maintaining a reputational value for each trainer (Cho et al. 2022). These are explored further in Sect. 5.1.

Currently, blockchain integrations into FML are largely academic and conceptual, however as greater practical adoption of FML increases, particularly by large technology companies, the critical challenges will require a solution, which BEFL may provide. It is critical to be cognisant that different applications will require different types of infrastructure, for example public, private or consortium blockchains (Ramanan and Nakayama November 2020; Kang et al. 2019). Fundamentally, the principles and standard design features of BEFL offer the solution to the data security challenges.

5.1 BEFL Explained

BEFL is an emerging paradigm in ML that integrates the principles of FML and the security features of blockchain technology. BEFL retains the existing benefits of FML but adds an additional immutable ledger to record the flow of data between trainers and the central server.

In particular, BEFL includes the following additional steps:

1. **Task Initialisation**: A trainer or device initialises a learning task by defining the initial parameters and cycle period. Some conceptual systems use smart contracts at this stage to establish conditions and rewards.
2. **Trainer Selection**: Following publication of the learning task, a client (or trainer) selection process is initiated. This process involves trainers, which satisfy certain computing or capacity requirements, nominating to contribute to the ML update and some algorithm or procedure determining which trainers are successful in selection. Some proposed models use data stored in a blockchain and smart contracts to evaluate trainer nominations and to direct selection (Goh et al. 2023: 7).
3. **Local Model Update and Verification**: The selected trainers train their local models on local, private data sets, and the updated parameters (as well as other data like computational time) are communicated to the miners. Miners (or pre-determined verifiers) conduct local model verification of the received parameters and store the updates in a candidate block. This is typically achieved through a verification algorithm, designed to retain the privacy benefits of FML, and continuously run until all model parameters are verified or the total set time has elapsed (Kalapaaking et al. 2023).
4. **Block Generation**: For each learning round, a consensus algorithm (such as proof-of-work) (Kim et al. 2020: 1281) runs and awards a miner the block generation right, which forces other miners to cease competing. The successful miner broadcasts their candidate block, and all miners append the block to their local ledgers. If a forking event occurs, the process is restarted (Kim et al. 2020: 1282).
5. **Local Model Aggregation**: The literature reviewed proposes alternative approaches for model update aggregation following acceptance of the block. In some cases, aggregation is conducted by the winning miner, which updates the global model parameters and stores the updated parameters on chain (Qu et al. 2023: 12). In other approaches, aggregation is conducted by a separate entity (often called an aggregator) or the original task publisher (Goh et al. 2023: 5–6). Typically, BEFL architecture stores only the local and global parameter updates in the blocks on-chain, but occasionally this is achieved through the use of a pointer to off-chain decentralised storage (such as the Interplanetary File System) (Qu et al. 2023: 12; Kim et al. 2020: 1282). Following this stage, rewards are distributed.

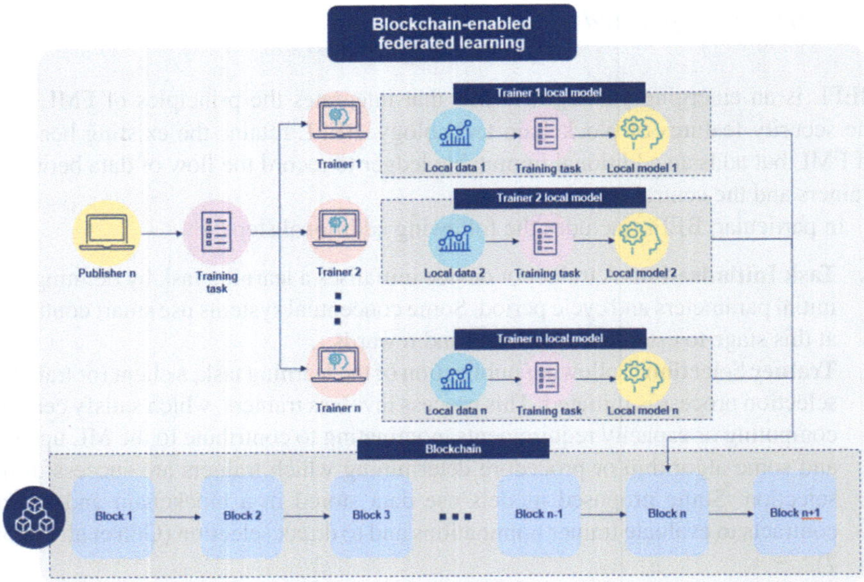

Fig. 2 Flow chart illustrating BEFL process

6. **Global Model:** Following this, the global model is available to download by anyone either from the blockchain (and the external, decentralised storage) or following the local aggregation.[3]

Figure 2 illustrates this process and presents the fundamental characteristics of many proof-of-concept BEFL constructions recommended in literature on this topic.

A review of the literature, which seeks to resolve specific privacy, data security and trust challenges of central or distributed learning or explore different applications (such as healthcare or IoT), explains that features and technologies used in the blockchain architecture can be designed for purpose. This includes selection of blockchain (or ledger) architecture, with some approaches proposing use of public, permissionless networks like Ethereum, for smart contract capabilities (Qu et al. 2023: 16; Shayan et al. 2018), and others leveraging private networks like Corda (Zarrin et al. 2021: 2842).

5.2 *BEFL Design Features*

The addition of the blockchain layer offers five fundamental benefits explained in Sect. 5.2.1 to 5.2.5 below.

[3] This generalised process follows the procedures in (Qu et al. 2023:12; Kim et al. 2020; Goh et al. 2023).

5.2.1 Decentralisation

Decentralisation is a core principle that aims to create a trustless, transparent, and permanent record system that does not depend on a single authority or intermediary (Zarrin et al. 2021: 2842). Decentralisation is achieved by using cryptographic methods, consensus algorithms, and peer-to-peer networks to distribute the data and functions of the system amongst multiple nodes (Zarrin et al. 2021: 2842).

BEFL decentralises the authority and power of the ML model by removing the role of a master server and enabling more than one participant in the distributed network to initiate learning tasks and operate as "task publishers". In some systems, it is proposed that any individual trainer can propose learning tasks to the trainer network and orchestrate the model update and aggregation (Zarrin et al. 2021: 2842). The probability of leading a training round is typically proportional to the trainer's available computational resources, including computing power, storage and local data quality. Sometimes, a consensus mechanism (like proof of stake) is used for selection (Qu et al. 2023: 16; Shayan et al. 2018).

By decentralising the function of the central, master server in traditional FML amongst trainers, BEFL may minimise security vulnerabilities susceptible to cyber-attacks and data breaches. BEFL's decentralised network increases network resilience because there is no single point of failure for attackers to target the model. Firstly, the distribution of trainers (including, for example, across business entities or geographically) also creates obstacles in distributed denial of service attacks and some collusion attacks, which threaten typical federated learning models. Secondly, unlike traditional FML, the global ML model will still be operational if an individual trainer is compromised, and development of the model will continue. Large-scale attacks are made significantly more difficult as attackers would need to compromise multiple nodes to effectively disrupt the ML model. Thirdly, local storage of raw data, siloed on devices (rather than communicated to a central server) enhances data security protections by compartmentalising data and avoiding transmission of sensitive information vulnerable to data breaches.

5.2.2 Verification Using the Consensus Mechanism

In lieu of a central server, a blockchain underpins the federated learning system which miners maintain and update. Miners can be trainers (sometimes called 'training miners') or can be an entirely separate group of participants in the BEFL network, responsible for block generation and propagation (Qu et al. 2023: 11). In the latter case, miners and trainers are paired up following local model updates (Qu et al. 2023: 11).

By leveraging the blockchain consensus mechanism deployed by miners to verify local model updates, and empowering enhanced auditability by recording the evolution of the global model, attacks by malicious actors that target local model updates can be detected and resolved. This is supported by key cryptography, built into blockchain technology, which requires trainers to digitally sign activity like uploading the local model update, and the immutability of the append-only chain (Qu et al. 2020).

An effectively designed consensus mechanism in BEFL can detect poisoning or backdoor cyber-attacks, where malicious data or functionality is inserted into the local model update (Mammen 2021), by using quality evaluation algorithms or privacy technologies such as zero-knowledge proofs (explored below) (Kang et al. 2019). This also creates resilience against attacks which intercept or interfere with the communication between the trainer and task publisher (for example man-in-the-middle attacks), which attempt to inject malicious model updates (Qammar et al. 2023: 3959). Furthermore, a BEFL's consensus mechanism also provides security against cyber threats unique to distributed computing, such as untrusted participants controlling or interfering with the network (e.g. Byzantine failures). Most proposed consensus mechanisms (such as proof-of-work) ensure sufficient resistance because of the cost of block generation or mining, the cross-verification of the block's data and the data's immutability (Hussein et al. 2023: 10–11; Zivic et al. April 2019: 3–4).

5.2.3 Audit Trail of Model Updates

Adopting the heightened transparency and enhanced auditability of blockchain technology, BEFL typically records the evolution of the AI model's parameters by storing model updates in individual blocks and securing the information through a consensus mechanism. This provides a chronological order of changes to the global model (Qu et al. 2020). Generally, proposed BEFL approaches timestamp and store local model parameters (prior to aggregation) and the global model parameters (following aggregation) on-chain.[4] This chronologically traces both the trainer's contribution and the evolution and history of the global ML model (Qammar et al. 2023: 3961). The ML parameters stored on the blockchain are generally available to all trainers, miners and network participants, depending on the characteristics of the distributed ledger. Tracking individual contributions facilitates detection of malicious trainers. Furthermore, as data storage using a blockchain is immutable, BEFL deters malicious actors from manipulating approved global model parameters, stored on-chain, without alerting the network of miners (Qammar et al. 2023: 3961).

5.2.4 Privacy Enhancement

Blockchain technology enables BEFL to inherently provide some enhanced privacy through pseudonymity, which can provide some initial resistance to certain cyber threats like background knowledge attacks, which target the identity and knowledge of individual trainers to retrieve local data. However, a more important component of BEFL is the integration of privacy enhancing technology ("PET") and tools, through

[4] As previously mentioned, this can also be achieved by storing unique identifiers of the parameters stored in decentralized services, off-chain see e.g.(Yuan et al. 29 March 2021).

cryptographic primitives and other protocols enabled, or enhanced, by blockchain (Li et al. 2021). These characteristics and enhancements mitigate cyber risk, enable advanced management and control of data and streamline and secure communication between network participants.

These PETs generally reinforce the communication layer of the federated learning network, securing transfers of the local model parameters and ensuring data privacy of individual training datasets. Many of these technologies have been researched in FML models, using different cryptographic or computing protocols to conceal trainer data or protect data leakage in transfers. Current literature on BEFL often proposes to integrate these other PETs into the blockchain solution, to fortify data privacy. Some key PETs are outlined below.

Zero-Knowledge Proofs

Zero-knowledge proofs ("ZKP") are a cryptographic protocol which involves a prover and a verifier, with the prover demonstrating the correctness of a promise or claim to the verifier without revealing any information about it (Li et al. 2023).

In a BEFL model, ZKPs can be used to achieve public verification of the local trainer contributions. It achieves this by transforming the localised training process, following publication of the learning task and selection of the trainers, into a corresponding "arithmetic circuit constraint" and enabling verification of the circuit satisfiability. This occurs by trainers generating corresponding verifiable ZKPs alongside the updated local models for each learning or communication cycle. These proofs can be verified by the task publisher and by all of the trainers in the network, mathematically demonstrating that the updated, local models have been computed using some local data (Xing et al. 2023: 3). Other approaches involve trainers providing an accompanying ZKP with model updates that verifies that the local model is free from specific poisoning attacks, for example by proving that a requested defensive protocol was used (Nguyen and Thai 2022). Alternatively, some papers have also considered trusted computing environments which deploy ZKPs and report heightened data privacy and security against malicious activity (Zhang et al. 2023: 1560–1570). Whilst some papers exploring ZKPs in some ML training highlight a comparatively high computational cost (Weng et al. 2021; Rückel et al. 2022), the continued development of succinct ZKPs (such as "zero-knowledge succinct non-interaction argument of knowledge" proofs) are offering practical relevance for industry and real-world use of BEFL.

Decentralised Identifiers

Decentralised identifiers ("DID") enable management of digital identity using a unique identifier that is verifiable, reliable and tamper-proof and independent of any central issuing authorities (Goh et al. 2023: 4). Personal or identifying information is stored in distributed, encrypted formats granting enhanced privacy and security.

Blockchain technology enables distributed, transparency mechanisms for storing and managing DIDs. This ensures data can also be shared with authorised parties. DIDs and blockchain also enable verifiable credentials ("VC"), which are digital records or attestations of a qualification (Weng et al. 2021; Rückel et al. 2022). Research in BEFL has explored the use of DIDs and VCs to enhance trainer privacy and in certification systems for selection and participation as a trainer or task publisher (Goh et al. 2023: 11). This can prevent malicious actors from participating in learning tasks, by eliminating unauthorised participants. This integration can also mitigate threats like Sybil attacks, where malicious actors create and distribute numerous fake identities to compromise systems.

Homomorphic Encryption

Homomorphic encryption is another PET explored in the context of federated learning and involves a form of encryption which enables algebraic operations to be performed using ciphertext, rather than plaintext.[5] Homomorphic encryption produces ciphertext outputs (following the calculations and operations) and therefore the operator is unaware of the corresponding plaintext, which conceals the underlying data. Full homomorphic encryption (which permits complex calculations as well as basic algebraic operations) was first proposed in 2009 (Gentry 2009), and has been conceptually applied to enhance privacy in federated learning models (Zhang et al. 2023: 1560–1570).

Integration of homomorphic encryption generally sees the task publishers or aggregators encrypt the initial model weights (extracted from the current version of the global model) and the trainers performing the learning task and submitting the updates in the ciphertext form. In this model, the trainers are unaware of the corresponding plaintext data involved in the initial weights of the global model, and data leakage is avoided because only ciphertext is communicated back to the task publisher or aggregator. In a BEFL solution, homomorphic encryption is effective in enhancing data privacy, particularly in the aggregating stages of the learning tasks. The updated weights produced by local training from the trainers, can be aggregated by the task publisher using homomorphic encryption, before updating the global model, to prevent data leakage and malicious activity. An example of this scheme is the conceptual design proposed by Xing et al., which proposes a secure sum protocol to aggregate updated models (Xing et al. 2023: 3).

5.2.5 Establishing Trust and Incentivising Active and Honest Participation

Successfully implementing federated learning models depends on active and honest involvement of all participants and individual trainers. Without incentives, the

[5] Ciphertext is encrypted text, which is the result of an encryption algorithm performed on plaintext.

successful training of the ML model is at risk (Toyoda and Zhang December 2019; Weng et al. 2019). Therefore, an incentive mechanism is crucial to motivate trainers to participate in the development of the model and to promote trainers' honest contribution to local AI model training, whilst also preventing unreliable or malicious contributions (Weng et al. 2019).

Previously, methods such as special hardware (i.e. trusted execution environments), or heavy computation (i.e. homomorphic encryption) were used to ensure rational contribution (Toyoda and Zhang December 2019). These methods facilitate secure communication but are not easily scalable with small or mobile end devices and don't completely prevent malicious activity.

BEFL systems offer a solution to this trust problem. Blockchains use consensus and voting mechanisms, smart contracts and economic incentives to reward validator participation, including rewards in cryptographic tokens and reduce malicious trainers (Toyoda and Zhang December 2019; Weng et al. 2019).

The trust problem in federated learning involves ensuring both "active" and "honest" participation (including preventing non-malicious conduct). The following section outlines some academic approaches to economic and non-economic incentives enabled by blockchain technology. A unified BEFL system that combines these methods can effectively address the trust issues.

Crypto Asset Rewards

Economic rewards derived from the blockchain consensus mechanism, or peer voting, can incentivise active and honest contribution based on the chosen measures in a network. Contributions to a BEFL system can be measured in a number of different ways with rewards being allocated accordingly.

Common measures of contribution include the value or reliability of the data used for training, the computational resources contributed (i.e. data size, bandwidth, internet connectivity), participation as a validator, and the increases to the accuracy of the ML model (Batool et al. 25 April 2022). Many theoretical designs elect to target the contribution of computational resources, as this often can correlate to accuracy of the federated model (Batool et al. 25 April 2022). In this approach, trainers specify their resources (i.e. data size, bandwidth, internet connectivity) and are selected through a 'multi-dimensional auction', conducted through smart contracts. Selected trainers receive corresponding rewards in cryptocurrencies (Batool et al. 25 April 2022).

Rewards can also be allocated based on participant voting. Toyoda and Zhang propose a competitive mechanism design which incentivises rational trainers to adhere to the learning protocol, make effective and honest contributions, and maximise profits. This system integrates a voting mechanism, where trainers in subsequent rounds evaluate, by reference to pre-established criteria (for example model performance values or data accuracy), and vote on the contributions of trainers in the previous training round, to the global AI model (Toyoda and Zhang December 2019). Rewards are distributed to trainers according to their vote rankings. To ensure honest contribution in the last round of the training task where no subsequent votes will be cast, the round in which trainers are participating is concealed until the global AI model is aggregated. To achieve this, the learning task publisher does not disclose the total number of rounds (using a one-time pseudo-random value in a commitment scheme). Additionally, the publisher must provide a larger reward deposit than is required for the total rewards for the total number of rounds, with the balance returned to the publisher after the learning task is complete.

Further, some theoretical models leverage the blockchain's consensus mechanism in the BEFL design to create a collaboratively incentivised network of trainers and validators, which receive crypto asset rewards for training the model and maintaining the network (Weng et al. 2019).

To further promote trust between participants, smart contracts can be also used to automate the distribution of rewards based on predefined rules (e.g. the proportion of the trainer's contribution). The transparency and immutability of reward distribution incentivises honest contributions and penalises malicious or unreliable trainers (Behera et al. 2021).

Blockchain-Supported Reputation Mechanisms

Reputation-based incentive mechanisms are commonly used to support reliability in various networks to support reliability (Liu et al. 2024; Noshad et al. 2021). Kang et al., propose using reputation as a measure of trustworthiness of participants in federated learning systems. This measure is used to select trainers in training rounds. The system also combines an incentive mechanism to stimulate high-reputation trainers, by providing correlative rewards based on the accuracy, computational efficiency and reliability of training data (Kang et al. 2019).

Reputation management involves calculating a measure of reputation based on multiple variables and storing it securely in a decentralised way using a consortium blockchain. (Kang et al. 2019). In this system, task publishers design "contract items", which outline the data and computation resource requirements for the ML update, and broadcast learning tasks to trainers. Trainers that satisfy these contract requirements, nominate themselves as candidates to participate in the learning task and train the ML model on their training data. The task publisher then selects qualified candidates based on their reputational values, which are determined by combining historical reputation opinion data from the blockchain and opinion values expressed from other task publishers. Trainer candidates exceeding a reputation threshold are selected to update the AI model. They are rewarded based on their resource contribution as outlined in the initial "contract items" and learning task. These rewards balance the task publisher's commitment to profits to the need to attract reliable trainers (Kang et al. 2019: 10706–10707). To evaluate the reliability of local model updates by trainers, task publishers use attack detection schemes like "reject on negative influence" ("RONI") and "FoolsGold". These schemes identify poisoning attacks and highlight unreliable trainers (Kang et al. 2019: 10704), allowing the task publisher to remove unreliable or malicious local model updates. These events are also recorded as "negative interactions" into the reputation opinion data stored on the blockchain. Following completion of the federated task, the task publisher updates the trainers' reputation opinions data on the blockchain.

6 Conclusion

FML promises to resolve some of the data security challenges of centralised ML, but several persistent and new data security, governance and processing issues emerge, creating vulnerability to data breaches and threatening cyber-attacks. BEFL offers an architecture which pre-emptively responds to these challenges, by effectively decentralising a degree of control and authority in the network of trainers, conducting verification, and keeping a record of local updates, to prevent poisoning threats, and by utilising PETs. These strategies and design features instil enhanced data security into the network. Furthermore, distributing computing (such as FML), challenges emerge regarding the trust required that network participants actively and honestly contribute to the computing or learning task. BEFL promotes built-in policy objectives regarding participation, to ensure that users comply with rules and effectively contribute, whilst deterring malicious actors from disrupting the system.

Whilst these technologies continue to evolve, there is a case for further experimentation with the convergence of DLT/blockchain to support the wide-scale adoption of machine learning.

References

Aledhari M, Razzak R, Parizi RM, Saeed F (2020) Federated learning: a survey on enabling technologies Protocols, and Applications. IEEE Access 8:140699–140725. https://doi.org/10.1109/ACCESS.2020.3013541

Batool Z, Zhang K and Toews M (25 April 2022) FL-MAB: client selection and monetization for blockchain-based federated learning. In: Proceedings of the 37th ACM/SIGAPP Symposium on Applied Computing, SAC '22: The 37th ACM/SIGAPP Symposium on Applied Computing, ACM, Virtual Event, https://doi.org/10.1145/3477314.3507050

Behera MR, Upadhyay S and Shetty S (2021) Federated Learning using Smart Contracts on Blockchains, based on Reward Driven Approach, https://doi.org/10.48550/ARXIV.2107.10243

Cho YJ, Jhunjhunwala D, Li T, Smith V and Joshi G (2022) Maximizing Global Model Appeal in Federated Learning, https://doi.org/10.48550/ARXIV.2205.14840

Gambetta D (1988) Can We Trust Trust? In: D Gambetta (ed) Trust: Making and Breaking Cooperative Relations. Blackwell

Gentry C (2009) A Fully Homomorphic Encryption Scheme (PhD Thesis), Stanford University, Stanford, CA, USA

Goh E, Kim Dae-Yeol, Lee K, Oh S, Chae J-E and Kim Do-Yup (2023) Blockchain-Enabled Federated Learning: A Reference Architecture Design, Implementation, and Verification, https://doi.org/10.48550/ARXIV.2306.10841

Hasan J (2023) Security and privacy issues of federated learning, https://doi.org/10.48550/ARXIV.2307.12181

Hasan M, Zhang Z, Guo K, Karami M, Zhang G, Chen X and Poupart P (2022) Robust one round federated learning with predictive space bayesian inference, https://doi.org/10.48550/ARXIV.2206.09526

Hussein Z, Salama MA, El-Rahman SA (2023) Evolution of blockchain consensus algorithms: a review on the latest milestones of blockchain consensus algorithms. Cybersecurity 6(30):1. https://doi.org/10.1186/s42400-023-00163-y

IBM (2024) IBM federated learning, IBM watsonx as a service, https://www.ibm.com/docs/en/watsonx-as-a-service?topic=models-federated-learning

Jochems A, Deist TM, Van Soest J, Eble M, Bulens P, Coucke P, Dries W, Lambin P, Dekker A (2016) Distributed learning: Developing a predictive model based on data from multiple hospitals without data leaving the hospital—a real life proof of concept. Radiother Oncol 121(3):459–467. https://doi.org/10.1016/j.radonc.2016.10.002

Kalapaaking AP, Khalil I and Yi X (2023) Blockchain-based Federated Learning with SMPC Model Verification Against Poisoning Attack for Healthcare Systems, https://doi.org/10.48550/ARXIV.2304.13360.

Kang J, Xiong Z, Niyato D, Xie S, Zhang J (2019) Incentive mechanism for reliable federated learning: a joint optimization approach to combining reputation and contract theory. IEEE Internet Things J 6(6):10700–10714. https://doi.org/10.1109/JIOT.2019.2940820

Kim H, Park J, Bennis M, Kim S-L (2020) Blockchained on-device federated learning. IEEE Commun Lett 24(6):1279–1283. https://doi.org/10.1109/LCOMM.2019.2921755

Kong S, Li Y and Zhou H (2022) Incentivizing federated learning, https://doi.org/10.48550/ARXIV.2205.10951

Li C, Yuan Y and Wang F-Y (2021) Blockchain-enabled Federated Learning: A Survey. IEEE 1st International Conference on Digital Twins and Parallel Intelligence, Beijing, China

Li T, Sahu AK, Talwalkar A, Smith V (2020) Federated learning: challenges, methods, and future directions. IEEE Signal Process Mag 37(3):50–60. https://doi.org/10.1109/MSP.2020.2975749

Li Z, Kong D, Niu Y, Peng H, Li X and Li W (2023) An overview of AI and blockchain integration for privacy-preserving, https://doi.org/10.48550/ARXIV.2305.03928

Liu J, Huang J, Zhou Y, Li X, Ji S, Xiong H, Dou D (2022) From distributed machine learning to federated learning: a survey. Knowl Inf Syst 64(4):885–917. https://doi.org/10.1007/s10115-022-01664-x

Liu Y, Liu Z, Zhang Q, Su J, Cai Z, Li X (2024) Blockchain and trusted reputation assessment-based incentive mechanism for healthcare services. Futur Gener Comput Syst 154:59–71. https://doi.org/10.1016/j.future.2023.12.023

Luo B, Feng Y, Wang S, Huang J and Tassiulas L (July 2023) Incentive mechanism design for unbiased federated learning with randomized client participation. In: 2023 IEEE 43rd International Conference on Distributed Computing Systems (ICDCS), 2023 IEEE 43rd International Conference on Distributed Computing Systems (ICDCS), IEEE, Hong Kong, Hong Kong, https://doi.org/10.1109/ICDCS57875.2023.00027

Ma C, Li J, Ding M, Shi L, Wang T, Han Z and Poor HV (2020) When federated learning meets blockchain: a new distributed learning paradigm, https://doi.org/10.48550/ARXIV.2009.09338

Mahmood Z, Jusas V (2022) Blockchain-enabled: multi-layered security federated learning platform for preserving data privacy. Electronics 11(10):1624. https://doi.org/10.3390/electronics11101624

Mammen PM (2021) Federated learning: opportunities and challenges, https://doi.org/10.48550/ARXIV.2101.05428

Martineau K (2022) What is Federated Learning?, IBM, https://research.ibm.com/blog/what-is-federated-learning

McMahan HB, Moore E, Ramage D, Hampson S and Arcas BA y (20 April 2017) Communication-Efficient Learning of Deep Networks from Decentralized Data. 20th International Conference on Artificial Intelligence and Statistics, arXiv, https://doi.org/10.48550/ARXIV.1602.05629

Melis L, Song C, De Cristofaro E and Shmatikov V (19 May 2019) Exploiting unintended feature leakage in collaborative learning. IEEE Symposium on Security and Privacy, arXiv, https://doi.org/10.48550/ARXIV.1805.04049

Nasr M, Shokri R and Houmansadr A (May 2019) Comprehensive privacy analysis of deep learning: passive and active white-box inference attacks against centralized and federated learning. In: 2019 IEEE Symposium on Security and Privacy (SP), 2019 IEEE Symposium on Security and Privacy (SP), IEEE, San Francisco, CA, USA, https://doi.org/10.1109/SP.2019.00065.

Nguyen T and Thai MT (2022) Preserving privacy and security in federated learning, https://doi.org/10.48550/ARXIV.2202.03402

Noshad Z, Khan AU, Abbas S, Abubaker Z, Javaid N, Shafiq M and Choi J-G (2021) An incentive and reputation mechanism based on blockchain for crowd sensing network. J Sens 2021(1): 1798256, https://doi.org/10.1155/2021/1798256

Qammar A, Karim A, Ning H, Ding J (2023) Securing federated learning with blockchain: a systematic literature review. Artif Intell Rev 56(5):3951–3985. https://doi.org/10.1007/s10462-022-10271-9

Qu Y, Gao L, Luan TH, Xiang Y, Yu S, Li B, Zheng G (2020) Decentralized privacy using blockchain-enabled federated learning in fog computing. IEEE Internet Things J 7(6):5171–5183. https://doi.org/10.1109/JIOT.2020.2977383

Qu Y, Uddin MP, Gan C, Xiang Y, Gao L, Yearwood J (2023) Blockchain-enabled federated learning: a survey. ACM Comput Surv 55(4):1–35. https://doi.org/10.1145/3524104

Ramanan P and Nakayama K (November 2020) 'BAFFLE : Blockchain based aggregator free federated learning. In: 2020 IEEE International Conference on Blockchain (Blockchain), 2020 IEEE International Conference on Blockchain (Blockchain), IEEE, Rhodes Island, Greece, https://doi.org/10.1109/Blockchain50366.2020.00017

Rückel T, Sedlmeir J, Hofmann P (2022) Fairness, integrity, and privacy in a scalable blockchain-based federated learning system. Comput Netw 202:108621. https://doi.org/10.1016/j.comnet.2021.108621

Shayan M, Fung C, Yoon CJM and Beschastnikh I (2018) Biscotti: a ledger for private and secure peer-to-peer machine learning, https://doi.org/10.48550/ARXIV.1811.09904

Shen S, Zhu T, Wu D, Wang W, Zhou W (2022) From distributed machine learning to federated learning: in the view of data privacy and security. Concurrency and Computation: Practice and Experience 34(16):1–19. https://doi.org/10.1002/cpe.6002

Song C, Ristenpart T and Schmatikov V (30 October 2017) Machine learning models that remember too much. ACM SIGSAC Conference on Computer and Communications Security

Toyoda K and Zhang AN (December 2019) Mechanism design for an incentive-aware blockchain-enabled federated learning platform. In: 2019 IEEE International Conference on Big Data (Big Data), 2019 IEEE International Conference on Big Data (Big Data), IEEE, Los Angeles, CA, USA, https://doi.org/10.1109/BigData47090.2019.9006344

Wen Y, Li W, Roth H and Dogra P (2019) Federated Learning powered by NVIDIA Clara, NVIDIA Technical Blog, https://developer.nvidia.com/blog/federated-learning-clara/. Accessed 10 Nov 2024

Weng C, Yang K, Xie X, Katz J and Wang X (2021) Mystique: efficient conversions for {Zero-Knowledge} proofs with applications to machine learning. In: USENIX Association (ed), Proceedings of the 30th USENIX Security Symposium: August 11–13, 2021, USENIX Security Symposium, USENIX Association, Berkeley, CA

Weng J, Weng J, Zhang J, Li M, Zhang Y and Luo W (2019) DeepChain: auditable and privacy-preserving deep learning with blockchain-based incentive. IEEE Transactions on Dependable and Secure Computing, 1–1, https://doi.org/10.1109/TDSC.2019.2952332

Wilkinson S (2022) Smart Contracts

Xing Z, Zhang Z, Li M, Liu J, Zhu L, Russello G and Asghar MR (2023) Zero-Knowledge Proof-based Practical Federated Learning on Blockchain, https://doi.org/10.48550/ARXIV.2304.05590

Yuan S, Cao B, Peng M and Sun Y (29 March 2021) ChainsFL: blockchain-driven federated learning from design to realization. In: 2021 IEEE Wireless Communications and Networking Conference (WCNC), 2021 IEEE Wireless Communications and Networking Conference (WCNC), IEEE, Nanjing, China, https://doi.org/10.1109/WCNC49053.2021.9417299

Zarrin J, Wen Phang H, Babu Saheer L, Zarrin B (2021) Blockchain for decentralization of internet: prospects, trends, and challenges. Clust Comput 24(4):2841–2866. https://doi.org/10.1007/s10586-021-03301-8

Zerka F, Urovi V, Vaidyanathan A, Barakat S, Leijenaar RTH, Walsh S, Gabrani-Juma H, Miraglio B, Woodruff HC, Dumontier M, Lambin P (2020) Blockchain for Privacy Preserving and Trustworthy Distributed Machine Learning in Multicentric Medical Imaging (C-DistriM). IEEE Access 8:183939–183951. https://doi.org/10.1109/ACCESS.2020.3029445

Zhang B, Lu G, Qiu P, Gui X, Shi Y (2023) Advancing Federated Learning through Verifiable Computations and Homomorphic Encryption. Entropy 25(11):1550. https://doi.org/10.3390/e25111550

Zhang J, Li M, Zeng S, Xie B and Zhao D (October 2021) A survey on security and privacy threats to federated learning. In 2021 International Conference on Networking and Network Applications (NaNA), 2021 International Conference on Networking and Network Applications (NaNA), IEEE, Lijiang City, China, https://doi.org/10.1109/NaNA53684.2021.00062

Zivic N, Ruland C and Ur-Rehman O (April 2019) Addressing Byzantine Fault Tolerance in Blockchain Technology. In: 2019 8th International Conference on Modeling Simulation and Applied Optimization (ICMSAO), 2019 8th International Conference on Modeling Simulation and Applied Optimization (ICMSAO), IEEE, Manama, Bahrain, https://doi.org/10.1109/ICMSAO.2019.8880419

Controlling Intangibles: The United States Approach to Digital Assets in Commerce

Juliet M. Moringiello

Abstract This chapter examines the new Article 12 of the Uniform Commercial Code, the American law that, when enacted by the states, governs a variety of commercial transactions. The article explains the uniform law drafting process in the United States, and the considerations that led to the drafting of Article 12, which provides a framework for the transfer of a category of digital assets called "controllable electronic records." It then discusses the key elements of Article 12, including the definition of control as the electronic analog to possession and the take-free rules that make controllable electronic records negotiable.

1 Introduction

In July 2022, the American Law Institute and the Uniform Law Commission approved the 2022 Amendments to the Uniform Commercial Code (UCC). The UCC is the United States law that governs a wide range of commercial transactions, such as sales and leases of goods, negotiable instruments, and secured transactions in personal property. The 2022 Amendments were the result of a three-year study and drafting process that involved members of the two sponsoring groups and hundreds of stakeholders and resulted in the addition of a new Article 12 of the UCC, covering a subset of digital assets called "controllable electronic records." This chapter will discuss Article 12 and the process by which the amendments were drafted as well as the choices made by the Drafting Committee in developing the amendments.

Former Associate Dean for Academic Affairs and Professor, Widener University Commonwealth Law School, Harrisburg, PA. The author was the Vice-Chair of the Uniform Law Commission/American Law Institute Drafting Committee for the 2022 Amendments to the Uniform Commercial Code. The views expressed in this chapter were the author's own and not the views of the American Law Institute or the Uniform Law Commission. The author thanked Widener University Commonwealth Law School for providing a research grant to complete this project.

J. M. Moringiello (✉)
Widener University Commonwealth Law School, Harrisburg, PA, USA
e-mail: paul.babie@adelaide.edu.au

P. Babie and M. Giancaspro (eds.), *Private Law, Digital Assets, and Infrastructure*,
https://doi.org/10.1007/978-981-96-7121-2_5

2 The Uniform Commercial Code

The UCC is a product of the American Law Institute (ALI) and the Uniform Law Commission (ULC). The ALI is an elected body of 4500 lawyers, judges, and law professors (The American Law Institute 2024a) from throughout the United States, with a handful of non-US lawyers. Its mission is to produce "scholarly work to clarify, modernize, and otherwise improve the law." The ALI is principally known for its Restatements of the Law, non-binding documents that have had in impact on the development of law in the US, and it is also responsible for some model and uniform laws, such as the Model Penal Code and, with the ULC, the UCC (The American Law Institute 2024b).

Members of the ULC are appointed by their states. State laws regarding appointments vary, and all US jurisdictions (states, the District of Columbia, the Virgin Islands, and Puerto Rico) have ULC delegations. The ULC's goal is to preserve federalism by providing uniform state laws in areas in which uniformity is desirable (Stein 2013: 2–3).[1] The organization has promulgated uniform state laws in a variety of areas including family law, unincorporated organizations law, wills and trusts law, and commercial law. The ULC works with the ALI on the UCC.

A uniform law is not the law anywhere until it is enacted by a state. The ULC and ALI have had tremendous success with the UCC, which has been enacted in every US jurisdiction.[2] Although states sometimes amend the uniform law in the enactment process, too many changes will make a law non-uniform. The goal is to have each law enacted in a substantially uniform way in every US jurisdiction.

The sponsoring organizations first promulgated the UCC in 1951, with Pennsylvania being the first enacting state in 1953. The first version of the UCC contained nine articles, including an article with general provisions such as definitions, and eight substantive articles covering the sale of goods, commercial paper (now known as negotiable instruments), bank deposits and collections, letters of credit, bulk transfers (repealed by most states at the recommendation of the ULC because many states had determined that the topic was obsolete), warehouse receipts, bills of lading and other documents of title, investment securities, and secured transactions (Stein 2013: 84–87).[3] The UCC has been amended several times, with new articles being added in 1987 and 1989 to govern leases of personal property and commercial funds transfers (Uniform Law Commission 2024).

The UCC is facilitative, not regulatory. This orientation is stated in the general provisions article of the UCC, Article 1, which sets forth the underlying purposes and policies of the UCC. The UCC was designed to "simplify, clarify, and modernize" the law of commercial transactions, and permit the "continued expansion of commercial practices though custom, usage, and agreement of the parties" (*Uniform Commercial Code* n.d.: § 1–103 (a)). It is also not the exclusive body of law that governs commercial

---

[1] Explaining the political background leading to the formation of the Uniform Law Commission.

[2] The one exception is Louisiana, which did not adopt Articles 2 and 2A of the UCC. *See* La. R.S. Title 10 (omitting Chapter 2, which would have included Articles 2 and 2A).

[3] Explaining the early history of the UCC.

transactions. Unless specifically displaced by statutory language, principles of law and equity supplement the UCC (*Uniform Commercial Code* n.d.:§1–103 (b)). Other state and federal statutes supplement the UCC's provisions, particularly in the area of consumer law (*Magnuson-Moss Warranty Act* 1975).[4]

3 The Study Process: Review the Entire UCC

In 2019, the ALI and ULC appointed a committee to study the impact of emerging technologies on the UCC. A study committee typically works for a year and then recommends whether or not to go forward with a drafting committee. The study committee, then named the Study Committee on the UCC and Emerging Technologies, had a broad charge: examine the entire UCC and determine what, if anything, needed to be changed to accommodate technologies that had emerged since the late 1990s. The late 1990s were a good starting point because the last major amendments to the UCC were amendments to Article 9, governing secured transactions in personal property, promulgated in 1998 with an effective date of July 1, 2001 (*Uniform Commercial Code* n.d.:§9–101 Official Comment (summarizing the 1998 Amendments)).

In the late 1990s, the major technological innovations enabled electronic transactions. The contracting process could easily move from a paper-based process to an electronic process save for one hurdle, the statute of frauds, which requires many contracts to be in writing and signed. The ULC and Congress solved that problem with two statutes, the Uniform Electronic Transactions Act (UETA) (Uniform Electronic Transactions Act 1999) and the Electronic Signatures in Global and National Commerce Act (E-Sign) (2000:§7001 *et seq.*). The key provision in both of these statutes is that a contract cannot be denied legal effect or enforceability solely because it is in electronic form. Both statutes also give effect to electronic signatures by stating that if a law requires a signature, an electronic signature satisfies the law (Uniform Electronic Transactions Act 1999:§7; *Electronic Signatures in Global and National Commerce Act* 2000:§7001). The revisions to Article 9 of the UCC were proceeding at the same time, and the UCC drafters included language in Article 9 that made electronic contracts and signatures enforceable under Article 9. To ensure that Article 9 could accommodate electronic transactions the drafters replaced the term writing with "record," using the definition of record from UETA and E-Sign (*Uniform Commercial Code* n.d.:§9–102 (a)(70) (2022 version)),[5] and replacing the term sign with "authenticate" (*Uniform Commercial Code* n.d.:§9–102 (a)(7) (1998

[4] Specifying standards for written warranties and establishing consumer remedies for breach of warranty in sales of goods for personal, family, or household use.

[5] Defining record as "information that is inscribed on a tangible medium or which is stored in an electronic or other medium and is retrievable in perceivable form.".

version)).[6] Those revisions also enabled electronic filing of financing statements, the statements that a secured creditor must file in a public office in order to establish priority over other parties claiming an interest in the collateral, by making the sections governing filing medium-neutral (*Uniform Commercial Code* n.d.:§9–516).[7]

Since the late 1990s, electronic property developed. Electronic, or digital, property refers to intangible assets that act like tangible assets. Before the 1990s, people often thought of intangible assets as intellectual property rights, or more accurately, the assets to which intellectual property rights refer (Moringiello 2007).[8] For example, copyright law gives a creator the right to exclude others from her creative work. That work, however, is non-rivalrous in that many people can enjoy it at once. If a painting is hanging in a museum, or in your living room, many people can enjoy it at once. The holder of the copyright gets to determine who can enjoy it.

Tangible assets are rivalrous in that only one person can enjoy the asset at a time. If I am sitting in a chair you cannot unless you invade my space in an unpleasant and likely unwelcome way. In the past 25 years, technology has developed to create rivalrous intangible assets. Internet domain names fall into that category. Only one person can use the name to refer to his website. Social media accounts are similarly rivalrous. More recently, cryptocurrencies and tokens maintained and transferred on distributed ledger systems are similarly rivalrous.

The emergence of electronic assets is of course not the only technological innovation that has an impact on commercial law. The goods we buy today are not the same as those that we bought 25 years ago (Elvy 2015). Many tangible goods are packed with software to enable their "smart" capabilities. Some of these smart goods can be remotely disabled, raising Article 9 enforcement issues (Moringiello 2022). Artificial intelligence has had an impact on how payment transactions are conducted. Although the committee decided to make small changes to most articles of the UCC, the committee's ultimate decision was to devote most of the committee's time and energy to drafting a law to accommodate the use in commerce of a type of digital asset that the UCC now calls Controllable Electronic Records (CERs).

Behind the decision to concentrate on a subset of digital assets were the moves by several states to enact laws governing the use in commerce of cryptocurrency and other assets tracked on a distributed ledger. These laws either explicitly amended the UCC or implicitly did so. The existence of non-uniform state laws that contained various definitions of the assets covered created a choice of law problem that could potentially vex courts, especially bankruptcy courts, which are called upon to determine the property rights of debtors and creditors in debtor assets. Because uniformity is key to smooth commercial transactions, the drafting committee chose to add a new Article 12 to the UCC, governing the transfer of Controllable Electronic Records. The addition of a new Article and a new asset category necessitated extensive revisions to Article 9 of the UCC, which governs security interests in personal property.

[6] The 2022 Amendments to the UCC removed this definition because they amended the definition of "sign" to include electronic signatures (*Uniform Commercial Code* n.d.:§1–201 (b)(37)).

[7] "communication of a record to a filing office . . . constitutes filing."

[8] Explaining the early doctrinal confusion surrounding intangible assets.

4 Why the Unamended UCC Does Not Work for Controllable Electronic Records

To explain why the unamended UCC is not satisfactory for CERs, this Part will use Bitcoin as an example. Although Article 12 does not use the words cryptocurrency, blockchain or distributed ledger, one of the reasons for drafting Article 12 was the fact that the rules in the unamended UCC did not work well for assets such as Bitcoin and other cryptocurrencies.

People want to use Bitcoin as a medium of exchange. The unamended UCC makes that difficult because it treats Bitcoin as a "general intangible." General intangible is a catch-all term in the UCC; it is the term used to describe assets that do not fall into any other asset category (*Uniform Commercial Code* n.d.:§9–102 (a)(42)). The UCC defines several categories of tangible personal property under the general category of "goods" (*Uniform Commercial Code* n.d.:§9–102 (a)(44)), and it defines several kinds of intangible and reified payment rights such as "accounts" (*Uniform Commercial Code* n.d.:§9–102 (a)(2)) and "instruments" (*Uniform Commercial Code* n.d.:§9–102 (a)(47)). An asset that is neither tangible nor a defined intangible or reified payment right is classified as a "general intangible." This category encompasses assets as diverse as copyrights, trademarks, licenses, and internet domain names.

Because Bitcoin is classified as a general intangible under the unamended UCC, an owner of Bitcoin can grant a security interest in it as collateral for a loan. To do so, the owner would sign a security agreement giving a creditor a lien on the Bitcoin (*Uniform Commercial Code* n.d.:§9–203). To obtain priority over other creditors and purchasers of the Bitcoin, the creditor would have to file a financing statement in a public place, usually the Secretary of State's Office in the state in which the debtor is located (*Uniform Commercial Code* n.d.:§9–310).

This process would give the secured creditor a priority interest in the Bitcoin, but it is undesirable for both debtors and creditors who deal in Bitcoin and other cryptocurrencies. An owner of Bitcoin wants to use it as a medium of exchange, and therefore would want it to be easily negotiable.

The UCC enables negotiability for other payment devices. These negotiability rules are grounded in possession, and recognize that payment devices are transferred in commerce by the transfer of manual possession. The UCC provides that when a secured party takes a physical transfer of money (*Uniform Commercial Code* n.d.:§9–332),[9] negotiable instruments, and chattel paper (*Uniform Commercial Code* n.d.:§9–330) in good faith, for value, and without notice of a competing security interest, that person takes priority over other creditors with security interests in those assets. A filed financing statement does not provide notice of a competing security interest. Article 3 of the UCC provides that a holder in due course of a negotiable instrument (someone who takes possession of the instrument for value, in good faith, and without

[9] The take-free rule for money allows the transferee to take free of a competing security interest.

notice of listed problems with the instrument), takes free of property claims to the instrument.

Because Bitcoin is not tangible and does not fall into any of the asset categories that benefit from the above-described rules, the unamended UCC rules are not desirable for parties who engage in commercial transactions involving Bitcoin. Anyone taking a transfer of Bitcoin as a payment or as collateral would take the Bitcoin subject to any security interest perfected by filing. To ascertain competing interests in the Bitcoin, a creditor or other transferee would be required to search the public records. The requirement to do so makes Bitcoin, and all other cryptocurrencies, unattractive as a medium of exchange.

To satisfy the market demand for negotiable assets, the drafters of the 2022 Amendments had to do three important things: define the intangible assets covered by Article 12, draft take-free rules for the assets, and develop an analog to possession for the take-free rules.

5 Focus on Digital Assets: Definitions and Technological Neutrality

As noted above, new Article 12 of the UCC governs the transfer of "Controllable Electronic Records." The words "crypto," "blockchain," "distributed ledger" and the like appear nowhere in the statute or in its Official Comments. Their absence is explained by the drafters' focus on technological neutrality. The goal is to have rules that work for today's digital assets and for those that will emerge in the future. The best example of a technologically neutral ULC act is the Uniform Electronic Transactions Act, promulgated in 1999 and enacted throughout the United States. At the time that act was drafted, electronic communications tended to be by e-mail and web sites on desktop computers. By providing that a contract cannot be denied enforceability solely because it is in electronic form or signed electronically and by defining "electronic" broadly (Uniform Electronic Transactions Act 1999:§2 (5)),[10] the statute has lasted 25 years so far.

"Digital Assets" is a term that the drafters could have used to describe the assets subject to Article 12, but that would have posed some problems. The ULC had already used that term in its Revised Uniform Fiduciary Access to Digital Assets Act (RUFADAA), and it is ULC policy to use definitions consistently throughout its acts. Another problem was that the term digital assets is sometimes (and is in the RUFADAA) used to describe a broad range of intangible assets, including social

[10] Defines "electronic" as "relating to technology having electrical, digital, magnetic, wireless, optical, electromagnetic, or similar capabilities.".

media accounts, e-mail accounts, and internet domain names (Revised Uniform Fiduciary Access to Digital Assets Act 2015:§2).[11] Although some of these assets are transferred and used as collateral for loans, they are not used in commerce in the same way that the assets that came to be known as CERs are.

To limit the assets covered by Article 12 to those used for payment and investment purposes, the drafters focused on the idea of control. In other words, to be classified as a CER, the electronic record must be susceptible to control, as defined in Article 12. The UCC defines Controllable Electronic Record as "a record stored in an electronic medium that can be subjected to control under Sect. 12–105" (*Uniform Commercial Code* n.d.:§12–102 (a)(1)).

The definition of control is designed to mimic possession. To have control of a CER, the person claiming control must have the power to enjoy all the benefits of the electronic record, to prevent others from enjoying all the benefits of the electronic record, and transfer control of the electronic record (*Uniform Commercial Code* n.d.:§12–105 (a)).

6 Possession and Control

One might ask why the UCC drafters did not concede that a CER could be possessed. The Article 12 definition of control mirrors the legal understanding of possession; just as a person in possession of a tangible item can include others in and exclude others from the enjoyment of that item, a person in control of a CER can do the same.

The classic first possession cases that are staples of law school Property casebooks define possession in terms of control. Law students learn that possession does not always mean manual possession of a tangible item. When discussing the concept of relative title, students read cases in which parties dispute rights in foxes (*Pierson v. Post* 1805), whales (*Ghen v. Rich,* 1881), and fish (*State v. Shaw* 1902). In *Pierson v. Post*, in which the parties fought over rights in a wild fox, the court explained that a person could establish first possession of a wild animal by wounding or ensnaring it "so as to deprive [it] of [its] natural liberty, and subject [it] to the control of [its] pursuer" (*Pierson v. Post* 1805:179). In *Ghen v. Rich,* in which the court had to decide the validity of a local custom for establishing first rights in a whale, the court upheld the custom because it required for first possession "the only act of appropriation that is possible in the nature of the case" (*Ghen v. Rich,* 1881: 162). In *State v. Shaw*, the court found the defendant guilty of larceny when he took fish out of a net belonging to another. The fish in that case were able to leave the net, but the court followed the rule that to acquire a property right in a wild animal, a person must bring the animal into "his power and control and so maintain his control as to show that he does not intend to abandon them again to the world at large" (*State v. Shaw* 1902: 876).

[11] Defining "digital asset" as "an electronic record in which an individual has a right or interest." The Comment to § 2 explains the wide range of assets that fall within this definition, such as "information stored on a user's computer and other digital devices.".

In all the above cases, the courts found possession when they found control. Although the assets in question were all tangible, the cases illustrate that possession can mean something less than taking an item in your hands. Yet discussions of possession tend to acknowledge that the "something" that is to be possessed is a tangible object,[12] likely because there was no such thing as a rivalrous intangible asset until recently. Moreover, whether or not one has experience in fox hunting, whale hunting, or fishing, it is easy to understand how one can capture such an asset so to establish first rights to it. One can see a wounded fox, a dead whale with a marking attached, and fish in a net. Possession has long been accepted as a signal of title, and signals are most effective when they can be seen (Baird and Jackson 1983: 180).[13]

Following the accepted view of possession, when the UCC says possession, it means manual possession. This is evident in several provisions of Article 9. For example, one way a creditor can perfect a security interest is by taking possession of collateral. A creditor can only perfect by possession if the collateral is tangible, such as goods, negotiable instruments, and documents (*Uniform Commercial Code* n.d.:§9–313). If the collateral is intangible, a creditor must perfect its interest by filing a financing statement (*Uniform Commercial Code* n.d.:§9–310).

More support for the "possession means manual possession" orientation of the UCC can be found in the Article 9 enforcement provisions. Article 9 allows a creditor after default to take possession of the collateral if it can do so without a breach of the peace. It also allows a creditor to "disable" equipment, which is a term of art that refers to goods used in a business (*Uniform Commercial Code* n.d.:§9–609). As "smart" and connected goods proliferate, creditor/sellers have the ability to remotely disable goods. Subprime auto lenders have been disabling consumer goods, an act not approved by the UCC, for more than 25 years (Moringiello 2022: 568–573).[14] Yet because the UCC is read to mean that possession is the manual possession of tangible goods, neither courts nor the drafters of the code have addressed the issue.

The modern UCC adopted the concept of control as the equivalent of possession for intangible assets. When Article 8, governing the transfer of investment securities was revised in 1994, the drafters introduced the concept of control to the UCC (Rogers 1995: 697). Control was an appropriate substitute for possession; under the emerging indirect holding system for securities, the ownership and transfer of rights in business entities was no longer evidenced by the existence and manual transfer of paper certificates. Instead, under the indirect holding system, evidence of ownership is maintained on the books of intermediaries, and the resulting asset, or the package of rights that one obtains when these accounting entries are made, is known as a securities entitlement (Anderson et al. 2001: 1452–1453). The attempt to analogize

[12] *See, e.g.,* Merrill 2017:114: "Possession 'refers to a claim by a person of exclusive control over a physical object.'"; Curtin 1978:25: Acknowledging that the classic first possession cases "all involve questions of title to tangible personal property.".

[13] "Since *Twyne's Case,* [decided in 1601] possession has been viewed as the best available source of information concerning ownership' of most types of personal property."

[14] Explaining the history of automated shutoff devices and the lack of judicial opinions analyzing the use of such devices under the UCC.

the holding and transfer of this asset to possession and delivery was described by one participant in the drafting process to "trying to insert an expanding multi-faceted peg in a round hole" (Aronstein 1990:429). The drafters of the 1994 version of Article 8 thus provided several definitions of control, a definition for certificated securities that incorporates possession and delivery, and a definition for securities entitlements that focuses not on possession, but on the purchaser's right to direct transfers of the securities entitlement without the consent of the purchaser's transferor (*Uniform Commercial Code* n.d.:§8–106 (a)-(d)). Article 9 allows a secured party to perfect its security interest by perfecting by control as defined in Article 8 (*Uniform Commercial Code* n.d.:§§9–106, 9–314).

The drafters imported control into Article 9 when the 1998 amendments incorporated security interests in deposit accounts as original collateral (Anderson et al. 2001: 221–223). The definitions of control for those assets mimic possession in some respects but not in others. For example, if the secured party is the bank at which the customer maintains the deposit account, the secured party has control over the deposit account (*Uniform Commercial Code* n.d.:§9–104 (a)(1)). Facially, this definition mimics possession, although what is being possessed is the customer's payment claims. A secured party can also gain control by an agreement with the bank and the debtor that provides that the bank will comply with the secured party's instructions regarding disposition of the funds in the account (*Uniform Commercial Code* n.d.:§9–104 (a)(2)). While this does not mirror possession, this method of control would be consistent with an ordinary understanding of the word control.

Because of the view that only tangible assets can be possessed and the UCC history of substituting control for possession when intangible assets are collateral, control became not only the method for transferring a CER, but a key part of the definition of CER. A digital asset is not a CER unless it is susceptible to control, as defined in Article 12 (*Uniform Commercial Code* n.d.:§12–102 (a)(1)).

A definition of control that mimics possession allows Article 12 to include take-free rules for CERs that are easily analogized to the existing take-free rules for negotiable instruments. A qualifying purchaser of a CER, defined as a purchaser who takes control of a CER for value, in good faith, and without notice of a property claim to the CER (*Uniform Commercial Code* n.d.:§12–102 (a)(2)), takes that CER free from competing property interests in the CER (*Uniform Commercial Code* n.d.:§12–104 (e)). This makes the CER negotiable; no one who takes Bitcoin as a form of payment would want to worry about other property interests in the Bitcoin.

Control is important in Article 9 as well. Because a CER remains a general intangible under the 2022 Amendments (*Uniform Commercial Code* n.d.:§9–102 (a)(42)), a secured creditor can perfect its security interest in it by filing a financing statement (*Uniform Commercial Code* n.d.:§9–312 (a)). Such a filing will give the creditor priority over a Trustee in Bankruptcy or other lien creditor. As it does for negotiable instruments, Article 9 contains a non-temporal priority for CERs. A secured creditor can take control of a CER to perfect its security interest (*Uniform Commercial Code* n.d.:§9–314). If it does so, its interest has priority over all prior security interests that were perfected by filing (*Uniform Commercial Code* n.d.:§9–326).

7 Tethering

While the UCC amendments were being drafted, the non-fungible token, or NFT, craze emerged. This craze led the drafters to consider whether NFTs are the kind of asset that falls within the definition of CER. Over the course of a few years, people claimed that they could tether NFTs to all sorts of assets, from drawings of apes to real estate, and that transferring the NFT could result in a quick and friction-free transfer of the underlying asset (Moringiello and Odinet 2021: 608–613).[15]

The problem with these claims is that there is no law that allows one asset to be transferred by the transfer of an NFT. Tokenization has a long history in United States law. Traditionally, tokenization refers to the reification of an intangible right in a tangible asset, usually a piece of paper. Negotiable instruments and corporate stock certificates are strong tokens, in that the transfer of the paper results in the transfer of the intangible right. Deeds to real estate are also tokens; in order to transfer rights in real estate, the transferor must deliver a piece of paper (the deed) to transfer an intangible right (fee simple absolute or another interest in the real estate). Bills of lading, which give the holder rights to goods, can also be considered tokens (Moringiello and Odinet 2021: 615–625).

All of the above tokens developed to solve specific problems. As the tokens developed, the law developed to recognize the relationship between the token and the underlying asset. There has been no such development with NFTs, nor has anyone made any compelling case for linking a token to an underlying asset.

The drafters of the UCC amendments recognized this gap in the law and decided not to fill it. They made two exceptions, for controllable accounts and controllable payment intangibles. Article 12 provides that an account (account receivable) or a payment intangible can be tethered to a CER so that the transfer of the CER will effectuate a transfer of the payment right (*Uniform Commercial Code* n.d.:§12–104). This creates an electronic analog to a negotiable instrument, which must still be in paper form.

8 Conclusion

At the time of writing, the 2022 Amendments to the UCC have been adopted in 24 United States jurisdictions. The slow adoption can be chalked up to the general political divide in the United States. Several high-profile politicians were convinced that the Amendments promoted and enabled a Central Bank Digital Currency,[16] something that, as state law, the UCC cannot do.

[15] Describing the NFT craze and the claims of those who promote NFTs.

[16] The most high-profile example is former South Dakota Governor Kristi Noem, now United States Secretary of Homeland Security, who vetoed a bill to enact the amendments in 2023, but ultimately signed a bill a year later that removed all mentions of electronic money (Strubinger 2024). Several other states have taken this approach proactively to head off political opposition to their bills.

Time will tell as to whether the definition of Controllable Electronic Record will stand the test of time in the same way the technology-neutral definitions in UETA did. The 2022 Amendments were designed to allow innovation in digital assets by providing a clear framework for their transfer, including their transfer as collateral. The coming years will tell us whether this clear framework achieved its goal.

References

Anderson TM, Culhane MB, Wilson CL (2001) Attachment and perfection of security interests under revised article 9: A Nuts and Bolts Primer. Am Bankr Inst L Rev 9:179

Aronstein MJ (1990) The new/old law of securities transfer: calling a spade a heart, diamond, club or the like. Cardozo L Rev 12:429

Baird DG, Jackson TH (1983) Possession and ownership: An examination of the scope of article 9. Stan L Rev 35:175

Curtin JS (1978) The concept of possession in commercial transactions: chasing the quick-Brown fox. Loy U Chi LJ 10:25

Electronic Signatures in Global and National Commerce Act 15 U.S.C. (2000)

Elvy S-A (2015) Contracting in the age of the internet of things: article 2 of the UCC and beyond. Hofstra L Rev 44:839

Ghen v. Rich, 8 F. 159 (District Court, D. Massachusetts 1881)

Magnuson-Moss Warranty Act 15 U.S.C. §§ 2301–2312 (1975)

Merrill TW (2017) Formalization, possession, and ownership. Brigham-Kanner Prop Rts Conf J (113) HeinOnline. https://scholarship.law.columbia.edu/faculty_scholarship/3318

Moringiello JM (2007) False categories in commercial law: the (ir) relevance of (in) tangibility. Fla State Univ Law Rev 35:141–150

Moringiello JM (2022) Automating Repossession. Nev Law J 22:563

Moringiello JM, Odinet CK (2021) The property law of tokens. Fla Law Rev 74(4):607–670. https://doi.org/10.2139/ssrn.3928901

Pierson v. Post, 3 Cai. R. 175 (N.Y. 1805)

Revised Uniform Fiduciary Access to Digital Assets Act (2015). https://www.uniformlaws.org/committees/community-home/librarydocuments?communitykey=f7237fc4-74c2-4728-81c6-b39a91ecdf22&LibraryFolderKey=&DefaultView=&5a583082-7c67-452b-9777-e4bdf7e1c729=eyJsaWJyYXJ5ZW50cnkiOiJlOWY4NWQ3Yy0xM2YzLTQ5MTgtYTAwMC0wYWJlN2ZhYjdmNjIifQ%3D%3D.

Rogers JS (1995) An essay on horseless carriages and paperless negotiable instruments: some lessons from the article 8 revision. Ida Law Rev 31:689

State v. Shaw, 65 N.E. 875 (Ohio 1902)

Stein RA (2013) Forming a more perfect union: a history of the uniform law commission. LexisNexis

Strubinger L (2024) Gov. Noem signs UCC updates she vetoed last year, with two changes. SDPB Radio. https://www.sdpb.org/politics/2024-02-27/noem-signs-ucc-bill-she-vetoed-last-year. Accessed 11 Nov 2024

The American Law Institute (2024a) Frequently asked questions. American Law Institute, https://www.ali.org/about-ali/faq/. Accessed 11 Nov 2024

The American Law Institute (2024b) About ALI. American Law Institute, https://www.ali.org/about-ali/. Accessed 11 Nov 2024

Uniform Commercial Code (n.d.)

Uniform Electronic Transactions Act (1999) https://www.uniformlaws.org/viewdocument/final-act-21?CommunityKey=2c04b76c-2b7d-4399-977e-d5876ba7e034&tab=librarydocuments.

Uniform Law Commission (2024) Uniform commercial code. Uniform Law Commission. https://www.uniformlaws.org/acts/ucc. Accessed 11 Nov 2024

Juliet M. Moringiello was a distinguished legal scholar and leader in law reform, whose contributions shaped both state and national legal landscapes. As Associate Dean for Academic Affairs at Widener University Commonwealth Law School, she played a pivotal role in the enactment of key revisions to the Uniform Commercial Code in Pennsylvania and contributed to numerous legal reforms, including the Uniform Voidable Transactions Act. Moringiello was a member of the American Law Institute, a Uniform Law Commissioner for Pennsylvania, and held influential roles such as Vice-Chair of the ALI/ULC Drafting Committee on the Uniform Commercial Code and Emerging Technologies. A respected scholar, her work on online contracting, digital assets, and bankruptcy law was widely cited, including in high-profile court cases and federal publications. Recognised for her excellence in teaching and scholarship, Moringiello was honoured with multiple awards, including the Outstanding Faculty Award and the Douglas E. Ray Excellence in Faculty Scholarship Award. Outside the classroom, she shared her passion for skiing as a certified instructor at Roundtop Mountain Resort. Sadly, on 27 February 2025, Juliet passed away after a courageous battle with cancer. She will be dearly missed. We are honoured to dedicate this collection to her memory.

Digital Assets and Contract

Why Should Contracts Be Smart?

Eliza Mik

Abstract This chapter enquires about the practical implications of making contracts smart. To many, any questions about the desirability of expressing contracts in code may seem like unnecessary academic nit-picking by someone who "clearly does not understand the unstoppable potential of the crypto economy." Code is, after all, supposed to remedy commercial uncertainty and guarantee performance. Code is, if one follows the dominant crypto-narrative, the solution to most of the world's problems! The simple question about the reason why contracts should be made smart may, however, lie at the very core of the misunderstandings surrounding smart contracts. Both lawyers and crypto-enthusiasts often overlook the important distinction between the source of contractual obligations and the expression of such obligations, not to mention the distinction between the *tools* used to perform an obligation and the contract itself. They also seem to assume that the manner of expressing a contract can guarantee its performance… In reality, the fact that an obligation or a contractual term are expressed in code can hardly be regarded as beneficial. Once a contract is expressed in code, the risk of breach is effectively replaced with the risk of programming errors, incorrect compilation or the unexpected execution of code.

> So many smart people had spent so many thousands of hours working on Crypto – and yet shockingly little of use had come of it. (Faux 2023: 237)

1 Introduction

Many scholars and regulators have been as nonchalant about contractual doctrine and technical terminology as Sam Bankman-Fried has been about the funds of his investors. Countless hours and dozens of academic articles have been devoted to the question whether "smart contracts" are or could be contracts in the legal sense of

E. Mik (✉)
Faculty of Law, Chinese University of Hong Kong, Hong Kong, China
e-mail: eliza@elizamik.io

P. Babie and M. Giancaspro (eds.), *Private Law, Digital Assets, and Infrastructure*,
https://doi.org/10.1007/978-981-96-7121-2_6

the term. The debates are often characterized by an uninformed use of both legal and technical terms as well as by a disregard of basic legal principles.[1] Hardly any analysis is devoted to the critical question *why* or *how* contracts should be made smart. To fill this gap, this chapter bypasses the debate as to the legal character of smart contracts. Irrespective of how many times it is demonstrated that comparing computer programs to legally enforceable agreements constitutes a category mistake, the idea that such programs can be contracts remains entrenched in many legal and technical analyses. Instead, this chapter asks: what would be the benefit of making a contract smart? How would this work in practice? What does it mean for a contract to be smart in the first place?

The term "smart" is traditionally associated with equipping objects with computer chips and/or connecting them to the Internet. Most readers are familiar with "smart TVs," "smartphones," or even "smart fridges." In such context, "smartness" denotes the additional functionality acquired by such objects due to their technological embellishment. The concept of smart contracts has, however, developed in the context of blockchains and the crypto economy.[2] Smart contracts are thus commonly associated with "programmable money," crypto-trading and decentralized finance (Eenmaa-Dimitrieva and Schmidt-Kessen 2019; Schär 2021). In such contexts, "smartness" seems to indicate that the "contract" is expressed in code (Werbach and Cornell 2017: 352). As smart contracts are said to "embody" or "execute" the terms of an agreement, their "smartness" is supposed to guarantee strict adherence to such terms and hence the performance of the agreement (Mark Verstraete 2020; Shin 2022: 146–148, 154). Once embodied in code, the obligations are set in stone and the contract cannot be broken. At least, this is what the mainstream smart contract narrative wants everyone to believe. It must be remembered that many discussions of smart contracts are difficult to follow given that the term has a myriad of inconsistent definitions (Mik 2019). It can, among others, refer to the embedding of legal terms in hardware and software to prevent breach (Szabo 1997), to transactional scripts (Cohney and Hoffman 2020: 323), or to a "collection of code and data (…) deployed using cryptographically signed transactions on the blockchain network" (Yaga et al. 2018: 54). Abstracting from strictly technical definitions, which generally associate smart contracts with distributed applications (Antonopoulos and Wood 2019; Guadamuz 2019), smart contracts are often described in legal terms and regarded as tools or mechanisms ensuring the performance of certain contractual obligations (Cieplak and Leefatt 2017)[3] or as programs implementing agreements (Governatori et al. 2018).

This chapter enquires about the practical implications of making contracts smart. To many, such enquiry may seem like unnecessary academic nit-picking by someone

[1] For recent examples, see (Dixon 2024; Bohyer and Hayajneh 2023); For a broader overview of the failure of legal scholarship to verify popular claims, see (Low and Mik 2020).

[2] The concept dates back to the mid-90 s but it has gained prominence with the introduction of the Ethereum blockchain, see: (Buterin 2015).

[3] For a more recent example, see: Article 2 (39) Regulation of The European Parliament and of the Council on harmonised rules on fair access to and use of data and amending (*Regulation (EU) 2017/2394 and Directive (EU) 2020/1828* 2024).

who "clearly does not understand the unstoppable potential of the crypto economy." It may, however, lie at the very core of the misunderstandings surrounding smart contracts. Both lawyers and crypto-enthusiasts often overlook the important distinction between the source of contractual obligations and the expression of such obligations, not to mention the distinction between the *tools* used to perform an obligation and the contract itself. They also seem to assume that the manner of expressing a contract can guarantee its performance…

1.1 Outline of Argument

To understand the challenges of expressing contracts (or parts thereof) in code, it is necessary to provide some technical background. The chapter commences with an explanation of the term "code" and its relationship with programming languages and computer programs. It demonstrates that expressing contracts in code creates multiple technical challenges related to the difficulty of ensuring that the *executable* code matches the source code and, more importantly, is error free. The chapter proceeds to present the legal background or, more specifically, the principles of contract law that are directly relevant to the legal analyses of smart contracts. The point is not to enquire whether smart contracts can be contracts in the legal sense, but to address two popular controversies: "can contracts be expressed in code?" and "is it legally permissible to automate the performance of contractual obligations?" Once the technicalities and the legalities are cleared, the chapter shifts its focus to the UK Law Commission ("UKLC") advice on so-called "smart legal contracts" ("Advice") (The Law Commission 2021). The document illustrates how the imprudent use of legal and technical concepts as well as the creation of nonsensical "solutions" to non-existent problems perpetuates a state of legal confusion. While the Advice devotes little time to explaining the benefits of making contracts smart, it simply assumes that it is not only necessary but possible for an entire contract to be represented in code. This assumption is ill-conceived—both from a technical and from a legal perspective.

In line[4] with the dominant smart contract narrative, the following discussion assumes that the aim of making contracts "smart" is to automate certain actions leading to or done in relation to the performance of contractual obligations.[5] Indirectly, it demonstrates the futility of placing "smart contracts" within a framework designed to analyze *human* actions and intentions in order to establish the existence of a legally enforceable agreement. Unsurprisingly, parts of the discussion will resemble forcing square pegs into triangular holes…

---

[4] But not in agreement!

[5] "Discharge" denotes the extinguishment of obligations (Furmston et al. 2017:696. 711).

2 Technical Background

To say that a contract is "smart" or "in code" means that the contract is written in a programming language. Programming languages are artificial languages used to instruct computers. Unlike natural languages, which are inherently ambiguous as they lack a formalized grammar (Russell and Norvig 2021: 270, 874, 875),[6] programming languages have a fixed syntax, strict rules defining the semantics and a pre-defined set of acceptable inputs (Russell and Norvig 2021: 269–272). Unlike natural languages, which resolve ambiguity by reference to context, programming languages are designed to preclude any ambiguity (Casalnuovo et al. 2019).[7] Consequently, to express contracts in code, any term that requires (or presupposes!) *human* interpretation and a reference to an external context, must be converted into a form that requires neither. The code will be unambiguous, self-contained—and unforgiving. An instruction written in code will not be open to debate or reinterpretation.

Broadly speaking, code can be said to exist at the programming level and at a machine level (Mitchell 2011: 170). On a programming level, it is common to speak of source code, which denotes human-readable instructions written in a high-level programming language, such as Java, Python or, in the case of smart contracts, Solidity. Source code is designed to facilitate programming. On a machine level, it is common to speak of machine code, which refers to low-level instructions that can be directly executed by the computer's central processing unit ("CPU"). Machine code is expressed in binary format (1s and 0s) and is specific to a particular computer architecture. While source code is human-friendly and relatively easy to write, machine code is hardware-friendly, and thus extremely difficult to write. It is, after all, incomprehensible to humans. As computer programs are generally written in source code but executed in machine code, source code must be converted into machine code. This is done through a process called compilation or interpretation. Compilation translates the entire source code into machine code in one go, creating an *executable* file. Interpretation translates the source code line by line into machine code while the program is running. This conversion can be a source of errors and affect the manner in particular smart contract executes. The distinction between source and machine code roughly translates into high-level and low-level programming languages. Smart contracts are generally written in high-level programming languages (that is: source code) and subsequently compiled into a lower-level language (that is: byte code) to run in the Ethereum Virtual Machine (EVM) (Kannengießer et al. 2021: 8). The latter provides a secure and isolated execution environment,[8] which is independent of the hardware a particular blockchain runs on. In sum, the smart contract is written in source code but executed in byte code, after undergoing a conversion by a compiler. To realize the implications of this conversion, it is worth quoting a technical paper:

[6] "there is no one definitive language model for English in the way that there is for Python 3.8."

[7] But see, in the context of smart contracts, (Grimmelmann 2019:9).

[8] A virtual machine is a software emulation of a physical computing environment.

> Smart contracts are typically developed in a high-level contract language and compiled to low-level virtual machine code before being committed to the blockchain. For a smart contract user to trust a given piece of low-level code on the blockchain, they must convince themselves that (a) they are in possession of the matching source code and (b) that the compiler has correctly translated the source code to the given low-level code. (Krijnen et al. 2022: 1)

Simply put, persons wanting to deploy an existing smart contract that is available on one of the popular permissionless blockchains (e.g. Ethereum) have a little assurance that its source code matches the low-level executable code. While both the high-level source code and the low-level byte code are transparent and can be inspected, (a) only the source code is human readable while the byte code takes the form of incomprehensible numbers and (b) it is the latter, not the former that is actually executed. The byte code is thus more important than the source code. The executable code may, in practice, differ from the human-readable code, be it due to a problem with the compiler itself or with the compilation process.[9] The average user will lack the technical skill to verify that the executable "version" of the smart contract is equivalent to its source code. Similarly, such user will lack the ability to evaluate the quality of the compiler or the compilation process. Many readers may regard these observations as unnecessary technicalities. It must be, however, remembered that transparency of the smart contract code is one of the central tenets of the "crypto-ideology" and, as discussed below, the entire smart contract narrative rests on the assumption that the expression of agreements in code renders them superior to their traditional equivalents. In reality, however, the ability to view the code is of little relevance and the problems of converting source into byte code are generally overlooked. The focus is placed, almost exclusively, on the generic term *code*—without any regard to the different of types of code.

The problems do not end here. As indicated, smart contracts are executed in the EVM, which operates "on top" of a blockchain. To be compiled into code that can execute in the EVM, smart contracts must be written in a specific type of programming language. Smart contract programming languages are relatively new, untested and often insecure (Rosu 2018). In principle, it is generally more beneficial to write programs in well-known, "tried and tested" programming languages and to use compilers with a proven track record. Smart contracts cannot, however, be written in any of the "older" programming languages such as Python or C because such languages cannot be compiled to the EVM (Parizi et al. 2018). The quality of a programming language affects the quality of smart contracts and many errors in their execution have, in fact, been attributed to the low quality or insecurity of the language they were written in.[10] This leads to the next point: the quality of programming. For smart contracts to guarantee performance (or the achievement of some agreed result), it is crucial that their code does not contain programming errors and/or vulnerabilities. It is practically impossible, however, to write code that is error

[9] Additional problems may derive from a "code substitution attack" where an adversary presents source code that does not match the executable low level code; see (Krijnen et al. 2022).

[10] See generally: (Antonopoulos and Wood 2019:128, 129).

free and, more importantly, the execution of which can be predicted. Contrary to popular belief, smart contracts are notorious for vulnerabilities and programming errors (Gupta et al. 2020; Atzei et al. 2017: 10). The latter are mistakes in the implementation of a system design that result in unexpected outputs. The former enable the malicious misuse of a system implementation to achieve effects contrary to its goals (so-called "exploits"). Smart contracts can be as unpredictable as humans.

Lastly, the fact that the contract is expressed in code need not mean that it becomes a computer program. Computer programs are executable.[11] This means that the instructions contained therein can be converted into sequences of actions. Computer programs are commands to *do* something. In contrast, some code is "only" machine-readable. This means that the specific file, such as an XML or a JSON file, can be parsed by a computer program. All executable files are machine-readable, but not all machine-readable files are executable. "Machine-readable" broadly refers to any data that can be interpreted or parsed by a computer, while "machine-executable" denotes instructions that result in actions. This is important in the present context because smart contracts are meant to "execute the terms of agreements" and such execution is supposed to guarantee the performance of contractual obligations (or, at least, the achievement of some agreed result). This positions smart contracts outside of the broader "LegalTech" narrative, which predominantly focuses on technologies used to facilitate certain aspects of contract management and analysis (Susskind OBE 2010). Automating the handling of contractual *documents* is unrelated to the automation of contractual *performance*.

3 Legal Background

When thinking of smart contracts, one of the first questions that comes to mind is: "can a contract be expressed in code?" Contrary to popular perceptions and subject to a small number of statutory exceptions dictating that some contracts be made or evidenced in writing, contract law does not prescribe how parties should express their agreement (UK Law Commission 2018: 20; Chitty and Beale 2015: paras 1–016, 2–001; Anson and Beatson 2010: 75). A contract can be formed orally or by conduct, it can be expressed in words (either spoken or written) or in actions. A contract can be formed in morse code, computer code or in smoke signals. In principle, there are no legal obstacles to agreements being written in code either in part or in their entirety. As contract law is largely indifferent to the issue *whether* or *how* an agreement is memorialized, it seems unnecessary to seek clarifications as to whether contracts can be expressed in code. Of course, the manner of expression (if any!) affects the difficulty of determining what has been agreed. The contents of an oral agreement will, by definition, be more difficult to prove than the contents of a written agreement signed by both parties.

---

[11] Executable" refers to files, often called binary executable files that contain machine code instructions that the computer's CPU can *understand* and *follow* directly.

There are also no legal obstacles to automate the process of contract formation and/or the processes involved in the performance of contractual obligations. In other words, it is legally permissible to use computer programs to form and/or perform contracts. Any obstacles are practical, not legal in nature. It may, for example, be impossible to automate the performance of strictly personal obligations that require human performance, such as teaching a course in contract law or cutting someone's hair. Much will depend on the type of contract and the nature of a specific obligation. As demonstrated by vending machines, parking meters and algorithmic trading, neither the automated formation of a contract nor its automated performance are legally problematic (*Thornton v Shoe Lane Parking Ltd* 1971). In practice, judges tend to gloss over the fact that the formation and/or performance of the contract is automated or involves computer programs (*Software Solutions Partners Ltd v Her Majesty's Commissioners for Customs and Excise* 2007).

4 Some Practical Considerations

What is important in the present context is not only that contract law is extremely liberal as to how parties express their agreement but that the expression of the agreement, be it words printed on paper or displayed on a screen, is not synonymous with the agreement (Kolber 2018: 219). The medium used to memorialize the contract constitutes proof of the parties' obligations, but it does not *create* them. Doubts concerning the enforceability of "smart contracts," which are written in code, and the resulting calls for regulatory intervention aimed at clarifying their legal status, derive from the failure to distinguish between the source of the rights and obligations and their expression. From a legal perspective, the source of the parties' respective rights and obligations is their agreement. Its written expression, if any, is of secondary importance. As illustrated by contractual templates that are prepared in advance to govern future transactions, it is possible to have a written contractual *document* that does not embody an *agreement*. In most instances, the parties will not *express* their agreement until they *are* in agreement![12] Once this distinction is firmly kept in mind, one must ask: if the parties have formed a contract, why would they go to the trouble of expressing such contract in code and not in a traditional manner?

The accompanying challenges will depend on whether the parties translate their agreement into a smart contract (e.g. "let's make our lease into a smart contract so that whenever you do not pay, I can disable your access with my smart lock!") or whether they decide to "use" an existing smart contract to govern their agreement ("I found this smart contract on Ethereum, it says it executes the terms of a lease—let's use it). In both instances, the parties *must agree* to "make their contract smart" or to use a smart contract…

In the first scenario, when the parties agree to "make their lease smart," they must convert their contract (or part thereof) into a computer program. Assuming

[12] They can either express the agreement themselves or customize a standard template.

that neither party knows how to code, they will hire a developer and instruct him or her what the smart contract should do or, assuming they have a written agreement in place, point the developer to the relevant parts of such agreement. In the first instance (no written agreement) the developer will rely on the parties' instructions, in the second (written agreement) the developer will rely on the document. Interestingly, in both instances the developer may find it difficult to establish the exact actions to be executed by the smart contract. The parties' instructions may be unclear or inconsistent, the written agreement may be ambiguous or incomplete. The developer may require additional information or more precise instructions. As the smart contract is supposed to execute automatically, irrespective of any change in the circumstances, the parties may realize the need to provide for more contingencies. They will not, after all, be able to rely on open-ended terms (Gergen 1992), such as "reasonable efforts" or "good faith" (Levy 2017: 11). They will also not be able to introduce any further amendments or interfere with the smart contract's operation. This will force them to express their obligations with unprecedented precision, in a manner that leaves nothing to interpretation or implication. Even if their agreement is originally not in writing, they may have to write down the instructions for the developer to ensure that the smart contract matches their agreement and addresses the greatest number of contingencies that might affect the commercial viability of the transaction. To aggravate matters, even if their instructions or the written agreement are perfectly clear it may still be difficult to write a smart contract that perfectly matches the agreed obligations.[13] Given the differences between natural- and programming languages, it is technically challenging to map natural language—including meticulously drafted legal prose—onto computer instructions. The problem is not that smart contracts cannot *remove* the ambiguity of natural language, an idea frequently mentioned in legal literature (Finck 2018: 27), but that such "removal" will lead to a situation where the smart contract does not accurately reflect the original agreement! With the exception of extremely simple payment obligations, ("on date X, transfer amount Y to account Z"), most terms drafted in legal prose will be imprecise to varying degrees—not due to bad drafting but because natural language is inherently ambiguous. Such discrepancies will be unavoidable and more pronounced in the case of complex obligations requiring lengthy descriptions. The more "legal language" must be translated into a programming language, the greater the risk of code not matching the original agreement.

In the second scenario, when the parties decide to use an existing smart contract to govern their relationship, they will most likely use one of the publicly available smart contracts on the Ethereum blockchain. Such smart contracts are usually accompanied by a brief description as to their functionality and their source code is available for inspection. The problem is that most publicly available smart contracts are written by anonymous developers who cannot be trusted as to their competence or motives. As indicated, the ability to inspect the smart contract's source code provides little assurance as to its quality and virtually no guarantee as to the manner it will execute

[13] There have been multiple attempts to create domain-specific programming languages for "smart contracts" that could capture the semantic richness of legal language, see: (Khalil 2017).

once it is compiled into byte code. Absent a direct contractual relationship with the developer, the parties have no assurance that the smart contract will do what it is supposed to do. More importantly, the parties will face great difficulty in ensuring that the smart contract matches their original agreement.

In sum, making a contract smart is legally permissible but technically challenging. This leads to the next point: the dangers of uninformed assumptions as to *why* or *how* to make contracts smart…

5 UK Law Commission Advice on Smart Legal Contracts

In a recent document titled "*Smart Legal Contracts Advice to Government*," ("Advice") the UKLC defined smart contracts as "computer code that, upon the occurrence of a specified condition or conditions, is capable of running automatically according to pre-specified functions" (The Law Commission 2021: vii). The UKLC elaborated that smart contracts can perform transactions on decentralized cryptocurrency exchanges, facilitate games and the exchange of collectibles on a distributed ledger as well as run online gambling programs (The Law Commission 2021: 1). Although these examples associate smart contracts with blockchains and although smart contracts gained popularity—and notoriety—with the introduction of the Ethereum blockchain (which was deliberately designed to enable their use), the UKLC decided not to permanently link them with any type of distributed ledger technology (The Law Commission 2021: 17). On one hand, such approach is technology neutral, on the other it abandons the *raison d'etre* of smart contracts—that of ensuring tamper-proof execution on a blockchain. It is also unclear why the definition refers to computer *code* instead of computer *programs*. All computer programs are expressed in code and all computer programs "run automatically" in response to specified conditions. Peculiar terminology aside, the definition seems to equate smart contracts with computer programs or with executable code (Giancaspro 2017: 831). If, however, smart contracts are "just" computer programs and if computer programs have been widely used for over 60 years to facilitate various aspects of commercial dealings (Mik 2022), then there simply is no legal problem. Why would anyone seek clarifications whether *computer programs* fit within the framework of contract law? Why would anyone debate whether executable code can be a contract? Seemingly then, the UKLC's somewhat awkward but simple and technology neutral approach provides some much-desired clarity and puts the entire "smart contract debate" to rest…

Regrettably, the UKLC proclaimed that "smart contracts can also be used to define and perform the obligations of a legally binding contract" (The Law Commission 2021: 1). This statement is confusing: how can a computer program *define* and *perform* obligations? To complicate matters, this particular type of smart contract was referred to as a "smart legal contract" and defined as a legally binding contract "in which some or all of the contractual obligations are defined in and/or performed automatically by a computer program" (The Law Commission 2021: 1, 8, 23). Following this "logic," smart contracts are computer programs but when they are used to "define and perform" contractual obligations, they become (?) smart *legal* contracts, which in turn are legally binding contracts in which some or all of the obligations "are defined in and/or performed automatically by a computer program" (The Law Commission 2021: 1, 8, 23). This approach is nonsensical.[14] How can computer programs become legally binding? How can "something" that is *used to perform* a contract become a contract? It remains unclear why the UKLC saw the need to introduce the concept of "smart *legal* contracts," especially given that it expressly acknowledged that it remained to be established how (and *whether*!) such "contracts" could "revolutionise the way we do business" (The Law Commission 2021: 1). In effect, the UKLC consulted the public on the legal implications of a phenomenon (for lack of a better term) that currently does not exist, may be unnecessary from a commercial perspective and technically impossible to implement in practice. Instead of clarifying the exact meaning and legal status of smart contracts (if any…) the UKLC sought advice about an abstract and convoluted *quasi*-legal construct on the assumption that it *will* gain relevance in the future (The Law Commission 2021: 1)!

Temporarily leaving aside "smart legal contracts," it is useful to inquire how smart contracts—or computer programs—can "define and perform" contractual obligations? Computer programs do not have the indispensable ability to reason, agree and act. They have neither the legal nor the technical capacity to define and perform contractual obligations. Admittedly, the UKLC was using a "linguistic shortcut" and referring to computer programs that *express* the relevant obligations in code or that can be *used* to automate the actions involved in their performance.[15] Such "shortcuts" seem, however, inadmissible in a document seeking to introduce clarity in a novel field, especially if such field is plagued by inconsistent terminology and a myriad of misunderstandings resulting from a conflation of legal and technical concepts (Reyes 2022: 89). It must be recalled that from their inception, smart contracts were associated with "self-executing" or "self-enforcing" contracts—*contracts* that ensured performance! There is, in other words, already plenty of confusion regarding the possibility of contracts performing or enforcing *themselves*! Instead of carefully framing the relevant definition, the UKLC's misconceived wording continues the absurd idea that contracts can act as discrete entities that define and perform "their" obligations.

It is uncontroversial that computer programs can be used to *automate* the performance of contractual obligations. It is nonsensical, however, to claim that computer programs can *define* and *perform* obligations. To define an obligation is to agree on the actions one will undertake (or refrain from undertaking) or to agree on the result to be achieved under a particular contract. Only the parties can define their obligations. "Of course," one might exclaim, "computer programs do not define obligations—they only expresses obligations in a programming language! The UKLC

[14] The UKLC's approach could be further distilled: smart contracts are computer programs and when such programs are used to perform contractual obligations, they are legally binding contracts.

[15] The same can be said with regards to "obligations *of* a legally binding contract"! Contracts cannot have obligations…

surely meant to say that computer code can be used to express obligations!" Given its rather nonchalant approach to terminology and a "discomfort" with the technologies involved, it is questionable whether the UKLC can be given the benefit of the doubt. Many important statements in the Advice require "creative" reinterpretations and additional clarifications.

The UKLC's approach also blurs the difference between performance and the *means* of performance. Only the parties can perform their respective contractual obligations. They can, however, perform such obligations by means of various technologies, including computer programs. To rephrase: computer programs can be used to automate the actions required to perform and hence to discharge contractual obligations. A typical example are automated teller machines, or ATMs, which automate the bank's contractual obligations to dispense funds on demand or to grant credit in pre-specified conditions. ATMs do not perform obligations. Another example is the Amazon platform. Arguably, Amazon can be regarded as an amalgam of smart contracts as it comprises thousands of computer programs that assist in the performance of Amazon's obligations. It cannot be suggested, however, that it is those smart contracts and not the e-commerce giant that perform the obligations deriving from the thousands of contracts that Amazon forms with its customers on a daily basis. In the above scenarios, computer programs are *tools* or *means* of performance. As I have described elsewhere (Mik 2022: 16, 17), in most circumstances, it is legally irrelevant whether the actions required to discharge a contractual obligation performed by a human or by a computer program. It is also irrelevant whether the orders placed on the Amazon website are processed by human employees or by software applications. What matters is the end result: is the order processed? Have the goods been delivered? In light of this, the UKLC's statement that smart contracts used to "define and perform" contracts are "legally binding contracts," seems particularly ill-informed. Computer programs cannot be contracts.

To provide fuel for endless academic debates, the Advice introduced three categories of smart legal contracts. Depending on the role played by code, these are: (a) natural language contracts with automated performance; (b) hybrid contracts and (c) solely code contracts (The Law Commission 2021: 11). Purportedly, such distinct categories were required to reflect "varying degrees of automation" (The Law Commission 2021: 22) and the role played by "code" (The Law Commission 2021: 23).

5.1 *Natural Language Contracts Performed Automatically*

The UKSC defined this category as a "contract in which all of the terms are recorded in natural language, either orally or in writing" (The Law Commission 2021: vi). In such contract, "some or all of the contractual obligations are performed automatically by the code of the computer program" (The Law Commission 2021: 22). Regarding such "traditional" contracts with automated performance, it is necessary to observe that this type of "smart legal contract" has pervaded commerce for more than 40 years.

There is nothing novel in automating the performance of contractual obligations, as exemplified by vending machines, parking meters and e-commerce websites. In the Amazon example, all contracts accompanying e-commerce transactions, especially those which involve the provision of digital content or services, can be regarded as smart legal contracts of the first category. Other examples are Netflix, Dropbox, Spotify as well as thousands of other online services that provide their services online, *by means of* a sophisticated infrastructure of hardware and computer programs. In such context, the "traditional" contract expressed in natural language takes the form of terms governing the use of an online service, usually available through a hyperlink placed on the bottom of the website or presented in a pop-up window during account set-up. Such terms create and describe the parties' respective rights and obligations—and the main obligations, such as payment and delivery are performed automatically. The terms can be said to exist *in parallel* to hundreds of electronic files containing the specific applications that enable the automated delivery of the requested content or service. Following the UKLC's approach, the aforementioned terms would constitute smart legal contracts. It remains unclear why such "novel category" is required, not to mention why such contracts would be regarded as "smart."

5.2 "Hybrid Contracts"

Most problems concern the second category, contracts that combine natural language and code. The UKLC defines such "hybrid contracts" as follows:

> A smart legal contract, some terms of which are defined in natural language and other terms of which are defined in the code of a computer program. Some or all of the contractual obligations are performed automatically by the code. In addition, the same contractual term(s) can be written in both natural language and in code. (The Law Commission 2021: vi)

As all computer programs are written in code, it is unclear why the UKLC chose to speak of "code of the computer program" when referring to contractual terms and of "code" in the context of contractual performance. It is also unclear what such "hybrid" smart legal contract would look like, especially given that some terms would be written "in both natural language and in code." One can, of course, imagine an electronic file—including a word document or python script—that contains provisions in natural language as well as executable code. The following questions arise: why would anyone express certain terms in code? What would be the purpose of a hybrid smart legal contract? Which terms would be defined by *in* code? Which obligations would be performed *by* the code? Only those which were defined in code? Would the contracting parties express some terms in natural language and some in code from the outset? Or would terms "defined in code" constitute a translation of natural language terms that were agreed to and written down earlier? If some terms are written both in natural language and in code, which expression would take precedence in case of conflict? How would the "encoded terms" be agreed upon if neither party knew how to code or understood code? Despite their importance, these questions have not been exhaustively addressed. The idea of hybrid smart legal contracts is so confusing that it deserves an extensive analysis—if only to illustrate the challenges of making contracts smart. Given space constraints, some points deserve brief mention.

First, the UKLC states that some *terms* are defined in code and "some or all" of contractual *obligations* are performed by code but does not clarify the reason for differentiating between terms and obligations. Why would anyone define terms in code given that it is not terms but obligations that are being performed? The contracting parties are generally more interested in the performance of the contract, not in the contractual document. Of course, the latter can provide conclusive evidence of what was agreed. It cannot, however, "perform anything." Assuming that the aim is to automate contractual performance, the focus should be on encoding of obligations not on encoding terms. There is often no direct mapping between terms and obligations as a single obligation can be defined in multiple terms. It would thus be necessary to "define in code" multiple terms that *taken together* would enable the automated performance of the relevant obligations. As smart contracts aim to guarantee performance, it seems more important for obligations to be performed than for terms to be defined in code.

Second, it is unclear *which* terms should be defined in code. As the definition of "hybrid" smart legal contracts mentions the automation of "some or *all* contractual obligations," it could be assumed that only those obligations that are described in the terms "defined in code" would be automated. A claim to the contrary seems illogical: what would be the purpose of encoding terms other than automating the obligations described therein? Nonetheless, given that the first category of smart legal contracts assumes that all terms are in natural language, but the performance of some obligations is automated, the idea of automatically performing obligations that are not expressed in code cannot be excluded. Irrespective of the foregoing, it must be acknowledged that not all contractual terms can be "defined in code" and "performed automatically." Before debating the definition of terms in code, it is necessary to establish which obligations can be performed by means of a computer program. It would, for example, seem pointless to "define in code" terms describing the governing law or force majeure provisions as the resulting obligations cannot be automated. Governing law provisions oblige the parties to resolve their disputes according to the rules of a particular legal system. Such rules are, however, primarily addressed to the relevant adjudicator, not to the parties. Similarly, force majeure clauses describe the consequences of an event beyond the parties' control that renders contractual performance impossible or fundamentally different from the one originally agreed. In principle, such clauses provide an excuse *not* to perform and may lead to the discharge of the contract. What actions could be automated when it comes to force majeure? Similarly, representations and warranties describe a particular legal state of affairs but do not necessarily oblige the parties to *do* anything specific. There being no obvious benefit of defining such "non-operational" terms in code, it must be assumed that only those terms that describe obligations that are to be performed by the parties should be "defined in code."

Third, oblivious to the challenges of "converting" legal prose into a programming language, the Advice states that "the same contractual term(s) can be written in both natural language and in code." Needless to say, the UKLC does not clarify the reason of such "dual expression" and seems unaware that there will be discrepancies between the terms expressed in both natural language and in code. It will be extremely challenging to ensure that the terms expressed in code will be identical to the terms in natural language, be it due to errors in the translation or the limitations of a given programming language. Consequently, hybrid smart legal contracts would require additional provisions allocating the risks resulting from the incorrect expression/translation of a term into code as well as the risks resulting from the incorrect execution of the code. It has already been suggested that smart contracts should be accompanied by traditional contracts that govern their operation (Lim et al. 2016). Such "legal wrappers" would contain terms that are unsuitable for automation and also allocate any risks resulting from the execution of the "smart contract."

5.3 "Solely Code" Contracts

Regarding "solely code" contracts, defined as smart legal contracts "in which all of the contractual terms are defined in, and performed automatically by, the code of a computer program," the UKLC overlooks the fact that such contracts are technically impossible and practically unnecessary. As indicated, there is little point in encoding terms that describe obligations that cannot be automated. Interestingly, while the UKLC admits that only a limited number of obligations is suitable for automation (The Law Commission 2021: 13),[16] it insists that a contract could be entirely in code. While the UKLC's conflation of "terms" and "obligations" renders any analysis extremely difficult, it can be assumed that if an obligation is to be "defined in code" it must be capable of precise description and that there must be a programming language that is sufficiently rich and expressive to correctly embody all types of obligations.[17]

6 Conclusion

The parties can agree to express their contracts in any manner—including by means of code. It is unclear, however, why such expression would be necessary, not to mention why it would warrant a separate legal category. It is equally unclear how smart contracts could improve upon traditional contracts. The expression of a contractual term—or obligation?—in code provides little assurance that the contract will be performed in accordance with the parties' agreement. It may be challenging to ensure

[16] Only those based on conditional logic.

[17] For a detailed explanation, see (Mik 2021:29).

that the code matches the agreement, that the terms expressed in the programming language are identical to the terms agreed by the parties. To complicate matters, both parties may lack the necessary technical expertise to verify whether executable code correctly reflects the source code and whether the source code correctly reflects the natural language agreement. Paradoxically, once contracts are expressed in code—or made smart—the parties will have *little control over* what the code does or, following the logic of the popular smart contract narratives, *how* the contract executes. Parties to smart contracts must worry about such technical issues like adequacy of programming language, the quality of the compiler and, most importantly, the quality of the smart contract code. Making a contract or a contractual term "smart" may thus have limited benefits. Once a contract is expressed in code, the risk of breach is effectively replaced with the risk of programming errors, incorrect compilation or the unexpected execution of code.

References

Anson WR, Beatson J (2010) Anson's law of contract, 29th edn. Oxford University Press, Oxford, New York

Antonopoulos AM, Wood GA (2019) Mastering Ethereum: building smart contracts and DApps, 1st edn. O'Reilly, Beijing, Boston, Farnham, Sebastopol, Tokyo

Atzei N, Bartoletti M, Cimoli T (2017) A survey of attacks on Ethereum smart contracts (SoK). In: Maffei M, Ryan M (eds) Principles of security and trust, lecture notes in computer science, Springer Berlin Heidelberg, Berlin, Heidelberg. https://doi.org/10.1007/978-3-662-54455-6_8

Bohyer K, Hayajneh T (2023) Modernizing contracts across industries: a review of smart contract applications and the evolving legal landscape. ICST Transactions on Scalable Information Systems. https://doi.org/10.4108/eetsis.3299

Buterin V (2015) Ethereum White Paper: a next generation smart contract and decentralized application platform. github.com/ethereum/wiki/wiki/White-Paper. Accessed 30 March 2024

Casalnuovo C, Sagae K, Devanbu P (2019) Studying the difference between natural and programming language corpora. Empir Softw Eng 24(4):1823–1868. https://doi.org/10.1007/s10664-018-9669-7

Chitty J, Beale HG (2015) Chitty on contracts, 32nd edn. Sweet & Maxwell Thomson Reuters, London

Cieplak J, Leefatt S (2017) "Smart contracts": a smart way to automate performance. Georg Law Technol Rev 1:414

Cohney S, Hoffman DA (2020) Transactional scripts in contract stacks. Minn Law Rev 105:319

Dixon C (2024) Read write own: building the next era of the internet, 1st edn. Random House, New York

Eenmaa-Dimitrieva H, Schmidt-Kessen MJ (2019) Creating markets in no-trust environments: the law and economics of smart contracts. Comput Law & Secur Rev 35(1):69–88. https://doi.org/10.1016/j.clsr.2018.09.003

Faux Z (2023) Number go up: inside Crypto's wild rise and staggering fall, 1st edn. Random House, New York

Finck M (2018) Blockchain regulation and governance in Europe, 1st edn. Cambridge University Press. https://doi.org/10.1017/9781108609708.

Furmston MP, Cheshire GC, Fifoot CHS (2017) Cheshire, Fifoot, and Furmston's law of contract, 17th edn. Oxford University Press, Oxford

Gergen MP (1992) The use of open terms in contract. Columbia Law Rev 92:997

Giancaspro M (2017) Is a "smart contract" really a smart idea? insights from a legal perspective. Comput Law & Secur Rev 33(6):825–835. https://doi.org/10.1016/j.clsr.2017.05.007
Governatori G, Idelberger F, Milosevic Z, Riveret R, Sartor G, Xu X (2018) On legal contracts, imperative and declarative smart contracts, and blockchain systems. Artif Intell Law 26(4):377–409. https://doi.org/10.1007/s10506-018-9223-3
Grimmelmann J (2019) All smart contracts are ambiguous. J Law Innov 2:1
Guadamuz A (2019) All watched over by machines of loving grace: a critical look at smart contracts. Comput Law & Secur Rev 35(6):105338. https://doi.org/10.1016/j.clsr.2019.105338
Gupta BC, Kumar N, Handa A, Shukla SK (2020) An insecurity study of Ethereum smart contracts. In: Batina L, Picek S, Mondal M (eds) Security, privacy, and applied cryptography engineering, lecture notes in computer science. Springer International Publishing, Cham. https://doi.org/10.1007/978-3-030-66626-2_10.
Kannengießer N, Lins S, Dehling T et al (2021) Trade-offs between distributed ledger technology characteristics. ACM Comput Surv 53(2):1–37. https://doi.org/10.1145/3379463
Khalil FA (2017) A solution for the problems of translation and transparency in smart contracts. Government Risk and Compliance Technology Centre
Kolber AJ (2018) Not-so-smart blockchain contracts and artificial responsibility. Stanf Technol Law Rev 21(2):198–234
Krijnen JOG, Chakravarty MMT, Keller G et al (2022). translation certification for smart contracts. https://doi.org/10.48550/ARXIV.2201.04919
Levy KEC (2017) Book-smart, not street-smart: blockchain-based smart contracts and the social workings of law. Engag Sci Technol Soc 3:1–15. https://doi.org/10.17351/ests2017.107
Lim C, Saw T, Sargeant C (2016) Smart contracts: bridging the gap between expectation and reality. Oxford Business Law Blog. https://blogs.law.ox.ac.uk/business-law-blog/blog/2016/07/smart-contracts-bridging-gap-between-expectation-and-reality.
Low KFK, Mik E (2020) Pause the blockchain legal revolution. Int Comp Law Q 69(1):135–175. https://doi.org/10.1017/S0020589319000502
Verstraete M (2020) The stakes of smart contracts. Loyola Univ Chic Law J 50:743
Mik E (2019) Smart contracts: a requiem. J Contract Law 38:70
Mik E (2021) Contracts in code? Law, Innov Technol 13(2):478–509. https://doi.org/10.1080/17579961.2021.1977220
Mik E (2022) 'Much ado about artificial intelligence or: the automation of contract formation. Int J Law Inf Technol 30(4):484–506. https://doi.org/10.1093/ijlit/eaad004
Mitchell M (2011) Complexity: a guided tour, 1 Iss. as an paperback. Oxford University Press, New York, NY,
Parizi RM, Amritraj, Dehghantanha A (2018) Smart contract programming languages on blockchains: an empirical evaluation of usability and security. In: Chen S, Wang H, and Zhang L-J (eds) Blockchain—ICBC 2018, lecture notes in computer science. Springer International Publishing, Cham, https://doi.org/10.1007/978-3-319-94478-4_6
Regulation (EU) 2017/2394 and Directive (EU) 2020/1828 (2024)
Reyes C (2022) Emerging technology's language wars: smart contracts. Wis Law Rev Forw 58:85
Rosu G (2018) Formal design, implementation and verification of blockchain languages (invited talk). In: 3rd international conference on formal structures for computation and deduction, FSCD, 108:2:1–2:6, https://doi.org/10.4230/LIPICS.FSCD.2018.2.
Russell SJ, Norvig P (2021) Artificial intelligence: a modern approach, 4th edn. Pearson, Hoboken, NJ
Schär F (2021) Decentralized finance: on blockchain- and smart contract-based financial markets. Federal Reserve Bank of St. Louis, 103(2), https://doi.org/10.20955/r.103.153-74.
Shin L (2022) The cryptopians: idealism, greed, lies, and the making of the first big cryptocurrency craze, 1st edn. PublicAffairs, New York
Software Solutions Partners Ltd v Her Majesty 's Commissioners for Customs and Excise (2007) EWHC 971

Susskind OBER (2010) The end of lawyers? Rethinking the nature of legal services, 2nd edn. Oxford University Press, Incorporated, Oxford
Szabo N (1997) Formalizing and securing relationships on public networks. First Monday 2(9). https://doi.org/10.5210/fm.v2i9.548
The Law Commission (2021) Smart legal contracts Advice to Government
Thornton v Shoe Lane Parking Ltd [1971] 2 QB 163
UK Law Commission (2018) Electronic Execution of Documents
Werbach K, Cornell N (2017) Contracts Ex Machina. Duke Law J 67:313–382
Yaga D, Mell P, Roby N et al (2018) Blockchain technology overview. National Institute of Standards and Technology, Gaithersburg, MD. https://doi.org/10.6028/NIST.IR.8202

Dr Eliza Mik teaches contract law, legal technologies and e-commerce law at the CUHK Faculty of Law in Hong Kong. Before joining academia, she worked in-house for a number of software and telecommunications companies in Australia, Poland, Malaysia and the United Arab Emirates. She advised on software licensing, technology procurement, digital signatures, and e-commerce regulation. Dating back to her PhD thesis, Eliza's interests have always centered on the private law aspects of the digital economy and on general problems of transaction automation, particularly with the use of technologies commonly referred to as Artificial Intelligence. Eliza is also one of the most cited authors on the topic of "smart contracts." In recent years, as part of a research grant, her academic explorations also include the use of large language models in the legal profession. At present, she is a member of the UNCITRAL Expert Group for the Digital Economy, a member of the Inclusive Global Legal Innovation Platform on ODR (iGLIP, Hong Kong), a Research Associate at the Tilburg Institute for Law, Society and Technology (TILT, Netherlands) and an Affiliate Researcher with the Centre for AI and Digital Ethics at the University of Melbourne (CAIDE, Australia).

Stealing Fire from the Gods: The Creation of Digital Assets and New Markets Derived from Legal Agreements—A Qualitative and Quantitative Exploration of Contract Value

Natasha Blycha, James Myint, and Lachlan McCalman

Abstract Contracts will be foundational in driving transformations in digital property (assets) like artificial intelligence (AI) systems, AI agents and authenticated data. This chapter explores the new notion of the "Live Contract" as a continuum of multiple, interconnected smart and legal contracts that acts as digital assets of value. It also explores the new notion of the Contract Bundle as a digitally connected and curated set of smart and legal Contracts (and/or Live Contracts) that can be traded for value.

1 Introduction

Contracts will be foundational in driving transformations in digital property (assets) like artificial intelligence (AI) systems, AI agents and authenticated data. The ability for the contract to bring contextual rules and remedies to these new digital assets can only happen if the legal integrity of the contract is protected through the "assetisation

N. Blycha (✉)
Perth, WA, Australia
e-mail: natasha.blycha@stirlingandrose.com

J. Myint
Sydney, NSW, Australia
e-mail: james.myint@stirlingandrose.com

L. McCalman
Canberra, ACT, Australia
e-mail: lachlan.mccalman@nooriam.com

P. Babie and M. Giancaspro (eds.), *Private Law, Digital Assets, and Infrastructure*,
https://doi.org/10.1007/978-981-96-7121-2_7

process".[1] A smart and legal Contract "…is a modern governance tool that needs to support, by design, the methodologies of both the legal and digital domains and their respective languages, while maintaining their effectiveness in both" (Blycha and Garside 2022: 145).

We explore the new notion of the "Live Contract" as a continuum of multiple, interconnected smart and legal Contracts that acts as digital assets of value. We also explore the new notion of the Contract Bundle as a digitally connected and curated set of smart and legal Contracts (and/or Live Contracts) that can be traded for value.

In Sect. 3 of this chapter, we introduce the Value Co-Efficient for a smart and legal Contract ($\mathbf{V_S}$) as a foundational empirical function that attempts to encapsulate various dimensions of value, cost, and risk arising from use of a smart and legal Contracts as compared to the rarely described notion of a Contract Value Co-Efficient ($\mathbf{V_T}$) that sets out to describe the realisable value, cost, and risk arising from a traditional contract.

In Sect. 4, we ground the contract, the smart and legal Contract, the Live Contract and the Contract Bundle in real-world examples to amplify some of the practical differences between the contract itself and the derived thing(s), namely the smart and legal Contract, Live Contract, or Contract Bundle,[2] (the new tradeable asset(s) of interest to financial markets). We go on to apply the V_S and V_T to a \$100 m invoicing factoring agreement, a standard managed service agreement and a bundle of contracts associated with a twenty-year mining operation to demonstrate the value that traditional contracting leaves on the table when compared to use of smart and legal Contracts.

In Sect. 5, we argue that the assetisation of contracts, if created and stored securely and with adequate legal guardrails,[3,4] is an important consideration (if not duty) in

[1] An advanced or second-generation digital asset offers more than just speculative value, it possesses intrinsic utility beyond collectability or profit potential. Smart and legal Contracts carrying underlying functionality and governance rights can be contrasted with crypto tokens such as Ethereum and NFTs, where value is derived from collective belief and a willingness of buyers to use certain systems (Zhang 2023; Schwiderowski et al. 2023).

[2] The authors consider that these are only initial foundational categories of contractual derived assets and that new categories will and should evolve over time.

[3] Sir Geoffrey Vos, Master of the Rolls and the Head of Civil Justice in England and Wales, writes in respect of smart and legal Contracts, "Another answer to the question of why end-to-end smart legal contracts have taken so long is, I think mainstream investors are unwilling to part with real money with the assurance that there is a legal foundation for their engagement" (Vos 2022: 54, 57). See also Estcourt (2022: 79) where he agrees with Sir Geoffrey Vos that smart and legal Contracts will only "be widely used for mainstream applications when they clearly provide for the legal enforceability of their contractual provisions".

[4] In the European Union, United States (mix of state, federal and industry specific consumer protection laws), India, Australia, and under the law of England and Wales, specific consumer protections apply to consumer contracts. These additional protections may necessitate further technical and legal requirements in the curation of smart and legal Contracts, Live Contracts and Contract Bundles as they pertain to assetisation of those things. "…consumer protections are principally set out in the Consumer Rights Act 2015 ("CRA 2015") and in various regulations implementing EU Directives. Under Sect. 68 of the CRA 2015, a trader must ensure that the written terms of a consumer contract are transparent. In order to be transparent, the terms must be expressed in plain and intelligible

modern corporate governance, particularly as a method in valuing and transacting proprietary (and shared relational) data sets in an artificial intelligence (AI) driven economy.[5]

In Sect. 6, we conclude that directors and officers should engage with smart and legal Contracts including in a granular way as per the V_S methodology.

2 Contracts as Universal Economic Tools with Unrealised Economic Value

There is currently something in the order of 340 million businesses around the planet (Statista Research Department 2024b). Within each business, the key relationships: finance, employment, procurement, leases and customers, are written down and recorded into contracts. This means that the number of extant contracts in the world measure in the billions if not trillions,[6] with billions being added each year. This colossal output is a considerable driver of annual global legal revenues being in the order of US$840 billion, or from the other side of the ledger, an expensive necessity (Statista Research Department 2024a).

Traditional contracts are recognised as expenses in terms of the costs required to produce the contract. While they may be liabilities (or conversely assets in the eyes of a counterparty) to the extent that they record choses in action which are realisable by a net present value calculation into present-day money, rarely does a chief financial officer get excited about the contractual assets sitting "within" their organisation. It is said that the opposite of legal spend in a corporation is not *"legal earn"*, rather it is to "*not spend*" on legal matters, or to minimise expenditure or save

---

language and be legible. The coded terms of a B2C smart legal contract may not be "transparent" to a non-code literate consumer in the absence of a natural language explanation of those terms. This is because the average consumer is unlikely to be able to read and understand code. From the consumer's perspective, code is unlikely to be readable, comprehensible or informative. Terms of a B2C smart legal contract which are drafted in code and not accompanied by a natural language explanation may be more susceptible to a finding of unfairness. Such terms may be considered contrary to good faith on the basis that they are not expressed fully, clearly and legibly, and serve to take advantage of the consumer's lack of familiarity with code. It is conceivable that a trader may seek to include statements in their pre-contractual literature that a transaction with a consumer is not intended to give rise to legally binding relations. In the consumer context, we consider that such statements may be at risk of being unfair consumer notices under Sect. 62(6) of the CRA 2015". See also Unfair Contract Terms: A Guide for Businesses and Legal Practitioners (March 2016) for an Australian perspective for businesses and legal practitioners on unfair contract terms in Australian Consumer Law ("ACL"). The ACL is contained in Competition and Consumer Act 2010 (Cth) sch 2 and is applied as a law of each state and territory by state or territory legislation.

[5] With many thanks to Ty Haberland, Associate at Stirling & Rose for drafting and editing assistance in preparing this chapter.

[6] It's worth noting that this estimate does not take into account contracts entered into by individuals. While it's challenging to provide precise statistics on the total number of legal agreements or contracts created each year, we can extrapolate from available data and consider various factors, such as business growth, population increases, and legal trends.

on legal activities.[7] We submit that the advent of smart and legal Contract supporting tools and infrastructure will rewrite this equation, moving executives from a focus on minimising the inherent V_T to maximising the V_S as set out below.

To make this point another way, rarely, outside of contracts which are cash or bearer and negotiable instruments, (or perhaps within law firm or corporate contract precedent banks), are contracts seen as valuable assets, or even the gateway to valuable assets, in and of themselves. This is understandable given that contracts as we currently use and understand them are most often bespoke instruments at least in so far as they contain the rules and remedies for private and confidential relationships between named parties.

We argue that the act of taking a contract and applying smart and legal Contract technologies to it, allows that contract, as the formative part of a smart and legal Contract, Live Contract or Contract Bundle, to create assets on the balance sheet.

2.1 The Contract, the Smart and Legal Contract, the Live Contract, and the Contract Bundle

There is already ample legal commentary on the digitisation of contracts including the Legal Statement on cryptoassets and smart contracts (UK Jurisdiction Taskforce, Lawtech Delivery Panel 2019), the Smarter Contracts report (UK Jurisdiction Taskforce, Lawtech Delivery Panel 2022), The Law Commission Smart Legal Contracts Advice to Government (The Law Commission 2021), the Oxford University Press Text on Smart Legal Contracts, Computable Law in Theory and Practice (Allen and Hunn 2022) and the Compagnucci et al. anthology on Smart Contracts, Technological, Business, and Legal Perspectives (2021) to name a few. There is less direct commentary or a framework for how smart and legal Contracts become assets, or what is different about a smart and legal Contract when seen through the lens of a legally binding agreement versus as an asset of value. Indeed, current discussion often interchangeably uses the words contract, smart legal contract, token, cryptoassets, and smart contract with little consideration for the considerable technical, legal, and potential value differences.

In this Part, we introduce some foundational concepts that include not just the smart and legal Contract, but also the Live Contract and the Contract Bundle. The separation of these concepts as nuanced and distinct categories will support the dual

[7] The opposite of "legal spend" in a corporation would generally refer to not spending on legal matters or minimising expenditure related to legal activities, which might include lawyers' fees, regulatory compliance costs, litigation expenses, and other legal-related financial outlays. This could be referred to as "legal savings" or "reducing legal expenditure". "Legal spend" typically encompasses all expenditures related to legal activities and compliance, while minimising or reducing legal spend would involve strategies to limit these costs, potentially through various means such as optimising internal legal processes, greater use of legal technology, adopting alternative fee arrangements with external counsel, or implementing preventive law practices to mitigate the risk of future legal issues.

Fig. 1 Contract

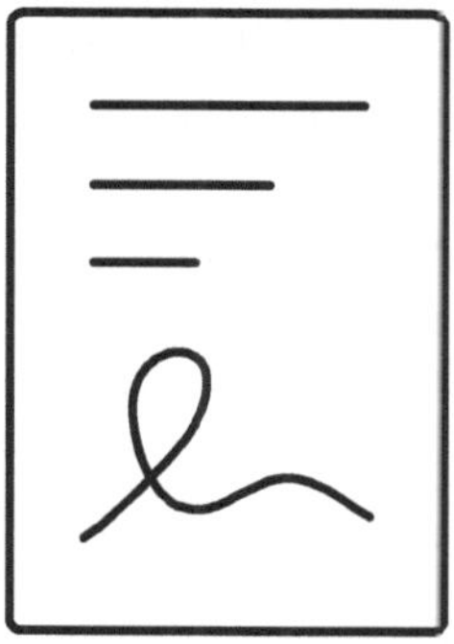

goals of continued legal permissibility and better assetisation of contracts (most often as contractual progeny) in the future. "Assetisation" in this instance involves turning non-physical assets (like contracts, which have intrinsic or acquired value) into a form that can be traded, invested in, or otherwise capitalised upon.

2.2 *What is a Contract?*

A contract is a legally binding agreement between two or more parties that is enforceable by law. It involves an exchange of promises or actions that the parties are obligated to fulfil. Contracts can be in writing or oral, although written contracts are easier to enforce due to the clear record of the agreed-upon terms.

Following from this definition (which has an inbuilt assumption of a static record of a binding agreement), and comparing the additional components required for the label of smart and legal Contract, we consider that a contract is an asset of less or little interest to financial markets as compared to a smart and legal Contract, Live Contract or Contract Bundle, except in so far as it is a part,[8] at least at some point in time, indeed a critical part, of a smart and legal Contract, Live Contract or Contract Bundle.

Figure 1 shows a diagrammatical representation or schema of a contract as a legally binding agreement.[9] See Fig. 1 Diagram.eps and Key.eps.

[8] A contract may still be a critical element of a smart and legal Contract, Live Contract or Contract Bundle (seen through the lens of an asset), even if it is not an enforceable contract in the legal sense.

[9] Readers should not overly concern themselves with the schema chosen to represent the legal agreement, it is of use only as a diagrammatic representation of comparison to the smart and legal Contract, the Live Contract and the Contract Bundle.

2.3 *What Is a Smart and Legal Contract? The Next Generation of Legally Binding Agreement*

A smart and legal Contract has been defined as: "…a legally binding, digital agreement in which part or all of the agreement is intended to execute as algorithmic instructions" (Blycha and Garside 2022: 147).[10] The Blycha and Garside model sets out five key components to a smart and legal Contract:

a. Status: legally binding—a smart and legal Contract must conform to the established rules of contract[11];
b. Form: the machine-readable or digital state;
c. Contents:
    i. Natural Language, as in any traditional legal contract being any typical contracting and business language used in the jurisdiction of the contract; and
    ii. Computer code, or other forms of machine-readable or algorithmic instructions intended to run digitally;
d. Active Function: the how, when, and why the digital components of a smart and legal Contract are triggered or affected by data or events generated from external or internal data sources, including the results of previously executed algorithms. This can include the data produced and accrued by the smart and legal Contract; and
e. Digital Execution Mechanism: the digital hosting or domain of the smart and legal Contract and how it integrates with the Active Function.

A smart and legal Contract should be distinguished from a Smart Contract, where a widely accepted definition of Smart Contract is some version of "Computer code that, upon the occurrence of a specified condition or conditions, runs on a distributed ledger (or blockchain)".

Equating a Smart Contract ipso facto with a legally enforceable contract because it contains the word "contract" is technically the same as suggesting that any software programme could be called a contract.

---

[10] See also the conceptual levels of Contract Automation where a smart and legal Contract is a continuum concept with increasing autonomous algorithm components that begins at Level 3 and ends at level 5, where there is "no human actions required for monitoring or performance…and contract actions are 'performed by machine", set out in (Wilkinson and Giuffre 2022: 182, 193).

[11] To reiterate, this is the legal contractual seed inside the smart and legal Contract. It is important to note that a smart and legal Contract, Live Contract or Contract Bundle may still contain good commercial value as a digital asset - even if it is not an enforceable contract.

2.4 What Is a Smart and Legal Contract? The Digital Asset

Having examined the smart and legal Contract through the model set out above, we can now deconstruct the model to introduce the relevant smart and legal Contract schema from the viewpoint of the smart and legal Contract as a digital asset. A critical element of difference between the legally enforceable smart and legal Contract set out above and the tabled schemas of the smart and legal Contract, Live Contract, and Contract Bundle set out below, is that the smart and legal Contract asset is of trading interest as both an enforceable or unenforceable contract and also as a smart and legal Contract that is on foot or no longer on foot (for termination, expiration, completion, or any other concluding act). An unenforceable smart and legal Contract is a useful governance data point for shaping future optimised relational behaviours (the asset) but not terribly useful for contractual parties motivated by ongoing relations (the contract). Moreover, the same point can be made as to the usefulness of the smart and legal Contract as a potential (data source) to another AI system or smart and legal Contract. Even at the conclusion of legal arrangements between the parties, the smart and legal Contract may be of ongoing use as a data source.

The distinction between the smart and legal Contract, the contract, and the smart and legal Contract, the asset (or data source), goes to the heart of what a smart and legal Contract is. As expertise in this area builds, we consider that the distinction between the smart and legal Contract, the (derived) asset, and the smart and legal Contract, the contract, may be considered so great—that it is likely that the nomenclature between the two will in time split. To possibly exacerbate this debate further, what is considered "in or out" of the four walls of the contract is a question of fact determined by the will of the parties. For now, we will persevere with the smart and legal Contract label to describe both the contract and the asset but ask that the reader continue to bear this distinction in mind.

A smart and legal Contract consists of a natural language contract body augmented with additional information used to enable automated activities. This may include specifications to connect to external APIs and retrieve data or execute commands, templates for automated notices, and other executable instructions specific to the contract. A smart and legal Contract may also capture data records of these automated activities, such as sent notices and data previously retrieved from external APIs.

See Fig. 2 Diagram.eps and Key.eps.

By digitising contracts and connecting these digitised contracts via application programming interfaces (APIs) with software platforms, data sources, the world and each other, two natural consequences flow:

a. A smart and legal Contract is able to self-perform key functions such as notifications, calculations, and payments, which would have otherwise been performed by humans alone or in conjunction with other technological and physical systems; and
b. The data trail of the contractual relationship and performance history between parties accrues to the smart and legal Contract.

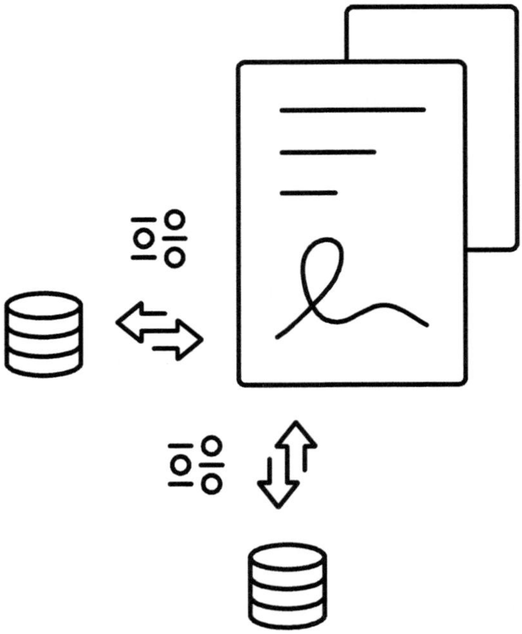

Fig. 2 Smart and Legal Contract

In this context, a smart and legal Contract evolves beyond a mere record of legal rights and obligations, but becomes a digital instrument or *digital asset*, which:

a. immutably captures the data mesh of the entire transaction history between parties;
b. is a performing legal agent self-referential to itself and other contractual legal agents; and
c. consequently becomes a reliable blueprint for future interactions between parties for the subject matter of the contract.

The data capture is not to be underestimated. Smart and legal contracts are a natural depot for all the information within or otherwise related to the contract. It does not take an extraordinary leap of the imagination to recognise that this means that such digitised contracts become digital twins of the particular relationship, and for a company or even an entire economy, a portfolio of such contracts is a digital twin of that company and that economy.[12] As we further examine the Live Contract and the Contract Bundle below, the reader will observe that points (a)–(c) are further validated as the complexity of interactions and audit trail (data) multiplies across aggregated numbers of contracts and accompanying algorithmic outputs like notices.

[12] For further discussion of the assetisation of the fluid digital twin of a smart and legal Contract see Blycha and Garside (2022b) 180-181.

2.5 *What Is a Live Contract?*

A Live Contract is a smart and legal Contract that runs over time and is hosted together with all variations to the original agreement between the originating parties, as well as any data accruing to the Live Contract from the outcomes of programmable coded instructions contained in each version of the contract. Notably, the set of data for a Live Contract would include each "layer" of data pertaining to each smart and legal Contract in the Live Contract but would also include the corpus of data relating to the Live Contract as its own phenomena.

This is a diagrammatic representation of the Live Contract in totality. It represents that a Live Contract comprises the smart and legal Contract with all variations to the agreement over time together with the data that may originate from the Live Contract or that may originate from external providers through the action of automations defined in the smart and legal Contract template, alongside the data sources.

See Fig. 3 Diagram.eps and Key.eps.

A Live Contract consists of a record of smart and legal Contracts and their implementation over time. This includes interactions between contracting parties such as proposed and accepted amendments and generated notices. It also includes data that may originate from the Live Contract or that may originate from external providers through the action of automations defined in the smart and legal Contract.

See Fig. 4 Diagram.eps and Figure-4-Key.eps.

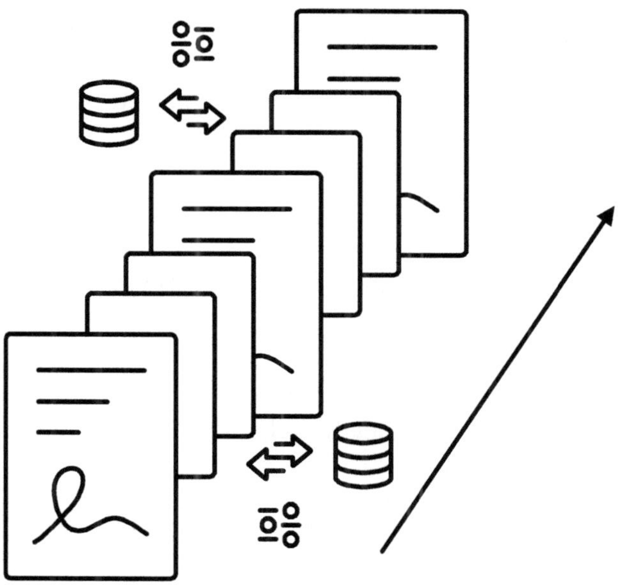

Fig. 3 *Live Contract*

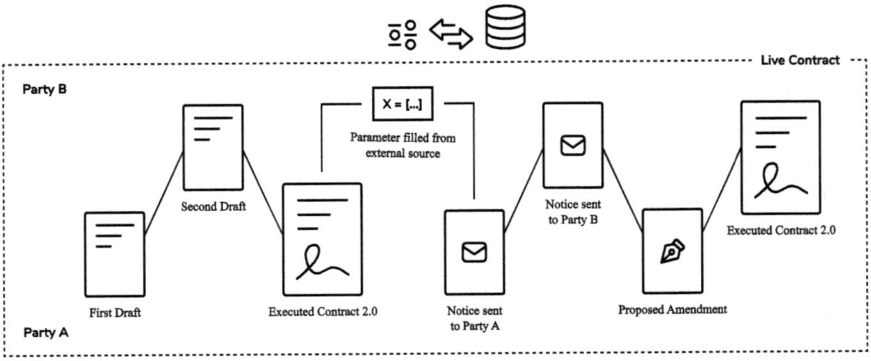

Fig. 4 *Live Contract in Operation*

2.6 *What Is a Contract Bundle?*

A Contract Bundle is a digitally connected and curated set of smart and legal Contracts (and/or Live Contracts) that runs over time, as well as any data accruing to the Contract Bundle from the outcomes of the programmable coded instructions produced from the contents of the Contract Bundle.

A Contract Bundle encapsulates multiple smart and legal Contracts and Live Contracts which may or may not be directly connected through data transfers or connected as a constituent part of an owner(s) or controller(s) directed set of interest. For example, the record of a notice sent in one Live Contract in the Contract Bundle may form external data input for another Live Contract or alternatively, the Contract Bundle may simply contain contracts relevant to the running of a particular type of business.

See Fig. 5 Diagram.eps and Key.eps.

2.7 *Traditional Contracting and the Contract as an Expense Model*

Before articulating the Contract Value Co-Efficient and the Smart and Legal Contract Value Co-Efficient in Sect. 3, we briefly explore the "how" of traditional contracts to understand their value and cost.

Contracts are increasingly created, amended, executed (and delivered), and stored in digital format. This is not to say that physical copies of contracts are not in use, but the majority of day-to-day contracting is electronic.

In either case, with perhaps the final stage of execution[13] and to a certain extent with the release of automated drafting solutions, Microsoft Office 365 Copilot being

[13] E.g. DocuSign or AdobeSign, or open source models such as DocuSeal.

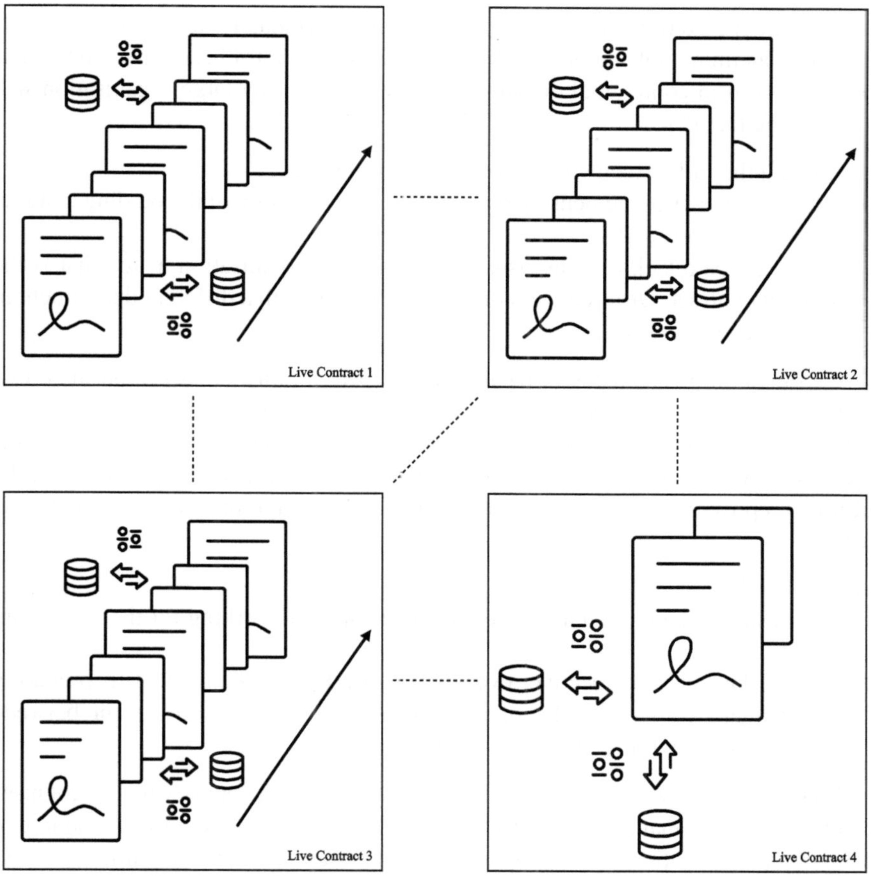

Fig. 5 *Contract Bundle*

perhaps the most notable development at the time of this chapter, contracting in the fullest sense of that word and the associated value chain, largely remain a manual process.

Storage is manual, and drafting still requires human input and will likely continue to require human input (at least for the foreseeable future). Most importantly, performance of the contract requires human involvement. This is not to say that humans don't use software tools to assist with the process, they do, but this is heavily dependent on organisational processes and software stacks and is not consistent nor readily interoperable across organisations.

Economically, from a user perspective, contracts are a material cost function[14] but organisations accept this as the price paid for an evidentiary record of their relationships, rights, and obligations. It is self-evident that there is material value in

[14] There are of course contracts which are bearer instruments and have inherent value in themselves, e.g. bank guarantees and letters of credit.

an accurate record of rights and obligations, but unfortunately in practice, contracts are rarely an immutable record let alone a single source of truth. Any person that has been involved in contractual disputes or has worked in any large organisation will attest to the fact that:

a. finding the fully executed contract can be problematic;
b. there is often disagreement as to what is the latest version of the binding contract between parties; and
c. there can be a lack of consensus even within an organisation as to what is the correct contract. Different versions may be sitting with a different department in the same organisation.

Certification mechanisms in legal systems speak to this. Notarisation in certain jurisdictions partly deals with this problem and in certain jurisdictions in a dispute setting, a solution will be affidavits to confirm (from the deponent's or declarant' (as the case may be) perspective) what is the most recent contract. Lawyers become the ultimate repository of contracting between parties, though this can be problematic as:

a. this is additional cost;
b. this assumes the particular lawyers involved are still working for the same firm; and
c. from a lawyer's perspective, even if the law firm was involved in preparing the primary contracts, a lot of ancillary contracting may still occur between counterparties without their involvement.

Fundamentally, while there may be an audited set of accounts which recognises an organisation's financial position each year, there is no audited universal source of truth of an organisation's legal position without extrapolation from multiple persons and data repositories, in circumstances where the persons may be in dispute. In this universe, shadow contracts—contracts (or waiver or amendments of contracts) entered into by a team or department without full transparency across the whole organisation, and zombie contracts—contracts which have no fulsome termination clauses and unknowingly bind organisations into perpetuity, are a live issue.

In summary, traditional contracting is a fragmented and costly system. The data indicates that the average cost of a single contract is US$6,900 (World Commerce and Contracting Association 2018). This figure may come as a surprise to readers, but demonstrates two things:

a. the majority of contractual cost is invisible to organisations and not embedded in the upfront initial costs of preparing the contract. Much like the proverbial iceberg, organisations neglect the subsequent and potentially more significant interpretation, management, and dispute costs; and
b. the challenge of traditional contracting is the truism that while relationships are dynamic, contracts are largely historical static constructs with limited means of updating for new circumstances and data.

Further cost dimensions of contracts are explored in Sect. 3 which explores the V_O and the V_S, and in real-world examples of smart and legal Contracts which are examined in Sect. 4 of this chapter.

3 Introducing the Contract Value Co-Efficient and the Smart and Legal Contract Value Co-Efficient

By introducing the Contract Value Co-Efficient (V_T) and Smart and Legal Contract Value Co-Efficient (V_S), institutional contract users can engage in greater quantitative analysis when making determinations as to whether they should adopt and use smart and legal Contract technological systems and processes going forward.

Traditional contracts are recognised as expenses in terms of the costs required to produce the contract. They represent liabilities (or conversely assets in the eyes of a counterparty) to the extent that they contain choses in action which are realisable into money.

This can be illustrated from the V_T of a traditional contract. The V_T for a single contractual party would be expressed as:

$V_T = V_I - \alpha_X \alpha_V (C_A + C_C)$

Where:

$\mathbf{V_I}$ = Inherent Value: the intrinsic value derived from entering into a contract with another party. Every contract records a particular dealing or series of dealings which has value to parties. V_I is a curious feature of a contract when measuring its value in the context of an organisation's wider balance sheet. This is because V_I is often attributed to a separate item on a company's balance sheet. For instance, as a receivable or intellectual property. It reveals an interesting property of traditional contracts: contracts have inherent value but they are not attributed value by an organisation. Accordingly, V_I may have notional value for a contract, but rarely is the full economic value attributed to the contract itself. There are exceptions to this, such as bearer and negotiable instruments where the contract is the asset.

$\boldsymbol{\alpha_X}$ = Contractual complexity: a scaling constant capturing length, tenor, cross referral with other contracts (and data sources), interconnected terms, if the contract spans dealings, property rights, and parties that are based across multiple legal jurisdictions etc.

$\boldsymbol{\alpha_V}$ = Contractual value: a scaling constant capturing the intrinsic value of the transaction underlying the contract. More valuable contracts tend to be more costly over time.[15]

$\mathbf{C_A}$ = Administration Function: these are the actual time and monetary costs of a contract and include but transcend the upfront and direct dollar costs which most

[15] Some contracts, such as derivatives documented on standardised terms, e.g. ISDA documentation may not be more expensive to create or manage. However, generally, a multimillion or multibillion-dollar contract, will have greater creation costs and management costs compared to a simpler contract.

people would recognise as the cost of a contract. These include the following, and may overlap with each other:

a. *Direct costs*—the external and internal costs of negotiating, producing, approving, and executing a contract, but also negotiating, producing, approving and executing variations, transfers (assignments and novations), and termination of contracts;
b. *Indirect costs—(mis)interpretation costs*: pre-dispute, there are the delays and costs associated with trying to understand what a contract does or does not mean;
c. *Indirect costs—contractual entropy*: the dollar value of the degradation of the contract over time. Circumstances change, relationships evolve, and contracts may cease to be fit for purpose over time. Parties may undertake actions or fail to take action which may result in a waiver (i.e. election or estoppel) or variation of the contract;
d. *Indirect costs—performance costs*: the dollar value of the resources involved in actually performing and operating a contract. The most visible costs are the salaries and wages paid to staff within an organisation to internally manage a contract and liaise with their counterparts at other organisations. But, it also includes the loss of efficiency in terms of delays and administrative burden in handling and managing a contractual sub-system within an organisation and distractions to management;
e. *Indirect costs—storage and audit costs*: the accuracy and veracity of contractual document management within an organisation is a cost leakage (with respect to time spent in finding documents, and missing documents requiring rectification or re-execution, or in the worst cases, dispute) as well as the overall costs in auditing all or part of the contractual suite, an exercise which tends to be event driven in expensive discovery or due diligence processes; and
f. *Indirect costs—other costs*: Costs which are specific to the organisation or the industry in which it operates. These may be considerable if an organisation or industry has unique compliance (e.g. ESG) or regulatory obligations, or unique approval processes in getting businesses done.

C_A is invariably a function of time (as distinct from F(t); see below). This is because the tenor of a contract will affect the overall costs associated with a contract. Longer term contracts will tend to be more expensive.

The costs of dispute are so significant that they are recorded separately below.

$\mathbf{C_C}$ = Contingent Costs: the expected value of the cost of potential disputes in respect of the contract, such as liquidated damages, indemnity amounts and/or the value of any reputational damage suffered in the course of dispute.

What is not included in V_T, which is a dollar amount, is the time cost of a contract, which we denote as F(t). F(t) represents the time taken to produce and manage a contract which is its own cost to an organisation.

In comparison, the Value Co-Efficient of a smart and legal Contract (V_S) would be expressed as:

$V_S = V_L + V_I - \alpha X \alpha V \ (C_A + C_C)$

Where:

$\mathbf{V_S}$ = Value Co-Efficient of a smart and legal Contract.

$\mathbf{V_L}$ = Smart Contract Value; the asset value of the smart and legal Contract or Live Contract, meaning that a smart and legal Contract or Live Contract (as the case may be) should have inherent value in itself and could sit as an asset on the balance sheet, because:

a. it is a richer form of "contract" than a traditional contract, as it encloses the data together with the digitised Contract;
b. once anonymised, is more liquid as an instrument in terms of useability by persons outside the immediate contracting parties as it and any associated data sets (or Contract Bundles) can be traded. The ability to transform contracts into digital assets with inherent value which can be traded is not to be underestimated;
c. forms strong internal networking effects when taken together with other smart and legal Contracts, Live Contracts, Contract Bundles and data, to form a data twin that is significantly richer than a particular smart and legal Contract in isolation;
d. the capacity to develop real-time contract and relationship graphs, enhancing partnerships, and allowing for immediate adjustments and improvements to relationships;
e. converts contract information into standardised, easily searchable, and machine-readable format enabling insight extraction which is valuable to the owner of such data from a machine learning (ML) perspective.

Using simple mathematical substitution, another way of expressing V_S in relation to V_T is:

$$V_s = v_l + v_t$$

Because V_L must be zero or greater than zero (assuming a rational organisation would not sell a digitised asset representing an anonymised smart and legal Contract or Live Contract for less than \$0 on any market),[16] then V_S must always equal or exceed V_T. The authors of this chapter would propose that due to the technological and productivity efficiencies of a smart and legal Contract or a Live Contract, and their ability to be traded, V_S will in reality almost always exceed V_T. That is, a smart and legal Contract or a Live Contract should almost always be more valuable than their traditional counterparts. By extension, V_S for a Live Contract will almost always exceed the V_S of a smart and legal Contract.

Taking this point further, the V_T that is a component of the V_S calculation for a particular smart and legal Contract is not the same as the V_T for the traditional contract corresponding to the smart and legal Contract. This is because:

a. First, the cost function of the smart and legal Contract tends to be less than the V_T of a traditional contract. There may exist organisations where existing contractual processes are highly efficient and internal staff are well trained to prepare, execute, perform, and manage each contract. Accordingly for such organisations, there is limited capacity in automating functions because C_A and C_C are

16 A conceivable exception to this is a negative V_L value where there are costs incurred at time of asset listing on market, but no asset sale is ultimately achieved.

optimised to be as low as possible. However, it is reasonable to assume that the vast majority of organisations have embedded inefficiencies and will benefit from automating contract management, reducing human intervention, reducing administrative burden, and expediting transaction and organisational timetables; and

b. Second, a smart and legal Contract should introduce new cost efficiency pathways that would not exist under a traditional contract. Path dependencies from adopting smart and legal Contract, include:

   i. Security: traditional contracting sees valuable contractual data shared across emails. Well-constructed smart and legal Contract platforms have robust security features that can protect transaction data and enforce access controls—system integrity, system trust and cybersecurity anxiety decrease;
   ii. Reduced disputes: Automated enforcement of contractual terms can minimise disputes related to non-compliance or misinterpretation of terms. Costs associated with expert witnesses recreating past real-world conduct slowly and with great expense reduce as the smart and legal Contract ecosystem is a digital twin of the relationship, meaning that recreation of common facts is easier;
   iii. Transparency and auditability: a single source of truth between counter-parties offers a clear audit trail of actions and transactions, enhancing accountability;
   iv. Compliance: Through a supply chain, greater transparency and auditability should result in enhanced compliance by an organisation;
   v. Trust: greater trust between parties. The nature of the relationship and greater transparency and auditability should result in greater trust and better faith contracting. Traditional contracting is fundamentally built on the assumption that parties may act in bad faith, and contracts and lawyers are implemented to prevent this. However, the continuing and greater transparency of a smart and legal Contract ecosystem should encourage better faith to be the default behavioural position adopted and expected to be adopted by parties; and
   vi. Reputation management: the above benefits of smart and legal Contracts together with generally improved contractual relations should enhance the reputation of a smart and legal Contract user.

The V_S should exceed the V_T in most scenarios. This is because the inherent data being produced by the smart and legal Contract, Live Contract or Contract Bundle (as the case may be) will always have inherent value, and thus be a point of value difference to traditional contracts. This is especially the case when supported by machine learning tools which means that the smart and legal Contract, Live Contract or Contract Bundle can be finetuned and optimised compared to their traditional counterparts over time, thus driving cost efficiency and value. Relevantly, what is being finetuned, improved, and optimised is not just the "contract" but the entire ecosystem and relationship that surrounds the contract.

There is an important caveat to the seeming conclusion of the above analysis which is that:

$$V_S \text{ (LIVE CONTRACT or LIVE CONTRACT Bundle)} > \sum V_T \text{ (Component Contracts)}$$

The caveat is that a smart and legal Contract and smart and legal Contract platform may introduce its own novel risks and costs to traditional contracting. Three obvious costs spring to mind:

a. the cost of maintaining smart and legal Contracts on the smart and legal Contract platform, namely the access and storage costs are an additional cost that will need to be included in C_A for each smart and legal Contract. This will be in addition to any data hosting and storage costs which an organisation maintains for their existing contracts;
b. the cybersecurity and operational risks associated with the smart and legal Contract platform. The smart and legal Contract platform and infrastructure connecting all parties on the smart and legal Contract platform will need to adequately protect their users otherwise the smart and legal Contract platform will present another risk vector; and
c. training costs associated with re-training staff to use the smart and legal Contract platform and also the behavioural changes associated with contracting with counterparties in an entirely different manner.

Over time we might expect risks and costs associated with (a) and (b) to increase and costs associated with (c) to reduce. There is of course precedent for reducing costs of technology over time with increasing economies of scale over time.

4 The Smart and Legal Contract, Live Contract, and Contract Bundle in the Real World

4.1 The Smart and Legal Contract—Invoice Factoring Arrangement

By applying both the smart and legal Contract Value Co-Efficient and traditional Contract Value Co-Efficient concepts to an invoice factoring arrangement we can better understand the underlying and marketable value of the arrangement between these parties. An invoice factoring arrangement is just one example that can be used to demonstrate the V_S and V_T methodology at work, in practice any contract hosted correctly can be a smart and legal Contract.

An invoice factoring arrangement is a type of debtor finance. In one form of this arrangement, a business sells its accounts receivable (invoices) to a third party (called a factor) at a discount. This is often used by businesses to improve their cash flow without being exposed to payment risk or payment delays from their own customers.

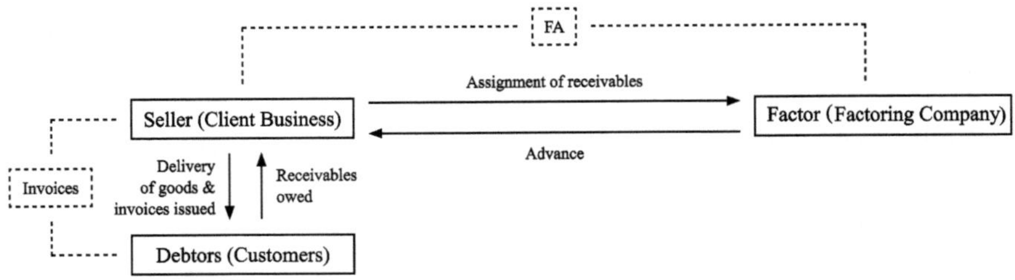

Fig. 6 A Basic Factoring Agreement Structure

There are generally three foundational parties involved in an invoice factoring arrangement:

a. the Seller (Client Business): The original business that has issued invoices to its Customers for goods or services provided. The Client Business may, for example, be a primary producer with little to no market power and an inability to absorb long payment terms from the Customers.
b. the Factor (Factoring Company): The third-party entity which purchases the invoices from the Client Business in exchange for an upfront cash payment. The Factoring Company is often a bank or a financial service provider; and
c. the Debtor (Customer): The customer who owes payment on the invoice to the Client Business. This may, for example, be a large supermarket chain with market power to only pay Client Businesses with long payment terms in the Customer's favour.

See Fig. 6 Diagram.eps.

Note, if this was an on-balance sheet factoring arrangement, the Customers would still pay the Client Business monies due under the invoices and the Client Business would be responsible for paying the Factoring Company and only two of the parties, the Client Business and the Factoring Company would be parties to the primary contract, the invoice factoring agreement (**FA**). In an off-balance sheet factoring, the Client Business could for instance, legally assign the receivables to the Factoring Company and the Customers would pay the Factoring Company directly.

A small value, repeat invoice factoring arrangement may not require external lawyers to be engaged to prepare the contracts by the parties. But assuming the face value of the receivables underlying the invoice factoring arrangement was $100 million and the FA was "vanilla", the contracts would still have sufficient complexity to require external law firms to review on behalf of the Client Business and the Factoring Company. The estimated legal fees of this arrangement is $15,000 for each party, with a month to negotiate and document the transaction (the lawyers here are efficient and the parties are constructive and prompt in negotiations).[17] The Factoring Company, being a bank, would require a legal opinion from its external

[17] This is based on direct legal quoting from partners at three law firms in Australia in terms of an efficient contractual negotiation and preparation process: two major top tiers and a boutique commercial practice. More complicated and structured factoring arrangements, e.g. for mining

counsel in relation to the validity of the FA (which would be a document that is not visible to the Client Business).

The V_T of the invoice factoring arrangement is a prosaic calculation. From the perspective of both parties, the V_T would be a negative figure representing the cost of the overall contracting arrangement. Importantly, the V_T would exceed the $15,000 that each of the Client Business and the Factoring Company would pay for their external lawyers. It would take into account:

a. V_I: the inherent value from the Client Business and the Factoring Company entering into an arrangement would notionally be $100,000,000, but in reality would be a far lower amount as the $100,000,000 would be recorded as a separate account receivable or account payable (as the case may be) on the relevant parties' balance sheets;
b. αX: In this case, the contracts are relatively simple as far as structured contracts go (cf., syndicated lending transactions or securitisation documents, which can run into hundreds if not thousands of pages across all transaction documents);
c. αV: this would scale against $100,000,000;
d. C_A: the cost of the transaction as a whole. To iterate, the "cost" of the transaction which parties focus on is often just legal fees, but it is apparent that (a) even the dollar cost of establishing the transaction must take into account the cost of staff members at each organisation being involved to make introductions, diligence, negotiate, review, draft, approve, and execute the deal, and (b) even the aggregate of such costs together with external legal costs, is one component of the overall C_A; and
e. C_C: the expected dollar value of disputes. While the Factoring Company's lawyers' legal opinion would (hopefully) confirm the validity of the FA, the human involvement in the entire invoice factoring agreement supply chain embeds potential dispute risk: fraud, human error, negligence, etc.

A practical takeaway from examining the V_T, is that even a deliberately basic factoring contract, involves multiple staff at the Client Business and the Factoring Company liaising and coordinating correspondence, checking calculations and financial statements, verifying ID numbers of the sold goods and payments, sending notices, and reviewing invoices.

The structure of invoice factoring arrangements lends itself to the smart and legal Contract format where each factoring agreement can, via the inclusion of programmable automations attached to the operable provisions, amongst other things, do the performance work of the Client Business and/or the Factoring Company or its agents in monitoring, calculating and verifying invoices, account management, and sending timely notifications associated with the FA.

Re-examining the V_S:

$$\mathbf{V_S = V_L + V_T}$$

companies, could take many months to negotiate, and external legal fees for one party could easily exceed $100,000.

First, in terms of the V_A, the automations embedded in the smart and legal Contract will reduce the C_A for each respective party. For instance:

a. The costs of actually performing the contracts are reduced as a result of API calls automatically collecting necessary data, payments being made and calculations being embedded and verified against the contractual obligations. Even with humans being involved in the loop to verify and approve the smart and legal Contract systems, the time cost is reduced. The inclusion of code to automate these administrative functions would see a reduction in time cost as well as direct monetary outlays to third parties.
b. Human error is reduced as the automations reduce the scope for mistakes with humans performing a low scale performance and verification role (which can also be technologically augmented) rather than a full-scale performance and verification role.

C_C should also reduce as the scope for disputes lessens with reduced human operational involvement in managing contracts (i.e. the risk of contractual performance failure, i.e. contractual breach should reduce). Further, the auditability of the digitally recorded performance of the running smart and legal Contract FA should lead to reduced risk of dispute as parties have a single source of evidentiary truth as to the administration of the smart and legal Contract. Ideally, C_C should approach close to zero.

Second, a new value is apparent for the smart and legal Contract: V_L. Over time, the smart and legal Contract which is the FA and associated performance data and payment data, should accrue value. This should be inherently valuable to organisations because the ability to anonymise the smart and legal Contract would provide a set of rules and data that could provide a blueprint to interested parties in operating an invoice factoring arrangement. In addition, it would be available as a dataset to further finetune generative AI models.

As a single invoice factoring arrangement, the smart and legal Contract may have minimal asset value, but as part of a Live Contract or Contract Bundle (being the invoice factoring arrangement in totality, i.e. including the invoice contracts, or alternatively and perhaps more interestingly, the Contract Bundle comprised of multiple invoice factoring arrangements undertaken by the Client Business or the Factoring Company's entire portfolio of invoice factoring arrangements with many different Client Businesses), there may be significant value (or derived value) as a blueprint for the running of such arrangements as a data input to an AI system. The contract within the smart and legal Contract structure allows the parties to also allocate risk and data ownership and/or control such that value can be allocated between the parties in a commercially nuanced and fractionalised way. This will be further explored in the examination of a Live Contract in respect of a managed services agreement in Sect. 4 and the Contract Bundle in respect of a long-term mining operation in Sect. 4.3 below.

In summary, in a real-world investment factoring example examined against the theoretical implications of the V_T and the V_S, a smart and legal Contract is a positive augmentation of traditional contracts. Smart and legal Contracts drive down costs and also recognise that smart and legal Contracts have inherent asset value.

4.2 The Live Contract—Managed Service Agreement with Variations

A Managed Service Agreement (MSA) is a contract between a company (the client) and a service provider, where the service provider manages certain aspects of the company's operations or responsibilities for a specified period. This type of agreement is commonly used in the technology industry, but it can also be relevant in various industries where outsourced services are used.

Again, any smart and legal Contract (and initiating contract type) may catalyse a Live Contract. Live Contracts will develop organically and will centre around complex contractual relationships that change over time and involve variations.

There are generally two parties involved in an MSA:

a. The Managed Service Provider (IT Business): The IT Business will generally be engaged by IT service users to handle IT needs such as network management, cybersecurity, data backup, and system maintenance;
b. The Corporate Client (Managed Service Client): The client may use managed services to gain IT expertise and capability without the need to maintain a full in-house IT team. Larger corporate clients may use managed services for specific tasks or projects or to streamline operations and focus on core business functions. They may also want to leverage the Managed Service Provider to mitigate IT risk.

MSAs are a good case study for understanding a Live Contract given that they often support long-term business relationships over multiple years and if curated correctly can yield high quality structured relational data to assist both traditional governance and AI supported governance in optimised decision making and relational modelling. Moreover, MSAs are regularly renegotiated and varied to match the evolving relationship and developments in the parties. Variations tend to follow initial phasing arrangements, unplanned events like cyber incidents, other significant events either external or internal, or changing business change needs associated with general technological advancements including pricing changes. These variations are intertwined with the agreed service levels (e.g. server uptime above 99.5% of the time) that are negotiated between the parties and will change as the Managed Service Client's needs develop.

It is worthwhile at this stage to distinguish between the individual MSA as an individual smart and legal Contract and the MSA as a Live Contract. In contrast to the MSA smart and legal Contract, the MSA Live Contract would comprise a stack of each MSA smart and legal Contract as varied over time between the parties, together with the data attributable and connected to the Live Contract.

In terms of the V_S analysis, all other things being equal, the V_S for the MSA Live Contract should be superior to the V_S for each individual MSA smart and legal

Contract.[18] All the benefits of an individual smart and legal Contract should accrue to the Live Contract (such as data accrual, automation of performance, improved transparency and auditability etc.). More importantly, the latest MSA smart and legal Contract within the Live Contract should build upon the advantages of each smart and legal Contract within the Live Contract. That is, it is an iterative improvement process which benefits from each individual data layer of each individual smart and legal Contract in the Live Contract together with the data layer of the entire Live Contract.

In practical terms, the data trail and data set associated with performance over time should also allow parties to identify and mitigate risk and optimise and finetune the contract system, business system, and relationship system that the smart and legal Contract represents in reality. For the reasons expressed above, this is optimal in an MSA setting and for any contract or class of contract that benefits from iterative improvement (which should be all of them—some individual contracts may be non-executory and not require iterative improvement, but the class of contracts to which a contract belongs, always benefits from improvement). A novel capability and advantage conferred from a Live Contract is the ability to use the data to optimise (model) and amend (or not amend based on modelling feedback) a contract between parties so that it is fit for purpose for dynamic and evolving relationships.

Further, a Live Contract that forms part of a Contract Bundle, for example, for a hospital, may provide significant value (or derived value) together with all the Live Contracts in that Contract Bundle as a blueprint for the running of a hospital (where the IT management is just one important variable amongst other important cost variables) including as a data input to an AI algorithm directed to the running of the hospital. The contracts (contract versions) underpinning the Live Contract allows the parties to also allocate risk and data ownership and/or control such that value can be allocated between the parties in a commercially nuanced and fractionalised way. We turn now to explore this in greater detail in the context of a mining project.

4.3 An Example: The Contract Bundle in Mining Operations

Managing a mining project from its inception to closure over time—here, twenty years—requires engaging numerous stakeholders, establishing a myriad of contracts, and ensuring regulatory compliance across exploration, development, operations, and eventual closure and rehabilitation (Mitchell 2023).

The Contract Bundle is not limited to a collection of agreements clustered around a mining operation, The Bundle concept can be applied liberally to any collection or constellation of smart and legal Contracts or Live Contracts that an individual can choose to curate.

---

[18] The T_A analysis for the MSA smart and legal Contract would be similar to the FA example for a singular smart and legal Contract.

In this respect, a mining project can be envisaged as a conglomeration of diverse and changing contracts and legal relationships (Gilbert + Tobin 2023). A medium to large mining operation would spend millions or even tens of millions of dollars on external legal services over the course of twenty years. On a large project, the administration costs of these contracts, being the costs of internal employees as supported by external consultants (including lawyers) and allowing for a minimum of one major and multiple minor disputes (PricewaterhouseCoopers 2023), could involve costs of $50 or $100 million for the mining operator alone (that is, ignoring the administration costs of the various counterparties) over the cost of the operation (PricewaterhouseCoopers 2023).

The contractual life cycle of a mining project might (at minimum) encompass:

a. Exploration and Feasibility Phase:

    i. Exploration Agreements and Land Access Agreements: Engaged with landowners or governmental entities for exploring and gauging mineral potential. Potential for contractual arrangements with Traditional Owners if native title is or may be relevant.
    ii. Joint Venture Agreements: Established with fellow mining enterprises or investors for collaborative exploration endeavours.
    iii. Consultancy Contracts: Formulated with specialists for executing geological surveys and feasibility analyses.
    iv. Environmental Impact Assessment Contracts: With environmental consultants for appraising potential impacts and rising ESG requirements across all contracts including scopes 2 and 3 emission requirements (PricewaterhouseCoopers 2023).

b) Development and Construction Phase:

    i. Financing and Investment Contracts[19]: Investment agreements with investors and stakeholders, alongside a suite of financing and security agreements with financial institutions.
    ii. Construction and Development Contracts: Encompassing design and construction contracts for infrastructural design and construction, equipment purchase and lease agreements for machinery acquisition, and supply agreements for construction material procurement.
    iii. Employment and Labour Hire Contracts: Entailing employment agreements for staff, management, and labour engagement, as well as contractor agreements for specialised task assignments.

c) Operational Phase:

    i. Production and Maintenance Contracts: Comprising Mining Services Contracts for mineral extraction, transportation, and processing, alongside

[19] The Roy Hill iron ore project is a useful example of the number of parties, advisors and value of financing during the development and construction phase all executed via complex contracts and contractual relations. See (Blott 2014).

Maintenance and Repair Contracts for operational efficacy and downtime reduction.

ii. Sales and Marketing Agreements: Various Offtake Agreements for pre-arranged mineral sales or purchases, and Transportation and Logistics Contracts for managing mineral transport to buyers or processors.
iii. Power Purchase Agreements: Long-term PPA with a utility provider for the supply of electricity to power mining operations.
iv. Environmental and Community Engagement: Featuring Environmental Management Contracts for ongoing environmental oversight, and Community Development Agreements for local community engagement and sustainable development facilitation.

d) Closure and Rehabilitation Phase:

i. Closure and Decommissioning Contracts: Including Decommissioning Services Contracts for safe mining operation cessation, and Asset Disposal Agreements for machinery and infrastructure sale or disposal.
ii. Rehabilitation and Environmental Contracts: Comprising Rehabilitation Services Contracts for mining site restoration and environmental impact mitigation, along with Monitoring Agreements for post-closure environmental and safety monitoring.

e) Ongoing across all Phases:

i. Insurance Contracts: Encompassing Insurance Agreements for operational, liability, and personnel risk management.
ii. IT hardware, IT software, and legal service contracts: Including the agreements for ongoing compliance, dispute resolution, and governance engagement.

The invoice factoring arrangement example in Sect. 4.1 demonstrated the ability of smart and legal Contracts to drive holistic cost reduction and efficiencies across a (literal) multifactorial arrangement of parties, even in circumstances where some parties (such as Customers) are not in direct contractual relationship with others (the Factoring Company). The managed service agreement example in Sect 4.2, built on the singular smart and legal Contract example to examine the capacity of a Live Contract to represent the iterative benefits of smart and legal Contracts longitudinally over time. A mining operation extends the concept to the Contract Bundle comprised of multiple smart and legal Contract and Live Contracts, data sets and relationship that are interconnected as part of a singular mining project.

For a mining operation, the V_S in aggregate across all involved contracts in the Contract Bundle is a complex calculation which scales from the complexity (αX), intrinsic value (αV), additional direct and indirect costs (C_A), and dispute costs (C_C). In turn, the V_S for the Contract Bundle will include the V_S of the smart and legal Contracts and Live Contracts for each party involved in the mining project. The time function F(t) is considerable across the multiple phases of the life of the project.

Critically, due to the complexity and scale of a mining operation, the benefits of smart and legal Contracts to traditional contracts is evident. V_S (smart and legal Contract) will exceed V_T. But in turn, V_S (Live Contract) will exceed V_S (smart and legal Contract), and V_S (Contract Bundle) will exceed V_S (Live Contract).

A medium to large mining operation would spend millions or even tens of millions of dollars on external legal services over the course of twenty years. On a large project, the administration costs of these contracts, being the costs of internal employees as supported by external consultants (including lawyers) and allowing for a minimum of one major and multiple minor disputes (Donaldson 2023), could involve costs of \$50 or \$100 million for the mining operator alone (that is, ignoring the administration costs of the various counterparties) over the cost of the operation.[20]

It is not a coincidence that higher complexity systems develop higher cost and audit requirements. Consequently, higher complexity contractual networks should benefit more from smart and legal Contracts, Live Contracts and Contract Bundles than lower complexity networks. The greater the scale of operations and contracts, the greater the number of potential contractual connections and steps which can be automated, reconciled to a single source of truth and data recorded and improved.

It is the capacity to improve the ecosystem rather than the discrete instrument, which is a major result of the V_S and V_T. The corollary of this is that while a singular smart and legal Contract may exceed a traditional contract in terms of value and efficiency, this calculus of value increases significantly when comparing the Live Contract to the traditional contracts, and moreover, comparing the sum of the V_T of each individual traditional contract in a portfolio or organisation against the V_S of the aggregated Contract Bundle corresponding to the portfolio or organisation.

In terms of the V_L, notwithstanding the extraordinary internal and external legal spend associated with mining operations, to date any contractual artefacts or mutually agreed contractual performance data is unlikely to be assetised or traded (on contractual or financial markets) by the contract purchaser or performer post use, with a resultant zero V_L.[21]

A Contract Bundle comprised of multiple digitally connected smart and legal Contracts and Live Contracts of the above list of mining related contracts allows parties to maximise their V_L, not least because a well-drafted contract together with a well-constructed smart and legal Contract tool or platform allows for each party to consent to the assetisation of their data in this way.

Essentially, the Contract Bundle for a mining operation is the blueprint to operating the entire mining commercial enterprise together with a data heatmap of the payments and operations of the project, and it indicates likely failure points (that is, not just commercial breach but also operational failure) which can be mitigated. This mining operation asset will be highly valuable to the mining operator and other project participants to optimise future or concurrently running mining operations.

[20] The size of these figures is of no surprise where the cost of mineral exploration alone in Australia for June 2023 is set at \$1,038.9 m. See (Australian Bureau of Statistics 2023).

[21] It can be argued that law firms and other consultants may recycle the collective intellectual property and know-how of traditional contracts even if their clients rarely (if ever) do.

Importantly, it can also be a digital asset for non-participants who are operating or will operate their own projects as a structured digital blueprint on good mining business, particularly in the post-AI world.

Finally, from a smart and legal Contract performance perspective, mining operations are a ready analogy to a corporate enterprise—they are both long-term endeavours, with high levels of contractual complexity and interconnectivity with data sources, human involvement and which involve significant operational requirements to implement and consistently require new contracts and amendments to existing contracts to manage the underlying commercial enterprise. If the V_S for the Contract Bundle representing a mining project has value, so too will the V_S for the Contract Bundle representing all or part of a corporation or even a corporate group. Complexity and scale increases the value proposition (the V_S) of the Contract Bundle.

5 Assetisation

The greater the use of smart and legal Contracts, rather than the traditional (no code) contracting process, the greater the opportunities that contractual parties will have to maximise and efficiently extract value and reduce risk in their business relationships (including compliance relationships).

In comparing output values of the V_T and the V_S across the case study of the smart and legal Contract invoice factoring agreement, the Live Contract and the managed services agreement, and the Contract Bundle for a 20-year mining operation, it appears that a failure to use smart and legal Contracts will in the majority of cases result in a declining bottom line as against a *ceteris paribus* competitor who does use smart and legal Contracts. A practical analogue for the importance of this decision as to whether (and when) to adopt smart and legal Contract technologies is akin to the decision to adopt electronic money or remain a user of physical money alone.

The "when" smart and legal Contract question is not insignificant given that the move to smart and legal Contracts will not be frictionless or without adoption costs and will likely take place across multiple years (if not decades) and will be a part of a larger digitisation, artificial intelligence story. Again a useful analogue for how this will play out is to look at the adoption timelines for electronic money and the accompanying shift in tools and behaviours to support that transition. It is also worth noting that the adoption of smart and legal Contracts as digitised and programmable instruments will introduce new risks like cybersecurity risks and deep fake contracts that may not have existed previously.

5.1 *Corporate Governance, Director Duties, and Use of Smart and Legal Contracts*

To conclude we briefly consider how decisions about implementation and use of smart and legal Contracts is likely to be considered a matter of mandatory corporate governance.[22] We note that corporate governance is a variable concept globally and may or may not include executives and officers but almost universally includes the board of directors.[23]

For now we will sidestep questions as to who might be "on the hook" for any potential failures in respect of smart and legal Contract adoption but note that the degree of board involvement in decisions about smart and legal Contracts might depend on various factors, including the size and nature of the organisation, the perceived strategic importance of smart and legal Contracts, and the specific governance model adopted by the company. Where corporate governance is the sole domain of the board, balancing the strategic oversight of technology adoption with the need to delegate operational and technical details to management will be relevant.

Directors' duties refer to the responsibilities held by the board of directors in a company to manage and oversee the organisation's activities in the best interests of its stakeholders (or the company). In this part, we focus on the globally recognisable director's duty to exercise care and diligence and how it may apply to an organisation's strategic or risk decisions to use (or not use) smart and legal Contracts.[24]

In the absence of any explicit case law that touches on the use (or not use) of smart and legal Contracts (including as part of a broader requirement to adoption of artificial intelligence) as a breach of directors' duties, we base the following comments

---

[22] In respect of corporate governance, many jurisdictions impose specific legal duties and liabilities on both directors and officers. In Australia, *Corporations Act 2001* (Cth) pt 2D.1 encompasses a wide range of provisions that pertain to directors and officers, not only boards. Duties and liabilities under the Corporations Act extend to individual directors and officers, emphasising their personal responsibilities and accountability. In the United Kingdom, the *Companies Act 2006* (UK) ss 171-177 does specify duties of directors, and there can also be instances where senior managers (officers) can be held accountable, particularly under certain regulatory frameworks, but this does not usually extend to the same comprehensive legal framework as for directors. In Germany the management board members (essentially executives/officers) are subject to direct duties and potential liabilities under German law, especially the Aktiengesetz (Germany) §§ 76-93. Corporate governance in the EU is influenced by both EU directives and individual member state legislation. Some member states may impose direct legal obligations and liabilities on officers, while others may not. Singapore imposes specific legal duties and liabilities on both directors and officers under its legal framework, notably Companies Act (Singapore) Part IX—Division 2.

[23] Our approach has been to consider a mix of both Australian director's duties as set out in the Australian Corporations Act and also Delaware's General Corporation Law (Del) as a good example of a state-based US laws setting out corporate governance expectations in the United States. Directors should look to the corporate laws of the particular jurisdiction(s) where their company is operating to determine the scope of their director duties. This section is not intended to be a full appraisal of Australian or other law in respect of director's duties and can only briefly touch on core concepts.

[24] We exclude for now the more granular operational questions of how to use smart and legal Contracts and other potentially relevant duties like the duty to avoid insolvent trading. In Australia, the duty to prevent insolvent trading is provided under s 588G of the *Corporations Act 2001* (Cth).

in analogous Australian and United States (State of Delaware) decisions as to the importance of optimisation of financial performance, prudent fiscal management, audit, supervision, and corporate stability. We also consider compliance and newer trends, for example, the expected increase in derivative actions in the US for director failures in respect of ESG standards to be relevant to the smart and legal Contract adoption decision.[25]

5.2 *Duty to Exercise Care and Diligence*[26]

The expectation that directors engage proactively and knowledgeably with crucial aspects of the business, can be said to extend to questions about the adoption and use of emerging technologies like artificial intelligence and smart and legal Contracts. This includes questions as to the director's explicit use of these tools in the real-time mapping of the company's relational, financial, and risk position.

In Australia, a notable case that addresses the theme of director's attention to the detail of a company's affairs, particularly relating to financial details, is the case of *Australian Securities and Investments Commission v Healey* (2011) 284 CLR 1, commonly referred to as the "Centro case" (*Australian Securities and Investments Commission v Healey* 2011). The case revolved around the directors of Centro Properties Group and its failure to accurately present its financial statements. The directors approved financial statements that misclassified short-term liabilities (amounting to billions of dollars) as long-term liabilities. ASIC claimed that the directors had failed to exercise due care and diligence, a breach of s 180(1) of the *Corporations Act 2001* (Cth). The Federal Court emphasised that directors must acquire a foundational understanding of the company and its financial statements, directors cannot merely delegate these responsibilities to management or external auditors and directors must actively engage with and scrutinise information presented to them, particularly relating to financial statements, to confirm their accuracy and compliance.

[25] "The new rules are also likely to give additional ammunition to activist shareholders in pushing pro climate-related practices or results. Activist shareholders may seek to inspect corporate books and records to prepare and file shareholder derivative litigation alleging that the board of directors breached their fiduciary duties by failing to implement adequate processes to tackle climate change issues or by otherwise failing to prevent an adverse climate change-related event" (Delikat et al. 2023).

[26] In Australia, fact patterns that suggest a failure to act with care and diligence (s 180, *Corporations Act 2001* (Cth)) may also raise questions about whether the directors acted in good faith and for a proper purpose (s 181, *Corporations Act 2001* (Cth)). For example, if a director fails to properly inform themselves before making a decision (potentially breaching s 180), it could also be questioned whether they acted in the best interests of the company (potentially implicating s 181). Legal claims brought by regulators or shareholders against directors often invoke both s 180 and s 181, arguing that directors failed to act with due care, diligence, and in good faith, with courts evaluating these claims through the lens of the directors' conduct, decision-making processes, and the purposes behind their decisions.

While the case does not address technology adoption per se, it underscores the expectation that directors should have a baseline of financial literacy and must be able to navigate and interrogate the company's financial affairs effectively. Extrapolating from the principles affirmed in this case, directors should similarly apply diligent attention and engagement to other critical aspects of the company, such as technological adaptation, cybersecurity, and digital transformation, to ensure that they are fulfilling their statutory and fiduciary duties. In certain industries, these obligations are enshrined in legally binding industry rules—for example, prudential standards imposed on Australian authorised deposit-taking institutions make clear that ultimate responsibility for operational risk (including cybersecurity) remains with the board.

In the United States, similar and analogous themes were explored in the 2006 Walt Disney Company Derivative Litigation (*In re The Walt Disney Company Derivative Litigation* 2005). The case revolved around the employment and subsequent termination of Michael Ovitz, who was hired as the President of the Walt Disney Company and departed with a severance package worth about $130 million. Shareholders initiated derivative suits, alleging that the directors failed in their fiduciary duties by not adequately scrutinising the terms of Ovitz's employment contract and the consequences of termination, amongst other things. The claim asserted breaches of fiduciary duty, specifically relating to the duties of care and good faith.

Although the directors were ultimately not held liable for damages (the business judgement rule shields directors from liability for decisions that harm the corporation if the directors acted in good faith), the court notably scrutinised their actions and decision-making processes, emphasising that directors should adequately inform themselves and deliberate thoroughly before making decisions. The concept of "good faith" was notably dissected in the case, affirming that fiduciary duties encompass an obligation to act with honest intentions and without the purposeful disregard of due processes.

Although the Disney case does not revolve around technological adaptation, it still illustrates the crucial principle that directors are expected to adequately inform themselves and diligently scrutinise significant decisions, especially those with considerable financial implications. Drawing from these principles, directors in the U.S. are also likely to be expected to diligently engage with and scrutinise decisions related to technological investments and adaptations, ensuring that they are in the company's best interests. Failure to adequately explore, understand, and deliberate on critical technological decisions could feasibly expose directors to scrutiny or potential claims of breaching their fiduciary duties.

5.3 Conclusion—Smart and Legal Contracts and Corporate Governance

It is not trite to say that it is difficult for a director to act in the best interest of a company that they cannot know. The maze of financial data, operational metrics, regulatory compliances, and stakeholder communications of the modern company (particularly in respect of publicly listed companies) can be seen as an unassailable fortress of complexity. A current director, irrespective of their acumen and experience, may find themselves unable to act in good faith. Smart and legal contracts (as part of a larger package of broad-spectrum AI) may provide real time and counterparty agreed data and compliance to reduce noise and complexity (*In re The Walt Disney Company Derivative Litigation* 2005). That is, smart and legal Contracts are not just a way to improve organisation efficiency and add value to the balance sheet, they may be a key tool to address corporate governance in a world where commerce, corporations, and technology become more complex.

An additional consideration for directors in any decision to engage with smart and legal Contracts (including smart and legal Contracts as AI tools) is the impact that adoption and use will have on organisational cybersecurity, including supply chain vulnerabilities and third-party cyber risk (Dempsey 2023).

Finally, it is unlikely that a director acting in the best interest of the company and with due care and diligence will be able to ignore the inclusion of digital assets on the balance sheet, particularly smart and legal Contracts with a positive V_L.[27]

6 Future of Smart and Legal Contracts as Digital Assets in New Markets

Together with broader AI adoption, lawful contracts will be foundational in driving transformations in digital assets, financial markets and legal markets. As we increasingly grapple with trust in what may be a post-truth "deepfake" world, the importance of the rules and remedies of contracting, coupled with the blockchain adjacent elements of timestamping characteristic of smart and legal Contract tools should be considered critical. The existence and positive comparative value as demonstrated by the application of the V_S as compared to the V_T across the smart and legal Contract, Live Contract and Contract Bundles is a compelling reason for directors and officers to investigate this emerging technology.

With the final caveat…those who seek to steal technological fire from the gods might also think to pray for a hearth.

References

Allen JG, Hunn P (2022) Smart legal contracts computable law in theory and practice. Oxford University Press, Oxford

[27] Another seminal Delaware Supreme Court decision of relevance is the landmark case of *Smith v. Van Gorkom*, 488 A.2d 858 (Del. 1985), often referred to as the "Trans Union" case. In this case, the directors of Trans Union Corporation approved a merger without taking the appropriate steps to inform themselves of the company's value, constituting a breach of their duty of care.

Australian Bureau of Statistics (2023) Mineral and Petroleum Exploration, Australia (Catalogue No 8412.0). https://www.abs.gov.au/statistics/industry/mining/mineral-and-petroleum-exploration-australia/jun-2023

Australian Securities and Investments Commission v Healey (2011).

Blott T (2014) *Roy Hill, Australia | Case Studies | IJGlobal, IJGlobal.* https://www.ijglobal.com/articles/91662/roy-hill-australia

Blycha N, Garside A (2022) 'A model for the integration of machine capabilities into contracts', in *Smart legal contracts.* Oxford University Press. https://doi.org/10.1093/oso/9780192858467.003.0008

Compagnucci MC, Fenwick M and Wrbka S (2021) *Smart contracts: technological, business and legal perspectives.* Bloomsbury Academic, https://books.google.com.au/books?id=jnrezQEACAAJ

Delikat M, Kray S, Frantz C (2023) Trends in ESG litigation and enforcement. Harvard Law School Forum on Corporate Governance. https://corpgov.law.harvard.edu/2023/08/10/trends-in-esg-litigation-and-enforcement

Dempsey S (2023) Regulators warn directors to step up on cyber threats. Australian Institute of Company Directors, https://www.aicd.com.au/risk-management/framework/cyber-security/regulators-warn-directors-to-step-up-on-cyber-threats.html.

Donaldson A (2023) Mining causes 24.7% of environmental conflict involving Indigenous people—mining technology. Mining Technology. https://www.mining-technology.com/news/mining-environmental-conflict-indigenous-people/.

Estcourt JS (2022) 79Smart contracts and dispute resolution: faster horses or a new car? In: Allen J, Hunn P (eds) Smart legal contracts: computable law in theory and practice. Oxford University Press. https://doi.org/10.1093/oso/9780192858467.003.0005.

Gilbert + Tobin (2023) Mining in Australia 2023. https://www.gtlaw.com.au/knowledge/chambers-mining.

In re The Walt Disney Company Derivative Litigation (2005)

Mitchell P (2023) Top 10 business risks and opportunities for mining and metals in 2024, EY. https://www.ey.com/en_au/mining-metals/risks-opportunities.

PricewaterhouseCoopers (2023) Mine 2023: The era of reinvention. PwC. https://www.pwc.com/gx/en/industries/energy-utilities-resources/publications/mine.html.

Schwiderowski J, Pedersen AB, Jensen JK, Beck R (2023) Value creation and capture in decentralized finance markets: Non-fungible tokens as a class of digital assets. Electron Mark 33(1):45. https://doi.org/10.1007/s12525-023-00658-z

Statista Research Department (2024a) Size of the legal services market worldwide 2015–2022. Statista https://www.statista.com/statistics/605125/size-of-the-global-legal-services-market

Statista Research Department (2024b) Number of companies worldwide 2000–2021. Statista. https://www.statista.com/statistics/1260686/global-companies.

The Law Commission (2021) Smart legal contracts advice to government.

UK Jurisdiction Taskforce, Lawtech Delivery Panel (2019) *Legal Statement on Cryptoassets and Smart Contracts.*

UK Jurisdiction Taskforce, Lawtech Delivery Panel (2022) Smarter contracts

Vos G (2022) '54end-to-end smart legal contracts: moving from aspiration to reality. In Allen J, Hunn P (eds) Smart legal contracts: computable law in theory and practice. Oxford University Press, https://doi.org/10.1093/oso/9780192858467.003.0003.

Wilkinson S, Giuffre J (2022) '182six levels of contract automation: the evolution of "smart legal contracts". In Allen J, Hunn P (eds) Smart legal contracts: computable law in theory and practice, Oxford University Press. https://doi.org/10.1093/oso/9780192858467.003.0009.

World Commerce and Contracting Association (2018) The cost of a contract

Zhang ZJ (2023) Cryptopricing: whence comes the value for cryptocurrencies and NFTs? Int J Res Mark 40(1):22–29. https://doi.org/10.1016/j.ijresmar.2022.08.002

Natasha Blycha is one of the world's pre-eminent Smart Legal Contract experts. She is recognised by Chambers as a global fintech expert with technical product design experience and deep legal understanding including as a contributing author of the 2022 Oxford University Press text on SLCs. Founder of Chambers ranked emerging technology firm Stirling & Rose, Natasha advises on SLCs, DAOs, digital assets and infrastructure and AI globally and has been awarded the Financial Times Most Innovative Lawyer and Thought Leader of the Year. Natasha received a Commendation in the Theology of Law with her thesis focused on the capacity for consciousness in and the application of natural law to Artificial Intelligence (AI) systems. Natasha has founded technology companies Nooriam and LexChip focused on democratic and lawful data and AI use.

James Myint is a senior finance lawyer and partner at Chambers ranked emerging technology firm Stirling & Rose. With a career spanning New York, Sydney and Tokyo, James has advised on some of the most novel funding and assetisation transactions, deploying legal technologies which were first in market. James founded technology company Nooriam alongside Natasha Blycha.

Digital Assets and Fraud

Third Thing or Sixth Sense? I See Ideational Objects?

Kelvin F. K. Low

Abstract With the publication of the Final Report of the Law Commission of England and Wales' project on Digital Assets, the English law of personal property seems poised to make a dramatic shift to recognise an "unbounded" category of third things (or *tertium quid*). The implications of such a shift will reverberate well beyond the realm of cryptoassets. However, since the push for this category was very much driven by the Law Commission's desire to accommodate cryptoassets within English law, this chapter proposes to critically analyse the Law Commission's proposal in relation to cryptoassets in particular, though some wider implications will be noted.

1 Introduction

With the publication of its final report on *Digital Assets* (Law Commission UK 2023), the Law Commission of England and Wales has kickstarted the process of propelling the English law of personal property into a new age. For more than a century, with the proliferation of then novel but now common types of personal property like shares and intellectual property, English law has resisted the introduction of a *tertium quid* (or third thing) between its division of personal property into things in possession (or tangible property) and things in action (or intangible property). The *locus classicus* of this resistance is Fry LJ's dissenting judgement in *Colonial Bank v Whinney* (1885) 30 Ch D 261, endorsed by the House of Lords on appeal (*Colonial Bank v Whinney* 1886). In the words of his Lordship (*Colonial Bank v Whinney* 1885: 285):

> All personal things are either in possession or in action. The law knows no tertium quid between the two.

Despite much agitation in the years to follow, as epitomised by the great debate over the nature of things in action in the *Law Quarterly Review* (Elphinstone 1893; Williams 1894, 1895; Sweet 1894; Pollock 1894; Broadhurst 1895; Sweet 1894), the English courts have until recently steadfastly maintained that English law knows

K. F. K. Low (✉)
The University of Hong Kong, Hong Kong, China
e-mail: fklow@hku.hk

P. Babie and M. Giancaspro (eds.), *Private Law, Digital Assets, and Infrastructure*,
https://doi.org/10.1007/978-981-96-7121-2_8

of no third thing distinct from things in possession and things in action (*Allgemeine Versicherungs-Gesellschaft Helvetia v Administrator of German Property* 1931: 704; *Your Response v Datateam Business Media* 2014). Prior to cryptoassets, there were only three exceptional instances that depart from this orthodoxy (or appear to do so). First, in *Attorney-General of Hong Kong v Daniel Chan Nai-Keung*, the Privy Council on appeal from Hong Kong (not technically an English decision) declared with no reasoning that export quotas for textiles, "although not 'things in action' are a form of 'other intangible property'" (*Attorney-General of Hong Kong v Daniel Chan Nai-Keung* 1987: 1342). There is no citation of any authority for this proposition and it has been suggested that it is "best regarded as decided per incuriam" (Low 2021: 198; Cf. Stevens 2023: 616). The second oddity is patents, which s 30(1) of the *Patents Act 1977* (UK) classes as personal property but not things in action. But this is not a judicial decision but rather statute overturning earlier authority recognising patents *as* things in action (*British Mutoscope and Biograph Co v Homer* 1901; *Edwards & Co v Picard* 1909: 905). As a leading intellectual property text remarks of this statutory declassification of patents as things in action, "why not, is a mystery" (Llewelyn et al. 2023: 263 fn 66). Finally, in *Armstrong DLW GmbH v Winnington Networks Ltd*, the English High Court appeared to classify regulatory carbon credits or European Union allowances (EUAs) as third things (*Armstrong DLW GmbH v Winnington Networks Ltd* 2013: para. 61). The keywords though are "appeared to," yet this apparition of a third thing will, it appears, soon be cast as law by the Law Commission.

2 The State of the Authorities

The case for a category of third things is a vigorously contested one. It is probably fair to say that a preponderance of opinions, driven at least in part by the apparent[1] innovation that is cryptoassets, supports such a category (Fox 2019: 139; Sarra and Gullifer QC (Hon) 2019; Michels and Millard 2022).[2] But some of these opinions are at least in part based on a strained reading of key authorities. For example, proponents often rely on *Armstrong v Winnington* but then omit to refer to Stephen Morris QC's statement in the same case that "ultimately I do not consider that it matters whether an EUA is a chose in action or merely some form of 'other intangible property'" (*Armstrong DLW GmbH v Winnington Networks Ltd* 2013: para. 61). It is true that his Lordship opined that EUAs did not fit the narrow definition of thing in action that he referenced but his Lordship also remarked that "to the extent that the concept encompasses wider matters of property, then it could be so described"

[1] In more than 15 years, despite promising much, cryptoassets and the underlying technology—the blockchain—has delivered little apart from speculation and as a vehicle for illicit activities: see, e.g. (Foley et al. 2019). See also (Matt Levine 2022a, b).

[2] See also the respondents to the Law Commission's call for evidence referenced in (Law Commission UK 2022: 69–73).

(*Armstrong DLW GmbH v Winnington Networks Ltd* 2013: para. 61). Unsurprisingly therefore, Stephen Morris QC never commits to a choice between the narrow and wider conception of thing in action despite references by both the UK Jurisdiction Taskforce (UK Jurisdiction Taskforce, Lawtech Delivery Panel 2019: paras. 82, 86) and the Law Commission (Law Commission UK 2023: para. 6.91) suggesting that he does. *Armstrong v Winnington* thus serves as a shaky foundation upon which the case for third things is built first by the UK Jurisdiction Taskforce, then by Bryan J in *AA v Persons Unknown* [2019] EWHC 3556 (Comm), [2020] 4 WLR 35,[3] building on the Taskforce's legal statement, and more recently by the Law Commission in its consultation paper and Final Report, relying on both the statement and the case. This is especially as it comes up not only against the House of Lords in *Colonial Bank v Whinney* (1886) 11 App Cas 426 but two subsequent Court of Appeal decisions affirming the twofold classification in *Allgemeine Versicherungs-Gesellschaft Helvetia v Administrator of German Property* (1931: 704) and *Your Response v Datateam Business Media* [2014] EWCA Civ 281, [2015] QB 41. Altogether, the three cases span three different centuries—the 19th, 20th, and 21st—so it is worrying to see the Law Commission so ready to cast aside established precedent on the basis of authorities built upon a misreading of a first instance judgement. It is also noteworthy that *AA v Persons Unknown* was an interlocutory decision in which all the defendants appear to have been unrepresented, a not uncommon state of affairs in many of the early litigation over cryptoassets. Nor, it appears, has "[t]he irony of courts allowing legal actions in respect of intangible property that are not choses in action because they do not entail rights enforceable by action" (Low 2020: 348) yet dawned on proponents of third things.

Other common law jurisdictions have been less enthusiastic about the necessity of a category of third things. In *Ruscoe v Cryptopia Ltd (in Liq)*, Gendall J sitting in the New Zealand High Court dismisses the debate as follows (*Ruscoe v Cryptopia Ltd (in Liq)* 2020: para. 123):

> On this, I am satisfied the argument here is in fact a red-herring. This is because cases which might be perceived to be problematic in this area are not about the limits of what can be recognised as 'property' but simply about the number of categories of 'property' one needs.

Many other common law courts, both English (*Danisz v Persons Unknown and Huobi Global Ltd* 2022) and others (*Re Gatecoin Limited* 2023), have likewise not considered it necessary to address the third thing debate, implicitly endorsing Gendall J's view in *Ruscoe v Cryptopia Ltd (in Liq)*. More recently, and regrettably not in time for the Law Commission's Final Report, Philip Jeyaretnam J sitting in the Singapore High Court remarked in *ByBit Fintech Ltd v Ho Kai Xi* (2023: para. 36):

> My conclusion is therefore that the holder of a crypto asset has in principle an incorporeal right of property recognisable by the common law as a thing in action and so enforceable in court. While it might be said that this conclusion has an element of circularity in that it could also be said that the right to enforce in court is what makes it a thing in action, this type of reasoning is not strikingly different from how the law approaches other social constructs, such as money.

---

[3] Criticised in (Low 2020).

It is true, of course, that every type of property, including a thing in possession, carries rights of enforcement in court. This should not be surprising since rights, broadly speaking, are the "fundamental legal conceptions" that the law deals in (Hohfeld 1913, 1917). But the object of a thing in possession is that which is possessed (typically a tangible object)[4] whereas the object of a thing in action is simply the right itself. As Crossley Vaines explained more than half a century ago (Crossley Vaines 1967: 14; Crossley Vaines et al. 1973: 14):

> Choses in possession are tangibles, choses in action intangibles: they are not rights over intangibles; the intangible thing or *res incoporalis* is the right itself.

Nor, despite the apparent unanimity of judicial opinions presented in the Law Commission's Final Report, is the record of cryptoassets before the English courts quite so uniform. In *Fetch.AI Ltd v Persons Unknown* (2021: para. 9), Judge Pelling QC appears to consider cryptoassets to simply be things in action, a reading even proponents of third things drew from the case. As Allen, Wells, and Mauer remarked, "it made a marked departure from the reasoning set out in the UK Jurisdictional Task Force's 2019 *Legal Statement* (endorsed in *AA v Persons Unknown*) which had stared down the *tertium quid* question and made a case for a third category of personal property beyond 'chose in possession' and 'chose in action'" (Allen et al. 2022). In the Law Commission's Final Report, this plain reading of *Fetch.AI Ltd v Persons Unknown*, which it acknowledged more openly in its consultation paper (Law Commission UK 2022: para. 4.36), is relegated to a footnote, in which it is recast to suit the Law Commission's proposal. According to the Law Commission (Law Commission UK 2023: 46 fn 171):

> [G]iven that Binance Exchange generally operates as a non-custodial holding intermediary, we consider that the better interpretation of the Fetch.ai judgment is that the court correctly classified the applicant's right against Binance Exchange as a thing in action (broadly, a personal contractual claim to the return of assets equivalent to those held).

In so recharacterising *Fetch.AI Ltd v Persons Unknown*, the Law Commission relies on the later case of *Piroozzadeh v Persons Unknown* (2023: para. 8 (Trower J)) to establish that the relationship between Binance and its customers was a non-custodial one, surely a questionable approach to interpreting a judicial opinion. There is no discussion of the nature of the relationship between Binance and its customers in *Fetch.AI Ltd v Persons Unknown* itself and in its consultation paper, the Law Commission had believed that the case entailed characterising Binance's relationship with its customers as a custodial one (Law Commission UK 2022: para. 4.46). The recharacterisation of Judge Pelling QC's reasoning though is not new and can also be found in the consultation paper (Law Commission UK 2022: para. 4.46), albeit in a slightly different form, alleging that it is a reference to Binance's customers' claims against it as a custodial (rather than non-custodial) exchange. But custodial intermediaries of intangible property in English law invariably operate as trustees (Cf. McFarlane and Stevens 2010: 33) and, without establishing that the underlying assets

---

[4] The result of the abstraction of right from object means that property in things in possession can be conceived of both as fact and as right: see, eg, (Gray and Gray 1998: 15).

are property of some sort, it is simply not possible to establish a trust relationship.[5] What exactly did Judge Pelling QC say?

> I am satisfied that the assets credited to the first applicant's accounts on the Binance Exchange are to be regarded as property for the purposes of English law. They are, to put it no higher for present purposes, a *chose in action*, and a *chose in action*, as a matter of English law, is generally regarded as property. (*Fetch.AI Ltd v Persons Unknown* 2021: para. 9)

If the court was referring to the exchange's customers' claims against it, it is curious that it didn't simply say so. The phrasing is also extremely curious if this were the case as it would be the account that would be the property (Cf. *Libyan Arab Foreign Bank v Bankers Trust Co* 1989: 748 (Staughton J)),[6] not the assets credited to the account since those would belong to the exchange on a non-custodial construction. The recharacterisation is even curiouser if the relationship was a custodial one, as the Law Commission surmised in its consultation paper, as it would entail concluding that the court failed to even consider if the underlying assets were even capable of being the subject matter of a trust (*B2C2 Ltd v Quoine Pte Ltd* 2019: para. 142 (Simon Thorley IJ); *Quoine Pte Ltd v B2C2 Ltd* 2020: para. 144 (Sundaresh Menon CJ for the majority)). The plain reading is also more consistent with other passages in the judgement, which speaks of "moving the assets out of the accounts of the claimant to third-party accounts" and "what is sought are a proprietary order which is designed to freeze ... the assets which were removed from the first claimant's account" (*Fetch.AI Ltd v Persons Unknown* 2021: para. 3).

It is convenient at this point to make another observation about the Final Report that some may find unsatisfactory. Despite repeated references to the opinions of "senior and specialist judges" (Law Commission UK 2023: paras. 1.14, 2.6, 2.11, 2.45, 2.53, 3.7, 3.70, 5.26), the number and identity of these judges are nowhere to be found. Unlike other consultees, who are identified and whose responses are publicly available (Law Commission UK 2024),we do not know who these judges are, how many they numbered, or what exactly they thought and why. All we are told is that statutory recognition of a third thing "was subject to significant discussion and received broad support" (Law Commission UK 2023: para. 2.53 fn 75, 3.70 fn 208). Broad, one suspects, is hardly unanimous.

---

[5] As Ben McFarlane remarked at a conference to celebrate the retirement of Sarah Worthington from the Downing Chair in Cambridge, one cannot declare a trust over a practical power, a point I regrettably missed in (Low 2021).

[6] Furthermore, despite popular misconceptions, a bank account is a single continuing contract (and hence a single asset) rather than a series of contracts referable to each fresh deposit: see (*Hart v Sangster* 1957: 337 (Lord Goddard CJ)).

3 The Case for Third Thing Categorisation for Cryptoassets

3.1 The Importance of Clear Boundaries to Rationalising Personal Property

Between its consultation paper and the Final Report, the Law Commission's case for a third thing categorisation evolved, and arguably not for the better. The key justification for a category of third things in the consultation paper had been that, unlike other intangible property such as debts, shares, or intellectual property, which "are purely creatures of the legal system" (Law Commission UK 2022: para. 4.27), cryptoassets had an independent existence apart from the law (Law Commission UK 2022: para. 10.64–10.68) and in doing so resembled tangible property or things in possession (Law Commission UK 2022: para. 4.10). This is debatable but it led the Law Commission in its consultation paper to set out a number of criteria for property to be categorised as third things (Law Commission UK 2022: para. 5.142):

a. it is composed of data represented in an electronic medium, including in the form of computer code, electronic, digital or analogue signals;
b. it exists independently of persons and exists independently of the legal system; and
c. it is rivalrous.

Reform along these lines would have ensured that much of the existing English law of personal property remained undisturbed by its proposals. But by the time of the Final Report, the Law Commission, apparently responding to the concern of some consultees, chose not to delineate hard boundaries of a third category of personal property (Law Commission UK 2023: para. 4.49). A very selective reading of *Armstrong v Winnington* was again pushed into service to justify the loosening of the boundaries (Law Commission UK 2023: para. 4.71–4.72). This of course necessitated a muddying of the waters as to what it was that was special about the category of third things. Was it an existence independent of a legal system, in which case the EUAs that were the object of dispute in *Armstrong v Winnington* would surely fail to qualify? Or was it the absence of Hohfeldian claim rights, in which case large swathes of personal property currently categorised as things in action, such as copyright (*Orwin v AG* 1998: 421) and registered design rights (*Ifeika v Ifeika* 2010: para. 25) may have to be recategorised as third things? Does this also mean that the classification of contractual rights—which debt, the original thing in action, exemplifies but does not exhaust—will now depend on whether they embody Hohfeldian claim rights or not? Where intangible property comprises a bundle of rights made up of both Hohfeldian claim rights and other Hohfeldian "rights" (privileges, powers, and immunities), how should these be classified?

As I have observed elsewhere (Low 2024: 463, 466–467):

> [I]t is undoubtedly the case that the category of things in action broadly defined is desperately in need of rationalisation, comprising as it does of a grab bag of intangibles ranging from purely personal rights (debt, being the classical thing in action), *erga omnes* rights (most intellectual property rights apart from patents), and rights against a fluctuating class of persons (shares). Some of these are positive rights (debt), others negative (intellectual property), and still others a complex mix (shares). ... If a rationalisation is in order, then the entire category of things in action needs to be carefully sorted.

Instead of doing so, the Law Commission considered it "not entirely clear how this would be practical or helpful for the development of the law. Nor is it obvious why, if such an approach were desirable, it has not been the position taken by the common law for the last ten years, despite the fact that the courts have considered the issue directly on multiple occasions" (Law Commission UK 2023: para. 3.36).

Taking the last point first, litigation is obviously not a conducive vehicle for categorical rationalisations since parties are only interested in their particular disputes. The failure of English personal property law to rationalise its mass and mess of intangible personal property is a failure of its academia, not that of its Bar or Bench. The rationalisation of legal subjects, as the recent experience of unjust enrichment demonstrates, has always relied upon academic endeavour.[7] Yet until 2011, when Sheehan published *The Principles of Personal Property Law* (2011), the last comprehensive English textbook on personal property was the 5th edition of *Crossley Vaines' Personal Property* (Crosslet Vaines et al. 1973),[8] published in 1973.[9] Since then, Bridge, Gullifer, McMeel and Worthington published *The Law of Personal Property* (Bridge et al. 2013) in 2013 and both *The Principles of Personal Property Law* (Sheehan 2017) and *The Law of Personal Property* (Bridge et al. 2022) have now seen newer editions. Long neglected, the almost four-decade gap between Crossley Vaines's last edition and Sheehan's first did the development of English personal property law no favours in terms of systemic rationalisation, especially as novel personal property—such as carbon credits—were introduced by the law during the intervening period.

But is such a rationalisation useful? It is submitted that it is because such an exercise would allow English law to recognise both similarities as well as differences within this entire category, regardless of label. A third thing category as proposed by the Law Commission emphasises differences without observing similarities and, particularly in the form it takes in the Final Report, is a bit of a muddle. The Law Commission recommends the creation of a new category but does not articulate any clear rules for categorisation. In the meantime, important questions—such as how judgement debts can be enforced against some of the newer (but not actually new)

[7] Being built on the foundations laid by (Goff and Jones 1966) (now (Goff and Jones 2022) and (Birks 1985a)) (see now (Birks 2005)).

[8] The last edition of the text to be fully written by Crossley Vaines' himself was the 4th edition in 1967.

[9] This excludes, of course, Michael Bridge's magisterial *Personal Property Law*, now in its 4th edition, as part of the Clarendon Law Series but the Clarendon Law Series was never intended to be comprehensive, prizing instead "concise, accessible overviews of major fields of law and legal thought.": see (Oxford University Press 2024).

forms of intangible property—remain unanswered (Low 2024: 463) and no obvious answer follows from the Law Commission's exercise.

3.2 *Relative Relativity of Title?*

Consider one key recommendation by the Law Commission: the introduction of relativity of title for control-based title to cryptoassets. Sheehan has convincingly argued that none of the justifications for relativity of title that apply to tangible property—such as discouraging violence and civil unrest (Rostill 2021: 128–129) –apply to intangibles (Sheehan 2024: 87–88) yet relativity of control-title is nothing more than the reinvention of the relativity of possessory title wheel (Sheehan 2024: 90–92). Relativity of title entails a trade-off as it risks subjecting defendants to double liability (Cf. *Attenborough v London and St Katharine's Dock Co* 1878: 454).[10] Without the corresponding justifications, how is that trade-off defensible for intangibles? Worse still, the Law Commission's Final Report appears to confuse two entirely different concepts altogether—relativity of title and competing claims. The Law Commission adopted Fox's articulation of relativity of title (Law Commission UK 2023: para. 5.77)[11]:

> To summarise then, relativity of title is about the respective enforceability of competing claims to vindicate the incidents of enjoyment inherent in some particular proprietary interest.

This is an unorthodox understanding of relativity of title. As Lord Diplock explained in relation to land (*Ocean Estates Ltd v Pinder* 1969: 24–25)[12]:

> At common law … there is no such concept as an 'absolute' title. Where questions of title to land arise in litigation the court is concerned only with the relative strengths of the titles proved by the rival claimants. If party A can prove a better title than party B he is entitled to succeed notwithstanding that C may have better title than A, if C is neither a party to the action nor a person by whose authority B is in possession or occupation of the land.

In other words, the rule that *jus tertii* (third-party rights) are not admissible is an essential element of relativity of title strictly so-called. As such, in English law, relativity of title to chattels is now "heavily qualified by the reforms introduced by ss. 7 and 8 of the Torts (Interference with Goods) Act 1977" (Bridge et al. 2022: paras. 2–034). Without the common law rule prohibiting a defendant from arguing *jus tertii*, any relative title that is successfully asserted because the defendant is unable to establish *jus tertii* is not meaningfully different from any other "wrongly" decided case owing to insufficient evidence. The same outcome can obviously follow in civilian systems despite their commitment to a unitary *dominium* (Birks 1985b).[13]

[10] See also (Bridge et al. 2022:paras. 33–044).

[11] Citing (Fox 2006: 334).

[12] See also (Bridge et al. 2022: paras. 2–033).

[13] See also (van Erp 2012: 224).

That this attenuated form of relativity is what Fox had in mind is clear from his analysis of equitable assignments (Fox 2006: 360):

> The historic approach of equity to the enforcement of a relative title would have been similar to the modern rule under the Torts (Interference with Goods) Act 1977 about pleading a *jus tertii* in actions for conversion or trespass.

Fox is also mistaken about the possibility of creating relative title by way of derivative transfers of pure intangibles if, by relative title, all he means is competing claims. Although governed differently than by the rule in *Dearle v Hall* (1828) 3 Russ 1; 38 ER 475, rules to determine the priority to competing claims to pure intangibles such as intellectual property rights do exist (Bridge et al. 2022: paras. 31-143–31-148), which should not be the case if relativity of title in this attenuated sense were not possible, as Fox suggests (2006: 361–364). Furthermore, the case relied upon by Fox to demonstrate his point—*Cronk v McManus* (1892) 8 TLR 449—is one in which the defendant managed to resist the claim by proving an earlier assignment, essentially *jus tertii*. How is this meaningfully different from what Fox describes as the modern rule of relativity of title for goods?

If we are truly concerned with relativity of title strictly so-called, then indeed there is case law to the effect that there is no relative title for intangible property, at least for some intellectual property rights (*Farmer v Moseley (Holdings) Ltd (t/a RTK Marine)* 2000: para. 45 (Neuberger J); *Rhone-Poulenc Rorer International Holdings Inc v Yeda Research and Development Co Ltd* 2006: 618). It is notable that the Law Commission makes no reference to any of these cases and its case for relativity of title rests on the slender weight of the much criticised (on this point) *Armstrong v Winnington* (Law Commission UK 2023 :para. 5.83).[14] Notably, no attempt is made to address these criticisms.

3.3 *Do Cryptoassets Exist and Does It Matter?*

It is a matter of some controversy whether cryptoassets exist in the real world in a manner similar to tangible property. As Fox correctly observed of cryptoassets, "[t]he coin is just an ideational construct" (Fox 2019: 139 [6.53]). But, as the Law Commission also correctly notes, it also exists "as instantiations in socio-technical systems" because it "relies on its technical instantiation as a data structure [whose] function is derived not merely from the abstract existence of the technical system in which it persists" (Law Commission UK 2022: para. 10.29, 2023: para. 4.16). Belief in the idea leads to the maintenance of the technical systems that instantiates the existence of these ideational objects. Yet the existence of such objects is quite distinct from real objects, which exist regardless of whether humanity suffers from mass delusion. The difference is not unlike the distinction the historian Harari draws

[14] This aspect of *Armstrong v Winnington* is criticised by (Goff and Jones 2022: paras. 8–70; Chambers and Buckingham 2013: 302; Low and Lin 2015: 395–396).

between inter-subjective and objective phenomena (Harari 2015: 116–118). In a way, *all* intangible property is inter-subjective in nature (Low 2024: 463, 473), though they are typically sustained by legal systems rather than collective socio-technical faith.

Does existence apart from the law matter then? It is submitted that it does not, and this can be proven by considering how the law relates to some unquestionably real objects. Property rights in water is not a particularly well-researched subject among modern property law scholars. Apart from a monograph by Getzler (2004), not much has been written about it in the past century (Cf. Moore 1924).[15] Gray and Gray remarked that "English property law remains relatively uncertain or incoherent in its conceptual treatment of the increasingly vital resource of water" (Gray and Gray 2009: para. 1.2.86). Perhaps most significantly for our purposes though is their observation that "English law persists in regarding water as incapable of being owned" (Gray and Gray 2009: para. 1.2.86).[16] But perhaps some clarification is in order. It is not so much that water is incapable of being owned as running water is incapable of being owned. Despite its apparent archaism, the old terminology of thing in possession carries some advantages to the modern one of tangible property because it emphasises that property in the law is less about *objects* and more about *relations* with them (Gray and Gray 2009: 15; Swadling 2013: para. 4.02; Stevens 2023: 628; Cf. Bentham 1948: 337 (Chapter XVI, sec. 26)). As Murphy J cautioned in *Dorman v Rodgers* (1982: 372), "In non-legal usage land or a thing (tangible or intangible) is referred to as property. In legal usage property is not the land or thing, but is *in* the land or thing."

The absence of a tort of visual trespass is again telling (*Victoria Park Racing and Recreation Grounds Co Ltd v Taylor* 1937).[17] We can have many extra-legal relations with rivalrous objects. Some of these (e.g. possession) are rivalrous. Others (e.g. sight) are not. The law protects the former, not the latter. The Law Commission was wrong therefore to focus, as lay observers often do (Swadling 2013:para. 4.02; Stevens 2023: 628; Cf. Bentham 1948), on whether cryptoassets are rivalrous. As Watts and I explain (Watts and Low 2024: 281, 287):

> Possession is rivalrous because A's possession of an object ipso facto means B is not in possession and vice versa. ... All forms of control are imperfect – A may be dispossessed by B – but their imperfection has no impact on the rivalrousness of possession as a form of control. When so dispossessed, B is in possession of the object and by definition A is not.

What then is the nature of extra-legal control over cryptoassets? "[E]xtra-legal control of cryptoassets via private keys is, unlike extra-legal possession which is rivalrous, non-rivalrous since private keys, as information, are non-rivalrous" (Watts and Low 2024: 281, 287). If one were to focus on the *use* of property to deduce

[15] Almost precisely a century old. See also (Wiel 1908). From a less doctrinal perspective, see (Smith 2008, Cf. 2016).

[16] Citing (*Alfred F Beckett Ltd v Lyons* 1967: 481–482; *Attorney-General ex rel Yorkshire Derwent Trust Ltd v Brotherton* 1992: 441, 445–446; *Thames Heliports plc v LB of Tower Hamlets* 1997: 169, 177).

[17] Though exceptionally visual intrusion can amount to nuisance: (*Fearn v Board of Trustees of the Tate Gallery* 2023).

rivalrousness, one might better argue that cryptoassets are rivalrous since (barring a fork[18] or a bug[19]) they can only be transferred once. But possession, both factual and legal—particularly the latter (Douglas and McFarlane 2013: 219)—is unconcerned with use. Possession of a book is rivalrous regardless of whether it is being read or not. The Law Commission attempts to paper over the essentially non-rivalrous nature of public key cryptography as a means of control as well as other technical frailties by coining the expressions "fragile rivalrousness" and "dynamic excludability" (Law Commission UK 2022: para. 10.100 et seq, 2023: para. 4.33 et seq) but both bear a striking resemblance to the state of being almost pregnant.

4 The Patchwork of Wrongs Without Rights

This brings us to the Law Commission's assertion that "crypto-tokens cannot be conceived of as rights or claims in themselves" (Law Commission UK 2023: para. 3.32, 3.34). As Watts and I explain (Watts and Low 2024):

> So long as the law does not recognise them as property, this is certainly true, but if the law chooses to accommodate them *as* property, it must do so through the creation of rights. The Law Commission's search for a patchwork of causes of action to protect these apparently non-rights-based properties necessarily entails the creation of rights, albeit viewed in reverse as wrongs and with any emergent rights obscured from view.

There are serious questions to be considered as to whether we ought to do so (Stevens 2023), and even if so, if the courts ought to be the branch of government that does (Grower 2024: 301; Contra Watts and Low 2024: 281), but the Law Commission (perhaps oddly) did not seem concerned to address either. Instead, the Law Commission's exercise in reasoning backwards results in another oddity: the patchwork of causes of action to protect cryptoassets. This differs from how intangible property, which are rights *as* things rather than rights *over* things, are conventionally protected (Low 2024: 463, 473):

> On this view, also, the question of remedies resolves itself since the right *ipso facto* clarifies its actionability. A breach of contract is determined by the terms of the contract and copyright infringement is co-extensive with interferences with the exclusive rights conferred on a copyright holder from time to time. There is accordingly no need to attempt to fashion a metaphorical equivalent to the tort of conversion, which arguably entails an exercise in using 'the tail to wag the dog'.

Where this simple picture appears to have been complicated is in the context of regulatory licences such as carbon credits but this is in part the persistent association lawyers make between property in its different conceptions (McFarlane and Douglas

[18] For which, see (Low and Mik 2020: 163). Although these inconsistencies eventually resolve themselves, temporarily some cryptoassets may find themselves effectively "duplicated."

[19] Perhaps most famously, the bitcoin overflow bug resulted in an output larger than the input: see (Sedgwick 2019).

2022),[20] and in part poor systemic design of the carbon trading system (Low and Lin 2015: 381–386). The resolution of *Armstrong v Winnington* was complicated by the absence of the relevant defendant (Low and Lin 2015: 391–394; Cf. Crawford 2023), which created the impression of a lacuna that Stephen Morris QC struggled valiantly to fill. Proprietary restitution is thus not so much a cause of action designed to protect third things[21] as a gap filler invented to fill a non-existent gap. As applied to cryptoassets, this gap filler is itself deficient as it supposedly left a further gap that necessitates the fabrication of an analogical cousin to conversion, which together with the controversial idea of a constructive trust in cases of theft (Chan and Low 2023), create a patchwork of claims akin to the patchwork of torts that the common law developed to protect chattels. According to *Clerk & Lindsell on Torts* (Andrew Tettenborn 2023: 1211–1212), there are about a half a dozen of these: (i) conversion; (ii) trespass to goods; (iii) negligence; (iv) reversionary injury; (v) rescous and pound breach; and (vi) replevin. This patchwork is mostly the result of historical accident, yet the Law Commission proposes that courts *intentionally* develop the law to create a similar patchwork for cryptoassets (and perhaps other third things). Yet it fails to explain why, if there is to be an intangible analogue to conversion, there are no similar analogues to the other property torts. Thinking backwards, it appears, does not engender clarity.

5 Conclusion

The Law Commission's proposal is riddled with flaws, particularly in the form it takes in the Final Report. First, and most importantly, there is no clarity as to when an intangible property is a thing in action and when it is a third thing. Secondly, its odd notion of relativity of title arguably confuses relativity of title strictly so-called with the idea of competing claims to property. In so doing, and especially in conjunction with its amorphous criteria for classification as third things, it fails to take English personal property law forwards in its rationalisation and classification of intangible property. If some third things have relative title and some third things don't, how is the category of third things remotely useful? Thirdly, it mistakes the law of property for being concerned with objects when it is concerned with relationships with objects. Thus, even if cryptoassets were objects, the extra-legal control over them is simply not rivalrous. Any comparison with possession, a rivalrous form of control, is simply inapt. Fourthly, despite its denial that there can be any rights to cryptoassets, its patchwork of wrongs necessarily creates rights, albeit in reverse and obscured from view. This then necessitates replicating for cryptoassets the patchwork of claims that exist for things in possession but which is hitherto alien to intangible property, however

[20] See also (Gretton 2007; Crawford 2023).

[21] It can't have been since *Armstrong v Winnington* relies upon the difficult decision of *Lipkin Gorman v Karpnale Ltd* [1991] 2 AC 548, which involved money, not third things, to craft its proprietary restitution claim.

classified. Classification as third things also does not even begin to address other important questions, such as how cryptoassets and many other intangible properties may be "seized" in order to satisfy a judgement debt.

References

Alfred F Beckett Ltd v Lyons [1967] Ch 449

Allen JG, Wells H and Mauer M (2022) Cryptoassets in private law: emerging trends and open questions from the first 10 years. https://www.ssrn.com/abstract=4206250. Accessed 12 Nov 2024

Allgemeine Versicherungs-Gesellschaft Helvetia v Administrator of German Property (1931) 1 KB 672

Armstrong DLW GmbH v Winnington Networks Ltd [2013] Ch 156

Attenborough v London and St Katharine's Dock Co (1878) 3 CPD 450

Attorney-General ex rel Yorkshire Derwent Trust Ltd v Brotherton (1992) 1 AC 425

Attorney-General of Hong Kong v Daniel Chan Nai-Keung (1987) 1 WLR 1339

B2C2 Ltd v Quoine Pte Ltd (2019) 4 SLR 17

Bentham J (1948) An introduction to the principles of morals and legislation. In: Harrison W (ed). Oxford University Press

Birks P (1985a) An introduction to the law of restitution. Clarendon Press, Oxford

Birks P (1985b) The Roman law concept of dominium and the idea of absolute ownership. Acta Juridica1

Birks P (2005) Unjust enrichment, 2nd edn. Oxford University Press, Oxford

Bridge M, Gullifer L, McMeel G, Worthington S (2013) The law of personal property, 1st edn. Sweet & Maxwell, London

Bridge MG, Gullifer L, Low KFK, McMeel G (2022) The law of personal property, 3rd edn. Thomson Reuters/Sweet & Maxwell, London

British Mutoscope and Biograph Co v Homer (1901) 18 RPC 177

Broadhurst S (1895) Is copyright a chose in action? LQR 11:64

ByBit Fintech Ltd v Ho Kai Xi [2023] SGHC 199

Chambers L, Buckingham C (2013) Intangible property and proprietary restitution in the high court. Lloyd's MaritE Commer Law Q 296

Chan WXT, Low KFK (2023) Post-scam crypto recovery: final clarity or deceptive simplicity? Law Q Rev 139:379. https://doi.org/10.2139/ssrn.4394820

Colonial Bank v Whinney (1886) 11 App Cas 426

Colonial Bank v Whinney (1885) 30 Ch D 261

Crawford MJR (2023) Contract as Property: Triangles and Tragic Choices. Camb Law J 82(1):83–109. https://doi.org/10.1017/S0008197322000903

Crossley Vaines J (ed) (1967) Personal property, 4th edn. Butterworth, London

Crosslet Vaines J, Tyler ELG, Palmer N (1973) Crossley Vaines' Personal Property, 5th edn. Butterworths, London

Danisz v Persons Unknown and Huobi Global Ltd [2022] EWHC 280

Dorman v Rodgers (1982) 148 CLR 365

Douglas S, McFarlane B (2013) Defining property rights. In: Penner J, Smith H (eds) Philos Found Prop Law, Oxford University Press, Oxford

Edwards & Co v Picard (1909) 2 KB 903

Elphinstone HW (1893) 'What is a chose in action? LQ Rev 9:311

van Erp S (2012) Cases, materials and text on property law. Bloomsbury Publishing, London

Farmer v Moseley (Holdings) Ltd (t/a RTK Marine) [2000] EWHC Patents 128

Fearn v Board of Trustees of the Tate Gallery (2023) 2 WLR 339

FetchAI Ltd v Persons Unknown [2021] EWHC 2254 (Comm)
Foley S, Karlsen JR, Putniņš TJ (2019) Sex, drugs, and bitcoin: how much illegal activity is financed through cryptocurrencies?'. Rev Financ Stud 32(5):1798–1853. https://doi.org/10.1093/rfs/hhz015
Fox D (2006) Relativity of title at law and in equity. Camb Law J 65(2):330–365
Fox D (2019) Cryptocurrencies in the common law of property. In: Fox D, Green S (eds) Cryptocurrencies in public and private law. Oxford University Press. https://doi.org/10.1093/law/9780198826385.003.0006.
Getzler J (2004) A history of water rights at common law. Oxford University Press, Oxford, New York
Goff R, Jones GH (1966) The law of restitution. Sweet & Maxwell, London
Goff R, Jones GH (2022) Goff & Jones on unjust enrichment, 10th edn. In: Mitchell C, Mitchell P, Watterson S (eds), Sweet & Maxwell, London
Gray K, Gray SF (1998) The idea of property in land. In: Bright S, Dewar JK (eds) Land law: themes and perspectives. Oxford University Press, Oxford
Gray KJ, Gray SF (2009) Elements of land law, 5th edn. Oxford University Press, Oxford
Gretton GL (2007) Ownership and its objects. Rabel J Comp Int PrivE Law 71(4):802. https://doi.org/10.1628/003372507782419462
Grower JA (2024) Better left to legislature? notes on a nagging doubt over the legal recognition of cryptoassets. In Agnew S, Smith M (eds) Law at the cutting edge: essays in honour of Sarah Worthington. Hart Publishing. https://doi.org/10.5040/9781509965182.
Harari YN (2015) Sapiens: a brief history of Humankind. 1st U.S. edn. Harper, New York
Hart v Sangster [1957] Ch 329
Hohfeld WN (1913) Some fundamental legal conceptions as applied in judicial reasoning. Yale Law J 23:16
Hohfeld WN (1917) Fundamental legal conceptions as applied in judicial reasoning. Yale Law J 26:710
Law Commission UK (1917) Fundamental legal conceptions as applied in judicial reasoning. Yale Law J 26(8):710–770
Ifeika v Ifeika [2010] FSR 29
Law Commission UK (2022) Digital assets: consultation paper
Law Commission UK (2023) Digital assets: final report
Law Commission UK (2024) Digital assets as personal property: responses to consultation on draft Bill
Libyan Arab Foreign Bank v Bankers Trust Co [1989] QB 728
Llewelyn D, Aplin T, Cornish WR (2023) Intellectual property: patents, copyright, trade marks & allied rights, 10th edn. Sweet & Maxwell, London
Low KFK (2020) Bitcoins as property: welcome clarity? Law Q Rev 136:345–349
Low KFK (2021) Trusts of Cryptoassets. Trust Law Int 34:191
Low KFK (2024) Cryptoassets and the renaissance of the *tertium quid*? In Bevan C (ed) Edward Elgar handbook on property law and theory. Edward Elgar. https://www.ssrn.com/abstract=4382599. Accessed 11 Nov 2024
Low KFK, Lin J (2015) Carbon credits as eu like it: property, immunity, tragiCO_2 medy? J Environ Law 377–404. https://doi.org/10.1093/jel/eqv020
Low KFK, Mik E (2020) Pause the blockchain legal revolution. Int Comp Law Q 69(1):135–175. https://doi.org/10.1017/S0020589319000502
Matt Levine (2022a) The crypto story. Bloomberg Businessweek. https://www.bloomberg.com/features/2022-the-crypto-story/
Matt Levine (2022b) How not to play the game. Bloomberg Businessweek. https://www.bloomberg.com/features/2022-the-crypto-story-FTX-collapse-matt-levine/
McFarlane B, Douglas S (2022) Property, analogy and variety. Oxf J Leg Stud 42(1):161–186. https://doi.org/10.1093/ojls/gqaa043

McFarlane B, Stevens R (2010) Interests in securities: practical problems and conceptual solutions. In: Gullifer L, Payne J (eds) Intermediated securities: legal problems and practical issues. Hart Publishing, Oxford
Michels JD, Millard C (2022) The new things: property rights in digital files? Camb Law J 81(2):323–355. https://doi.org/10.1017/S0008197322000228
Moore HS (1924) Coulson and forbes' the law relating to waters, sea, tidal, and inland, 4th edn. Sweet & Maxwell, London
Ocean Estates Ltd v Pinder (1969) 2 AC 19
Orwin v AG [1998] FSR 415
Oxford University Press (2024) Clarendon law series. Oxford University Press, https://global.oup.com/academic/content/series/c/clarendon-law-series-cls/?cc=au&lang=en&
Piroozzadeh v Persons Unknown [2023] EWHC 1024
Pollock F (1894) What is a thing? LQ Rev 10:318
Quoine Pte Ltd v B2C2 Ltd (2020) 2 SLR 20
Re Gatecoin Limited [2023] HKCFI 91
Rhone-Poulenc Rorer International Holdings Inc v Yeda Research and Development Co Ltd [2006] RPC 24
Rostill L (2021) Possession, relative title, and ownership in English law. Oxford University Press USA—OSO, Oxford
Ruscoe v Cryptopia Ltd (in Liq) (2020) 2 NZLR 809
Sarra J, Qc G, (Hon) L, (2019) Crypto—claimants and bitcoin bankruptcy: challenges for recognition and realization. Int Insolv Rev 28(2):233–272. https://doi.org/10.1002/iir.1346
Sedgwick K (2019) Bitcoin history part 10: the 184 billion BTC Bug. Bitcoin.com. https://news.bitcoin.com/bitcoin-history-part-10-the-184-billion-btc-bug
Sheehan D (2011) The principles of personal property law. Hart Publishing, Oxford
Sheehan D (2017) The principles of personal property law, 2nd edn. Hart Publishing, Oxford
Sheehan D (2024) Digital assets, blockchains and relativity of title. J Bus Law 78
Smith HE (2008) Governing Water: the Semicommons of Fluid Property Rights Ariz L Rev 50:445
Smith HE (2016) Semicommons in fluid resources. Marq Intell Prop L Rev 20:195
Stevens R (2023) Crypto is not property. Law Q Rev. 139:615. https://doi.org/10.2139/ssrn.4416200
Swadling W (2013) Property: general principles. In: Burrows A (ed) English private law. Oxford University Press. https://doi.org/10.1093/acprof:oso/9780199661770.003.0004
Sweet C (1894) Choses in Action. LQ Rev 10:303
Tettenborn A (2023) Wrongful interference with goods. In: Tettenborn A, Clerk JF, Lindsell WHB, Junes MA, and Bagshaw R (eds) Clerk & Lindsell on Torts. The Common Law Library, Sweet & Maxwell, London
Thames Heliports plc v LB of Tower Hamlets (1997) 74 P & CR 164
UK Jurisdiction Taskforce, Lawtech Delivery Panel (2019) Legal statement on cryptoassets and smart contracts
Victoria Park Racing and Recreation Grounds Co Ltd v Taylor (1937) 58 CLR 479
Watts P, Low KFK (2024) The case for cryptoassets as property. In Agnew S, Smith M (eds) Law at the cutting edge: essays in honour of Sarah Worthington, Hart Publishing. https://doi.org/10.5040/9781509965182
Wiel SC (1908) Running water. Harv. Law Rev 22:190
Williams TC (1894) Is a right of action in tort a chose in action? LQ Rev 10:143
Williams TC (1895) Property things in action and copyright. LQ Rev 11:223
Your Response v Datateam Business Media [2014] EWCA Civ 281

Through the Looking Glass: We All See Ideational Objects Here

Jason Grant Allen

Abstract In this chapter, I explore the property law treatment of cryptoassets—and, presumably, other digital artefacts that are not clearly rights to anything or against anyone. I argue that such artefacts are well described as "ideational objects" and draw together insights from private law theory and social ontology to explore how we should think about complex objects with a social and a technical dimension. I then examine how the law of property can accommodate ideational objects as objects of property rights (including the right of ownership) and dealing such as transfer, and what challenges and implications this poses for the traditional doctrines and concepts of property law. The chapter aims to contribute to the emerging literature on cryptoassets (and digital assets more broadly), as well as to the broader debate on the nature and boundaries of property in the digital age. In particular, it defends the Law Commission's suggested approach of recognizing a "third category" of personal property from criticisms made by Professor Kelvin Low, and introduces a

Thanks to David Fox, Jasper Verstappen, Louise Gullifer, Johan David Michels, and Peter Hunn for their comments on the draft. Peter and I have had various conversations on this topic in the course of our collaboration on a forthcoming handbook on digital assets in the law (among other projects), and this chapter could be read as a parallel contribution to his manuscript on "Bits and Atoms" (working title). Thanks also to Amy Held for her review of the Christian von Bar's Foundations of Property Law: Things as Objects of Property Rights, which I have seen in draft and which helped me to understand the book much better myself. I translated that book (from Volume I of his Gemeineuropäisches Sachenrecht) during 2020–2022 while serving on the UNIDROIT Working Group on the Private Law Applicable to Digital Assets, and this chapter provides the occasion to set out some of the thoughts I had during the Working Group's discussions which have not been published elsewhere. Thanks also to Kelvin Low for generously sharing a draft of his chapter in this volume—a courtesy I was not able to reciprocate given the tardiness of my own drafting—and to the editors for their indulgence. The usual disclaimer applies: I am responsible for all errors. All URLs were last accessed at 3 September 2024.

J. G. Allen (✉)
SMU Centre for Digital Law, SMU Yong Pung How School of Law, Singapore, Singapore
e-mail: jgallen@smu.edu.sg

School of Law, University of Tasmania, Sandy Bay, Australia

Cambridge Centre for Alternative Finance, University of Cambridge, Cambridge, UK

P. Babie and M. Giancaspro (eds.), *Private Law, Digital Assets, and Infrastructure*,
https://doi.org/10.1007/978-981-96-7121-2_9

new conceptual framework from Professor Christian von Bar's seminal treatise on "things as objects of property rights".

1 Introduction

> "But I don't want to go among mad people," Alice remarked. "Oh, you can't help that," said the Cat: "we're all mad here. I'm mad. You're mad." "How do you know I'm mad?" said Alice. "You must be," said the Cat, "or you wouldn't have come here." (Carroll 1865: Chap. 6)

A good deal has now been written on the property law treatment of cryptoassets.[1] This emerging literature can and should be read in the context of earlier (but ongoing) conversations about digital artefacts such as game objects and digital data structures, as well as older (and often neglected) conversations about intangible legal artefacts such as company shares and the various objects of intellectual property rights.[2] Indeed, the treatment of cryptoassets in the law of property is perhaps interesting less for its own sake than because it has forced us to confront questions we have fudged for some time. These questions are potentially relevant to a broader raft of digital artefacts of increasing importance in the global digital economy: at least plausibly, a central bank digital currency (CBDC) could fall into the same category,[3] as could digital artefacts such as game objects or even digital files.[4]

Debate has focused on cryptoassets like Bitcoin that (i) *clearly are* some kind of "digital artefact" to which subjects of the legal system ascribe value but (ii) *are not clearly* a "right" in, to, or over anything or against anyone. Cryptoassets like "stablecoins" or "tokenized company shares", on the other hand, raise interesting questions about the link between some asset or value external to the distributed ledger (in particular, whether it is legally robust). "Category (ii)" cryptoassets may present a *refoulement* to (i) in the case that the "link" fails under the applicable law, however, as the cryptoasset unsuccessfully linked to a "real-world" asset could simply be an unbacked, "Category (i)" cryptoasset.[5] Further, they raise interesting

---

[1] I will leave this term broadly defined for now as "digital assets represented in a blockchain data structure". Of course, "digital assets" is also in need of a definition.

[2] See Allen (2018a: 70–72) and the various sources cited there. I would not use the same terminology around "coins" and "tokens" today, and introduce a number of refinements in terms of the different types of blockchain system. However, at core the argument was sound and is reflected, with refinements, in this chapter.

[3] Central bank money does not represent anything meaningfully like a "liability" of the central bank; a unit of CBDC, like a unit of central bank reserve money or indeed a unit of cash, would plausibly be a "digital asset" that is *not* a digital representation of a debt obligation; it is therefore potentially a candidate for the "third category" approach. See discussion in Kumhof et al. (2020).

[4] On the classification of different types of "digital asset", broadly defined, see Wendehorst (2023a: 102).

[5] This is the position taken in the UNIDROIT Principles on Digital Assets and Private Law Principle 4; see the commentary at (International Institute for the Unification of Private Law 2023: para. 4.5).

questions parallel to, but distinct from, those pertaining to intangible financial assets "embodied" in paper, which we traditionally refer to as "documentary intangibles".

My purpose in this chapter is to examine the challenges (and opportunities for conceptual development) that cryptoassets present for the law of property. In particular, I ask whether cryptoassets can be placed into our existing categories of property or whether they require a new category. In so doing, I engage directly with Professor Kelvin Low, who has been an outspoken critic in the "*tertium quid* debate". This chapter presents an equally outspoken critique of his position. In short, it is necessary to reject Low's framing of the issue, which confuses the terms of the debate and obscures the questions we should be asking. My hope is also that, by spelling out some points of difference explicitly, any future engagement by Low (and others working in a similar vein) will address what I see as the important issues more directly.

I focus on Low's more recent writings and take my immediate point of departure from his chapter in this volume. This chapter is not, however, only (or even primarily) a refutation of Low's position. My goal is rather to present my own view of cryptoassets in property law, and in particular to present the concepts and theoretical resources that I have found most useful in thinking about the problems they present. These include social ontology, institutional legal theory, and Christian von Bar's scheme of property law. On the latter view, "property law" is a product of the reflexive relationship between property rights and their objects, which he calls *things*. This fundamental insight, I argue, breaks some of the deadlock (and reduces some of the noise) around the *tertium quid* debate.

The chapter comprises four sections. Section 2 sets the scene, providing a brief background of what I see the debate to be about: where we are, and how we got here. Section 3 sets out the most important substantive points of difference, as I see them, between myself and Low and introduces some of the conceptual resources that we could use to find an answer. Section 4 presents my substantive view of the property law treatment of cryptoassets, which in particular sets out von Bar's conceptual scheme. Section 5 concludes.

2 Setting the Scene

For better or worse, there is no generally accepted definition of cryptoassets or their sub-types; it is easy to speak at cross-purposes and beg questions (for example, whether the reference asset of a "tokenized company share" should determine its transfer rules, or whether the blockchain "container" should do so). Heuristically, my own approach has been to focus on "unbacked" cryptoassets like Bitcoin in the first instance (Allen 2021a). The legal treatment of a ledger entry with no external referent should, I think, provide a starting point for reasoning about ledger entries that have some external referent. I will adopt that same approach here.

On the other hand, it seems generally accepted that we *should* recognize cryptoassets like Bitcoin as "property". Discussion has focused on *how* we should recognize them as such, which in part means where we should place them in our taxonomy of "objects in which a person may hold property rights". (Spoiler alert: questions surround both "What type of objects are cryptoassets" and "What type of rights are property rights"; these two questions are easily conflated but must be kept distinct, and taken in turn.) In particular, a proposal has been made by the Law Commission of England and Wales to place cryptoassets in a "third category" of personal property rather than in the traditional, mutually exclusive categories of "choses in possession" and "choses in action".[6] This chapter will focus on cryptoassets' *ontology*, and the importance of an accurate understanding of this ontology to a proper analysis of their legal treatment. I use "ontology" in both senses of that term: (i) their "true nature" and mode of existence and (ii) their categorization relative to other types of objects that (the legal system recognizes to) exist. On that basis, I will make some arguments about where cryptoassets belong and, in so doing, how we should approach wider questions about property, property rights, and property law.

At the outset, I should state clearly that a purely doctrinal analysis of this subject matter is impossible. Legal systems (including the common law) operate with a "positive–negative dualist logic", by which a primary category is stipulated and everything which is *not that* falls into a residual category.[7] This approach works in a tiered cascade: for example, "real property" is posited and everything else is, necessarily, "personal property"; "choses in possession" are posited and everything else is a "chose in action". While there is debate about the turn of phrase used in the leading case of *Colonial Bank v Whinney* (1885) 30 Ch D 261, this logic animates Fry LJ's famous *dictum* that "the law knows no *tertium quid*" between choses in possession and choses in action. However, the taxonomy that results from this logic is in dire need of rationalization. (If nothing else, the unitary category of "choses in action" would include both choses in action where there is an obligor of some kind and where there is none, so there is an important distinction *within* the supposedly unitary category.) In particular, intangible objects are not well accommodated within the scheme, and a historical perspective shows that the treatment of intangibles has long been a sticking point in the law of personal property—in all legal systems. This is simply a consequence of rigid categories that do not track to the reality they purport to categorize. Thus, while we should ensure that our conceptual enquiry is historically grounded, historical-doctrinal debates must serve that conceptual enquiry, and not be allowed to capture it.

The common law is not unique in this respect. For example, German law distinguishes "moveable" and "immoveable" things and recognizes no third category between them; consequently, things connected to a parcel of land belonging to another through the exercise of a right over that land are classified as "moveable things" in

[6] The traditional taxonomy is a little more complex than this still: personalty is itself divided into chattels "real" and "personal", the latter category breaking down to the familiar choses in possession and choses in action. "Real chattels" are temporary interests land (ie, leasehold estates). I will discuss another relatively neglected category, "incorporeal hereditaments", in due course.

[7] Christian von Bar criticises this approach roundly: "Nearly all Continental codifications work with a main category and a residual category. They define the former, and put everything that remains into the latter. It is difficult to imagine a cruder method" (Bar 2023: [5.56]). See also Palka (2017).

the German Civil Code. As Christian von Bar observes: "[e]ven a monumental structure, then, is transformed by §95 German Civil Code (despite all appearances) into a *Mobilie*" where in truth "it is as immoveable as an object can be; the classification leads to mysteries" (Bar 2023: [5.29]).[8] Equally mysterious is the Napoleonic approach of treating reified rights—*res incorporales*—as "moveable" by dint of law:

> Art. 516 of the French, Belgian, and Luxembourgish Civil Codes provide: "*Tous les biens sont meubles ou immeubles.*" All goods are either moveable or immoveable; *tertium non datur*. Such a *summa divisio* of all goods (or things) employs a legal term of art; *it purports to state a matter of physical reality, but is minded, in the end, only towards a legal ordering.* (Bar 2023: [5.29])[9]

As I will explain in due course, there is a nuanced, reflexive relationship between the concept of "property rights" and the objects in which those rights can be held: rights and things are distinctive, and must not be conflated, but they are *mutually constitutive*. Ultimately, von Bar argues (rightly) that "thing" as a legal concept means "those objects in which the legal system grants persons property rights". I will turn to a more detailed explication of (and gloss on) von Bar's conceptual schema below. For now, it is important to note that while property rights are constitutive of "things" *qua* legal category, this does not mean that all things are just "reified rights"; further, if we follow the traditional pathways of reasoning (whether in the common law or civilian tradition), we wander in circles. The secret is to recognize "things" as a legally constituted category and to describe, with as much rigour as possible, the relation between the legal "thing" and whatever object of extra-legal reality the "thing" implicates. It is possible that certain phenomena of extra-legal reality simply *should not* be recognized as objects of property rights (ie, granted "thing status"). And so, it appears necessary to define what kind of phenomena should be recognized as things, on what basis. It may be, for example, that there are logical criteria arising from the nature of property law as a system of *erga omnes* monopoly rights that should limit the type of extra-legal objects that can count as things. There are certainly policy criteria to limit the objects of property rights; classical examples include human body products, for example. But in my view it is important to keep the arguments distinct, and to avoid dressing up legal-policy arguments as legal-technical ones.

The short point of this chapter is thus to urge common lawyers to approach the present debate as one that turns on the question of whether cryptoassets are the kind of object in which a legal system should grant me "property rights" (and, if so, which "property rights" it should give me in or over them) rather than as a question of whether the rights I have to my cryptoassets are "property rights"—or, worse still, what remedies I should have and what rights must be reverse-engineered to rationalize those remedies. These are valid and important questions, but the order of things makes a difference.

Methodologically, my suggested orientation is less familiar, though not entirely foreign, to common lawyers. Although it is a somewhat stylized description today,

---

[8] See also discussion on the division of "things" into moveables and immoveables from [5.56] onwards.

[9] Emphasis mine.

the traditional approach sees property law as a system based on particular types of rights and remedies. The abstract question: "In which objects those rights can be held?" is hardly ever posed (Bar 2023: [8.8]). "[T]he notion that such a definition *in abstracto* for all objects would even be possible is somewhat 'un-English'" (Bar 2023: [5.62]). The English case of *National Provincial Bank v Ainsworth* [1965] AC 1175, which has been influential in the debate about cryptoassets so far, was concerned to determine whether a right was a "property right" or a "personal right", not whether the relevant *object* was one fitting for "property rights".[10] Thus, in addition to the infamous circularity of the reasoning (Gray and Gray 2009: 97), it was simply asking the wrong question.[11] True, the criteria of definability, identifiability, transferability, and stability may tell us something about whether an object is a "fitting object of property rights"; several judges and scholars have attempted to repurpose them functionally in this way (Michels and Millard 2022).[12] But the *Ainsworth* criteria do not really say that much, and are by no means the final word.

There is a strange situation in the current development of property law, then, that is only evident if we zoom out to a comparative view. It should be clear from the above that I am not suggesting that the civilian legal systems get it "right" (let alone "righter") than the common law. The truth is more paradoxical (Alice would say "curioser") than that: while the civilian lawyers more naturally *ask the right question*, they are often dogmatically prevented from *giving it the correct answer*; the common lawyers, on the other hand, have all the tools ready to hand to get the right answer, if they would *only ask the right question.*[13]

2.1 Enter the Law Commission

Whatever its substantive merits or demerits, therefore, one noteworthy and praiseworthy aspect of the Law Commission's report on digital assets is the overt focus on cryptoassets as "things". As alerted to, "thing" is not a term of art in English legal

[10] "Before a right or an interest can be admitted into the category of property, or of a right affecting property, it must be definable, identifiable by third parties, capable in its nature of assumption by third parties, and have some degree of permanence or stability. The wife's right has none of these qualities, it is characterised by the reverse of them." *National Provincial Bank v Ainsworth* [1965] AC 1175, 1247–1248.

[11] As Lyria Bennet Moses rightly argues, the criteria describe *property rights* rather than *objects of property*, so they are not relevant to determining what things can be owned: (Moses 2008).

[12] See, for example, (UK Jurisdiction Taskforce, Lawtech Delivery Panel 2019; *AA v Persons Unknown, Re Bitcoin* 2019).

[13] This is related to the "deeply anti-intellectual streak in the common law tradition which cares little for grand or abstract theories of ownership": see Gray and Gray (1998: 17), with reference to *Commissioner for Railways v Valuer-General* [1974] AC 328. A similar conclusion on "asking the right question" is reached by Jasper Verstappen in a manuscript on file with the author, "Ownership, Possession and Control of Digital Assets: Common Law and Civil Law Comparison" (working title) to be published in a forthcoming handbook on digital assets and the law.

parlance, and common law property lawyers do not generally ask whether cryptoassets (or digital files, or cartoon avatars, or whatever) are "fitting objects of property rights". This has to change: we have to intentionally approach property law as the "law of things" and, as a corollary, to define "things" more technically. As von Bar writes:

> English common law, which is fascinating for its much greater historical continuity, would never have allowed [a move such as that in the German Civil Code §90 to define *Sache* as a *terminus technicus*]. A "thing" has, in England [and Wales] and Ireland, remained a colloquial term for the most part, and one to which jurists pay little attention. The common law does not use the term; to define it, therefore, was not and is not necessary. One takes as one's point of departure not the objects in which *erga omnes* rights subsist, but rather the rights themselves, and therefore starts with the terminology and the concept of "property." (Bar 2023: [5.41])

Lately, however, a literature has emerged among Anglophone private law theorists that casts the "law of property" as the "law of things" (Smith 2012; Fairfield 2022). But it is by no means (yet) the dominant school of thought in the common law world. We are still caught in a swirl of rights-and-remedies-oriented reasoning. This is so even though scholars, including Low, do speak of "things" and "thingness" (sometimes even using the Latin terminology of *res*) and make comparative references in their arguments. At base, however, their approach tends to remain rooted in the common law's traditional orientation, categories, and modes of thought. Through it all, we often use different words to articulate our arguments, leaving an empty matrix, or use the same words for different concepts, speaking at cross purposes.

3 Where to from Here?

> "Would you tell me, please, which way I ought to go from here?" "That depends a good deal on where you want to get to," said the Cat. "I don't much care where—" said Alice. "Then it doesn't matter which way you go," said the Cat. "—so long as I get somewhere," Alice added as an explanation. "Oh, you're sure to do that," said the Cat, "if you only walk long enough." (Carroll 1865: Chap. 6)

At the time of writing, it looks increasingly likely that the law of England and Wales will take the "third category" approach to the classification of cryptoassets—which may well pave the way for "third category" treatment of other types of assets associated with conventional information architectures, or indeed future ones that have not yet been conceived. In early 2024, the Law Commission proposed a Draft Bill that would provide:

> A thing (including a thing that is digital or electronic in nature) is capable of being the object of personal property rights even though it is neither—
>
> (a) a thing in possession, nor
>
> (b) a thing in action (Law Commission UK 2024).

The effect of this is to abandon the binary scheme implicit in the conventional law and to define the category of "choses in action" not just as a residual catch-all (without any organizing logic of its own—ie, "everything that is not a chose in possession") but as a category with borders that tracks the notion of a "reified right" (ie, a right, or bundle of rights and other jural incidents, treated "as if" it were an object of property rights). This requires a third category in which to put apparent things that are *neither* physical, tangible chattels *nor* reified rights, including "digital objects" that are phenomenologically (or ontologically) "real" but "odd" or "queer". As the Law Commission explains in its recent report:

> A strong majority of our consultees in response to our original consultation agreed that either a third category of things to which personal property rights can relate has already developed in England and Wales at common law, or, to the extent it has not, that one should be recognised as existing. Some consultees, including senior and specialist judges, said to us that the explicit recognition of such a category would confirm the existing law, facilitate the law's future development and lay to rest any lingering uncertainty as to whether such a category exists. It also would have a further beneficial effect in demonstrating the flexibility and forward-looking nature of the law of this jurisdiction in respect of digital assets. (Law Commission of England and Wales 2024: [2.3])

An intermediate court in Singapore recently hinted that it might characterize all "cryptoassets"—including unbacked ones—as choses in action, disavowing the third category approach.[14] But the main points of the Law Commission's proposed approach have been incorporated into the law of at least one common law jurisdiction, namely that of the Dubai International Financial Centre (DFIC), enacted in early 2024. Section 8 of the DIFC Digital Assets Law defines a "Digital Asset" as a thing that:

(a) exists as a notional quantity unit manifested by the combination of the active operation of software by a network of participants and network-instantiated data;
(b) exists independently of any particular person and legal system; and
(c) is not capable of duplication and use or consumption of the thing by one person or specific group of persons necessarily prejudices the use or consumption of that thing by one or more other persons (Dubai International Financial Centre (DIFC) 2024).

Section 9 of the law provides that a Digital Asset is intangible property but is neither a thing in possession nor a thing in action.

The Law Commission's suggested approach will leave much work to be done by the common law courts. As a joint response to the Law Commission consultation by the Commercial Bar Association and Chancery Bar Association muses:

[14] See *ByBit Fintech Ltd v Ho Kai Xin* [2023] SGHC 199, [35], [36] per Jeyaretnam J. The suggestion that *all* cryptoassets could be seen as choses in action was *obiter*, as the case concerned stablecoins (which are clearly amenable to characterization as choses in action, because they represent rights in the assets "underwriting" the value of the stablecoin); it was not necessary for Jeyaretnam J to suggest (and in truth he may not have suggested or intended to suggest, though it is likely that he did) that "unbacked" cryptoassets should be so characterized, too. See also Ben Chester Cheong and Kunhe Lin, "Crypto assets are property, specifically, choses in action, that are capable of being held on trust" [2024] *SAL Practitioner* 2, [19]–[23].

> In the context of further categories of rights, is the "thing" an object, or a right, or something else? The draft bill gives no guidance on how wide this definition of a "thing" is: does it include an email address? What about an idea for a book? Is happiness a "thing"? To date the Courts have not considered it necessary to determine whether cryptocurrencies are "things", or what that concept may mean, but the draft Bill could force the Courts to do so, creating disputes and litigation where currently there is none. After all, prima facie, all "things" are capable of being the object of personal property rights under the draft Bill. (Law Commission of England and Wales 2024: [2.15])

Surely, a clear framework and orientation is going to be necessary in the near to medium term—a critical period during which that work is to be done. This chapter could be read as an effort to allay such concerns about the advent of a new technical concept as a reference point for the common law of property.

In my view, the Law Commission's recommendation is a positive development. Indeed, it has been, for the most part, well-received. Beyond its explicit "thing" orientation, the Law Commission approach is characterized by three substantive features. First, it clearly posits "digital objects" as *socio-technical* objects—that is, complex objects comprising both technical artefacts, networks of users *and those users' beliefs and intentions*. Secondly, however, to prevent the category just collapsing into either its technical or its social component, it clearly stipulates that the object must *exist independently of persons and the legal system*. The point is subtle, as a socio-technical object is *in part* observer-dependent, that is, ontologically dependent on the states of mind of the agents that make up the community of the relevant legal system. But only in part: there has to be something "there" beyond just human mental states.[15] Likewise, independence from the legal system keeps the category distinct from traditional choses in action, that is, reified rights, that are pure creatures of the legal system.[16] I will discuss these notions of independent existence in due course below. Finally, the Law Commission's approach stresses the features of *rivalrousness and excludability* as threshold characteristics for "object" status (despite being composed of digital data). As I will discuss in due course, these characteristics are important for ensuring that only "fitting" digital candidates become objects of "fitting" property rights.[17] Data per se—let alone information—are not fitting objects of property rights (or necessarily "objects" at all), and only become *object-like* in virtue of some kind of technical-functional constraint in combination with the shared understandings of a community of users. Getting this story right is crucial to a principled advancement of the law in the digital age.

---

[15] I think of (Stein 1937: 289): "there is no 'there' there".

[16] Astute observers will notice that the *legal system itself* is a social contrivance built on convention and shared beliefs and intentions. See further, for example, (MacCormick 2008).

[17] There are shades of Continental reasoning here, in particular of *Typenzwang* and *Typenfixierung*, the notion that there is (i) a limited set of objects of property rights, (ii) a limited number of property rights that can be held, and a (iii) need to restrict certain property rights to appropriate objects even within that category. The approach need not be a list-based closed catalogue, however; it could be open-ended, but based on logical criteria (such as those suggested by the Law Commission).

3.1 A Prolific Dissentient

Kelvin Low has written prolifically in favour of treating all cryptoassets (including unbacked ones) as choses in action. Fighting the good fight against what he regards as a historical wrong-turning, Low is outspoken in his criticism of the Law Commission's proposed trajectory for English law. His contribution to this volume makes a characteristically witty pop culture reference and, at the same time, riffs on David Fox's claim that a Bitcoin is an "ideational object".[18] While my intention is to set out my own approach to property in cryptoassets, rather than a refutation of his approach, it is convenient to identify the main points of divergence.

The first point is that, while it might seem counter-intuitive, "seeing ideational objects" fingers the live issue before us rather nicely—and deserves to be taken seriously. Our own twist is that "ideational objects" are the stock-in-trade of the legal guild. The furniture of our legal world is, by and large, composed of ideational objects, and the law has a fundamental role in their constitution and maintenance.[19] In my view of property law and its objects, *all* objects are a little bit "ideational". My own title includes a reference to Lewis Carroll's famous children's stories, and implicitly argues that there is something fictive about even the most concrete objects of property law.[20] We must engage systematically with the interplay between (i) the digital artefact and (ii) the ideational object that together comprise "a bitcoin" (for example) and ask whether the complex (ie, socio-technical) object so described is a fitting object of property rights. This is best done in the context of an open-minded enquiry into the foundations of property law itself and the relationship between property rights and their objects.

The second point to note is Low's singular consistency in arguing that cryptoassets should be seen as choses in action because the asset they represent or comprise is, properly seen, really a *right* to make a register entry (Low and Teo 2017: 253; Low 2020a: 81; Kurtz et al. 2018: 8-050).[21] On this view, cryptoassets—including unbacked ones—really are just choses in action in the conventional sense: the *res* in question "just is" the *jus*. As Timothy Chan writes, "[t]he main difficulty with Low's view is identifying a base for the proposed right" (Chan 2023: 491). Working through the possibilities (including contract, statute, and a common law copyright analogy) Chan comes up empty-handed, and instead prefers to characterize the subject-matter (I would say "object") of property rights as a "practical transactional ability" rather than a "right" or "power" (Chan 2023: 491). Likewise, in his abrupt (and in many respects baffling) foray into the debate, Robert Stevens gets this much right: "Within a common law system", he asks, "what rights (or privileges, powers or immunities)

[18] Namely, to the M. Night Shyamalan film *The Sixth Sense*, Other references include the Bard and Japanese director Akira Kurosawa: see, eg, (Low and Lin 2015; Low 2016).

[19] I borrow the language of "furniture" from (Mäki 2011: 8); see also (Mäki 1996).

[20] I am not the first to use a Lewis Carroll analogy; see also Solinas (2019). Of course, Carroll's tales are also sophisticated plays on logic and possibility and also on the contingency of convention.

[21] See also Chan (2023: 491) for discussion.

does the correct holder of a key to a Bitcoin wallet have?" (Stevens 2023: 625). Again, he comes up empty-handed:

> It is impossible to identify any [cause of action to enforce a primary right or one to correct any infringement]. No tort applicable to things… is operative as these are all dependent upon the claimant having a right in relation to a physical thing that can be possessed. The holder of the key has no contractual rights against anyone, the whole point of the system is to do away with intermediaries such as banks who would owe such a duty. There are no statutory rights of enforcement, such as those of someone who holds a patent, copyright or trade mark. Unlike the holder of a milk quota, the string of numbers that gives access to the Bitcoin wallet does not, without more, acquire a privilege not to perform any duty or an immunity from any suit. (Stevens 2023: 625)[22]

We will discuss the "substance" of a cryptoasset again below; the short point is that in my view—and in the view of the majority of commentators, even those otherwise sympathetic to Low's position—a cryptoasset gives its holder something akin to a *functional ability* rather than a legal "right" or "power" to do something. This makes it inappropriate to describe cryptoassets as "reified rights". A similar point has been made by Johan David Michels and Christopher Millard. Rather than reifying a supposed right, they argue that "there is only a thing, but no right" (Michels and Millard 2022: 353):

> Low and Teo suggest that a Bitcoin could be conceived as the legal right of the holder to have the Bitcoin "locked to their chosen… address on the blockchain", so that they can exercise exclusive control. This right could qualify as a thing in action. In sum, on this view, with intangible property, there is only a right; there is no thing. We argue the opposite for Bitcoins and digital files: there is a thing, but there is no right. In particular, a Bitcoin or a file is a virtual thing that can be subject to exclusive control at the logical layer of a computer system. But there is no right to that virtual object that could qualify as a thing in action. (Michels and Millard 2022: 353)

A third noteworthy point of difference has emerged more recently, as Low has drawn on Ben McFarlane and Simon Douglas's argument against the "property syllogism". This really boils down to the proposition that, just because a bicycle is "property" and a dematerialized company share is "property", it does not necessarily follow that I have all the same rights and remedies *vis-à-vis* my share as *vis-à-vis* my bicycle (McFarlane and Douglas 2022). The point is well taken: we should be clear when we are talking about *different types of object* protected by property rights, as they may *attract different kinds of property rights*, and otherwise behave differently "downstream". I do not, however, think that this argument says very much about the present debate—unless we've already got ourselves in a muddle. If we adopt the right point of departure, and stick to the right path, the problem McFarlane and Douglas criticize does not arise. That is to say, McFarlane and Douglas are correct that the holders of chose in action (reified rights) *do not need* and *should not have* all the same legal rights and remedies as holders of choses in possession (physical objects like bicycles)—even though we might call both "property". These are different *types of object* that logically require and merit different *types of legal protection*. Property law

[22] Stephens here mentions a number of "Hohfeldian incidents" beyond claim rights.

grants rights in objects to persons—but it does not grant rights to *all types* objects in the universe, and it does not grant all the same rights in *every type* of object. Far from being a knock-out argument, the property syllogism only underscores the importance of *taking objects seriously*, and working outwards from there.

3.2 A Matter of Approach

From these substantive points, the real divergence relates to our approach. To be fair, Low does (try) to engage with the nature of the object in question and has more than once engaged in comparative analysis (Low and Hara 2024). However, although we traverse similar terrain, we seem to be using very different maps.

This is in large measure, I think, because his point of departure remains very much the common lawyer's familiar one: rights and remedies. The Law Commission gets it wrong, he says, by "mistak[ing] the law of property for being concerned with objects when it is concerned with relationships with objects" (Low 2025). In my view, the law of property is concerned with persons' relationships to each other *vis-à-vis* objects. However, to do this, property law has to determine what objects it recognizes (or takes cognizance of) in the first place. It does so primarily through establishing categories from which legal consequences follow and stipulating criteria for inclusion of phenomena in the relevant category. That's just how legal systems work (Honoré 1977: 117). As I wrote in my first foray into the topic (which was not cited by, but substantively reflects the position taken by the UK Jurisdiction Taskforce (UKJT)):

> When confronted with an entity that defies straightforward placement in our catalogue of all that exists and is the case, we have three options: (i) we can deny the intuitive fact that it exists (i.e. that it is a legally cognizable entity) at all; (ii) we can shoehorn it into an existing category; or (iii) we can reform our catalogue. As a general principle, it is undesirable for the law to diverge too far from the expectations of the community that uses it, so I reject (i) as a viable approach. While 'bodging' what we've got is a serviceable approach in many cases, there is no guarantee that our existing categories... will provide a rational framework for digital coins, and we may be trapped in the path-dependencies of our legal system's inherited categories before an optimal solution is achieved. This cautions against (ii). I would therefore advocate for option (iii). In my view, adjusting private law specifically to incorporeal objects would not only help us to describe the legal nature of digital coins, it would also make our law of property in general more future-ready. (Allen 2018a: 76)

Low criticizes the opinion set out in the UKJT's *Legal Statement* that "if a cryptoasset does not embody a legally enforceable right or obligation then it is neither necessary nor useful to classify it as a thing in action" (UK Jurisdiction Taskforce, Lawtech Delivery Panel 2019: 22). To many of us, the UKJT's proposition makes sense because the paradigmatic case (and historical origin) of the chose in action was a reified right-duty relationship—a "right" transmuted through legal alchemy into a "thing". The problem presented by unbacked cryptoassets, then, is one of positing a third category and describing it—and of justifying how objects that are intangible, but not pure creatures of the legal system, could be considered "objects of property rights" at all. (This is the preliminary first step before we can get to the equally important question: Should we grant subjects property rights in these objects? If so, why? And if not, why not?)

Low's arguments are always complex, and we sometimes talk at cross-purposes. The following is based on my best efforts to understand his position and articulate it in my own terms. In the first step, Low glosses the view of the opposing camp. In short, he says that we (who support a third category approach) would limit the category of choses in action to only *certain* types of rights, namely "enforcement rights", which he identifies as "claim rights" in the Hohfeldian sense (Low 2024: n. 20). His touchstone is the late nineteenth century debate in the *Law Quarterly Review* about the property law treatment of artefacts like patents and company shares.[23] Low argues that a "conceptual concern appears to have firmly taken root", namely that "only Hohfeldian claim rights would fall within the category of choses in action".[24] This is, he thinks, incoherent: "The irony of courts allowing legal actions in respect of intangible property that are not choses in action because they do not entail rights enforceable by action", he observes, "appears to have eluded proponents" of the *tertium quid* approach (Low 2020b: 348). Low's desired check-mate argument, however, elides the all-important starting question: Is a "cryptoasset" a fitting object of property rights? If so, is it (i) a right masquerading as a thing in a manner that conforms to the historical (more importantly) conceptual requirements of the category of "chose in action" in the common law tradition? Or is it (ii) something in which the legal system can grant property rights even though it cannot be treated as a reified right?

If my reading of his argument is accurate, he has set the frame of reference to suit his argument and desired conclusion. That is, the "chose in action = Hohfeldian claim right" position he ascribes to the *tertium quid* camp is a strawman. Parking that complaint for the present, the position is wrong, Low says, in a two-fold sense. Here, his conventional rights-and-remedies driven approach resurfaces:

> [S]uch a view of things in action both overemphasises the necessity of a right in action and underestimates the panoply of remedies available to a modern court. As to the former, the right of action serves the purpose of securing performance and in the vast majority of cases,

---

[23] Low claims that "[t]he more considered proponents [of the *tertium quid* view] at least reference Blackstone's *Commentaries on the Laws of England* but no proponent has referenced either the late nineteenth century debate over the nature of things in action in the *Law Quarterly Review*... by the foremost property law scholars of the that era or Holdsworth's historical study of the same for the *Harvard Law Review* in the early twentieth century" (Low 2024: n. 37). This is not correct; I discussed Blackstone as well as the seminal articles by Howard Elphinstone and William Holdsworth in Allen (2018a).

[24] The 1890s debate predates W.N. Hohfeld's influential schema of fundamental legal conceptions, which was published in the 1910s. The Hohfeldian concept of a "claim right" *avant la lettre* is presumably something like the German concept of *Anpsruch*, ie a demand against someone rather than a *Recht* as an entitlement to something. I have never been a great fan of Hohfeld's schematic of fundamental legal conceptions; in particular, I have been critical of the category of "no-rights", the lack of articulation between the two "boxes" in the schema, and the lack of an express logic of action in the schema. On the problems with the Hohfeldian schema for understanding property law and property rights, see also (Penner 2020: pt. II).

things in action, even in the limited sense, are enjoyed in their performance rather than by way of action... As to the latter, the availability of declaratory and *quia timet* injunctive relief also severely blunts the force of criticism that no rights of action exist prior to infringement (Bridge et al. 2022: 175).

I had to read this repeatedly to decipher where the argument was going. The key is to remember that Low is trying to convince us that *all* crypotasses are choses in action, so he needs to convince us that the holder of a bitcoin (for example) has some kind of *legal right* to change the Bitcoin ledger (rather than just a *factual-technical ability* to do so). Arguing from concerns that I share—namely that the law should *prima facie* recognize and protect social (including market) expectations, including through recognizing the objects of market dealings as objects of property rights—Low seems now to argue that the right being reified belongs to a parallel normative order: "the case for treating cryptoassets as property is more helpfully explicated by the notion that the law, including the law of property, entails the institutionalization of extra-legal conventions" (Low 2024: n. 99).[25] In making this bold argument, Low makes passing reference to Neil MacCormick's institutional theory of law, but does not develop it.[26] This is unfortunate because MacCormick's approach holds many useful resources for thinking through these sorts of questions which, if taken seriously, would help bring order to Low's account.[27] In any case, there is a lot to unpack in the proposition. While the notion of blockchain networks as norm-generating communities is plausible,[28] I harbour reservations about the straightforward importation of "cryptolaw" norms into state law; in particular, I do think that we should make such a move just in order to save a pet argument that bitcoins are just reified rights. As Rosa Lastra and I observed previously, in a broadly Lessigian framework:

In effect, a new source of... norms is emerging—those implicit in the digital architecture of DLT systems. Some of these norms, *but only some of them*, are translations of state law into code, or code recognized as state law. Others seem to be a result of "bleeding" from technical architecture, designed by coders rather than lawyers, into state law. Whether law is encoded, or code simply becomes law (or its functional equivalent), any cross-over should be subject to scrutiny against the core legal and political values of the relevant society. In our view, this demands that anything like "cryptolaw" must be jurisprudentially grounded in a respectable framework—ideally, one that is continuous with the framework on which

[25] This appears to be adopting one of the possibilities set out—and rejected—in Michels and Millard (2022: 353).

[26] Low further asserts, citing an earlier piece co-authored with Peter Watts, that cryptoassets are a modern example of the law "adding flesh to extra-legal bones", See Watts and Low (2024). This assertion follows a rambling just-so story of property's origins in the physical occupation of territory and some armchair conjecture about whether normative order or physical force came first in the primordial dawn. It does not move the present debate forward in any meaningful sense.

[27] The institutional theory of law is at base a marriage of Searleian social ontology, and Oxonian language philosophy in a broadly Hartian concept of law. For a more expanded treatment, see Allen (2021b).

[28] For example, see Reed and Murray (2018), arguing *inter alia* that at least some Internet-based communities should be recognized to possess legitimate norm-generating authority. Personally, I would not ascribe this status to the Bitcoin network, and I don't think that doing so is consistent with Low's normative commitments, either.

> similar phenomena of interstitial (ie non-state) "law" have been grounded. (Lastra and Allen 2023: para. 7.23–7.24)

Getting back to the framing of Low's main argument, notice again that he first grasps at remedies to save his approach, using the fact that courts are granting remedies to prove the existence of some right (though not a Hohfeldian claim right) that can be reified. Again, this is presented as a "gotcha" argument: If the view posited by the UKJT (ie, that a bitcoin embodies no legally-enforceable right or obligation) were true, Low asks, how did the English High Court in *AA v Persons Unknown* grant a remedy in the case? Here, his approach reveals itself *to* be entirely remedies-driven:

> Most lawyers are familiar with the maxim *ubi jus, ibi remedium* [where there is a right, there is a remedy], but the reverse—*ubi remedium, ibi jus*—arguably sits on firmer foundations. Right holders are often left effectively remediless if they cannot locate those that have infringed their rights within the jurisdiction, or if they are strawmen unable to satisfy whatever judgment is ordered against them. These considerations are particularly acute in the context of cryptoassets given the pseudonymity and immutability that are a feature of the community. *Ubi remedium, ibi jus*, however, is a more immutable truth... Given the various remedies that the English courts have granted to cryptoasset holders, is it seriously arguable that they have no legal rights (Low 2024: n. 27)?

Again, the argument is not about whether the category "choses in action" is coterminous with "intangible personal property", but about whether the holder of a bitcoin has a "legal right" rather than a "factual ability" grounded in the technical features of an information system with certain (eg, cryptographic and game theory) design features. And again, Low's approach effectively precludes the kind of enquiry that I (and the other third category proponents) think is important: describing how something which is both (i) not tangible and (ii) not obviously "just a reified right" can be an object of property rights in the first place—which rights may, in turn, attract remedies. In my view, Low's treatment of rights-*as*-things and rights-*in*-things rather confuses the enquiry than advances it. In particular, he seems to confuse (i) the idea of a remedy to protect the proprietary right *in or to* an asset and (ii) a remedy given to enforce the right that *is itself* an asset. If a bitcoin is a type of asset that is an object of property rights but is not a reified right itself, as we think, granting remedies to protect property rights in the bitcoin does not transmute it into a chose in action.

I take it as uncontentious (i) that bare cryptoassets are not paradigmatic choses in action and (ii) that the category of choses in action needs conceptual and doctrinal development. In my first foray into the subject matter, I noticed the obvious attraction of choses in action as a pigeon-hole for cryptoassets, and the plausibility of expanding the category to accommodate them, but cautioned against path-dependent habits of thought.[29] Low's more recent contributions, too, recognize that the chose in action category needs a more or less radical clean-up:

> [I]t is undoubtedly the case that the category of things in action broadly defined is desperately in need of rationalization, comprising as it does a grab-bag of intangibles ranging from purely personal rights (debt, being the classic thing in action), *erga omnes* rights (most intellectual property rights apart from patents), and rights against a fluctuating class of persons (shares). (Low 2024: n. 27)

There is still some distance between his position and mine in terms of what "rationalization" might entail, and whether it would differ materially from the creation of a third category. Low seems to accept that cryptoassets could be used as a starting point for a broader cleanup, but seems ambivalent about that project,[30] whereas that is the position I have advocated enthusiastically.[31] Low would, I think, say there is no "expansion" of the category of choses in action entailed in his position—that, properly understood, the category *already is* wider than I think it is. (This gets messy, as Low imputes a narrower view to the third category camp than any of us, to my knowledge, actually hold, as set out above, so I will not pursue any more blind chess here.) But even taking that point for the sake of argument, it would dodge the central issue: If cleaning up means imposing of internal distinctions between choses in action of different types—including some that are reified rights and others that are not—that would be tantamount to recognizing a third category. (If there is a "gotcha" argument in my case, this is the most likely candidate.)

The real insight to be gained from an exploration of choses in action has, meanwhile, been largely ignored in the debate—namely, the relation between a reified right, which is generally the product of a speech-act, and the documents that fix its existence and allow dealings with it over time.[32] Some theory of *documentality* is implicit in any conception of reified rights in the modern context—as so often in

---

[29] I listed a number of reasons, including the historical non-assignability of choses in action and their complex relationship with maintenance and champerty. Further, I argued: "[B]oth choses in action and incorporeal hereditaments are incorporeal, but they straddle English property law's basic dichotomy of real and personal property. This is not necessarily problematic, but it is odd that a classification of things by type should treat some incorporeal objects as tantamount to land and others as tantamount to chattels, and perhaps points to the general serviceability of the system" (Allen 2018a: 82).

[30] "One problem with concluding that cryptoassets should be regarded as *tertium quid* because they do not entail [Hohfeldian] claim rights against another is that much the same criticism could be made of many other intangible property [sic] currently classified as things in action such as intellectual property law rights. Why should we do so for an 'innovation' that is increasingly looking like 'all hype, no substance' following the cascade of crypto failures of 2022? If a rationalisation is in order, then the entire category of things in action needs to be carefully sorted" (Low 2024: n. 27).

[31] "Reforming a category of property law requires a basic consideration of the conceptual structure of property law itself… I argue that we should recognize incorporeal objects directly as objects of property rights… As digital coins present both novel problems and variations on familiar themes, they provide a challenging and topical context for [an enquiry into the qualification of structured information into a separate object as to which subjects can have legal relationships]" (Allen 2018a: 66, 70).

[32] On this point, see also Koepsell (2022).

private law, doctrinalists leave their theories implicit. In particular, this remains as a topic for focused attention when we consider the relation between the digital record ("token") of a linked ("real world") asset and that asset itself. This important enquiry is still in its relative early days. In the case of documentary intangibles, we treat the chose in action like a chattel in virtue of its paper "wrapper" and apply the property law rules governing chattels that "drag along" the chose in action when the paper is dealt with; we have not, in my view, really satisfactorily dealt with choses in action represented in a *traditional* ledger, let alone with the new types of data architecture that present object-like (eg, "controllable") electronic records.[33]

3.3 Looking Beyond Choses in Action

I think it is helpful to look past the category of choses in action—beyond the nineteenth century debate about the borders of that category in the *Law Quarterly Review*, and even beyond the category of personal property. Examining the law's treatment of intangible objects of property rights across the *summa divisio* ("realty/personalty") of our taxonomy illuminates both (i) the (in)coherence of the taxonomy's historical categories and (ii) the nature of intangible "objects" of different kinds, including complex socio-technical artefacts such as cryptoassets. In Sect. 4, I will argue that real property—"land", properly understood—actually provides us with the closest cognate to "third category" digital objects. To tilt us down the rabbit-hole, a brief examination of the common law category of incorporeal hereditaments is useful.

Incorporeal hereditaments are intangible objects of property rights that were classified as "realty" for inheritance purposes, reflecting the feudal system's characteristic fusion of legal, economic, and social relations. Incorporeal hereditaments were thus transferable (subject to that system's restrictions) for a long time during which choses in action were (categorically) not. Beyond the obvious point about the common law's historical continuity and the vestigial nature of many of its appendages, there is much to be learned from the category. Much of my prior work has been on one category of incorporeal hereditaments, *offices*, and the story of how they came to be neglected in both public law and the law of private associations (even though they continue to do significant heavy lifting behind the scenes).[34] Offices were long considered a form of property—in fact, the law has not actually changed, so formally at least they must still be so considered.

Low is generally critical of Blackstone's treatment of personalty in his *Commentaries on the Laws of England*, and in key respects rightly so (Low 2024: n. 41). (Bentham earlier criticized Blackstone for ignoring things like company shares and

[33] See also Wendehorst (2023b: 102–103).

[34] See, for example, (Kershaw 2020). In broad terms, I define an "office" as a role that an individual assumes within a broader social institution (be it ecclesiastical, eleemosynary, or secular) that enables her to perform actions she could not perform in her own right, that exists as an enduring entity distinct from the occupant, and that serves interests broader than the occupant's own. See Allen (2018b: 309); see also Finn (2017) and Allen (2024, 2022).

money in his treatment of personal property, and these objects would not be fully incorporated into the commentaries until far too late in the nineteenth century (Sokol 1994).) But he does not mention Blackstone's treatment of incorporeal hereditaments. While the eighteenth century framing is not free of difficulties, it does make clear some things that later commentators miss. Blackstone tells us that an "incorporeal hereditament" is a "right issuing out" or otherwise related to "a thing corporate (whether real or personal)", without *being* the thing corporate itself:

> In short, as the logicians speak, corporeal hereditaments are the substance, which may be always seen, always handled: incorporeal hereditaments are but a sort of accidents, which inhere in and are supported by that substance; and may belong, or not belong to it, without any visible alteration therein. *Their existence is merely in idea and abstracted contemplation*; though their effects and profits may be frequently objects of our bodily senses (Blackstone 1766: bk. II, Chapter III).

To understand incorporeal hereditaments, Blackstone says, "we must be careful not to confound together the profits produced, and the thing, or hereditament, which produces them"; an annuity, for instance, is an incorporeal hereditament, "for though the money, which is the fruit or product of this annuity, is doubtless of a corporeal nature, yet the annuity itself, which produces that money, is a thing invisible, has only a mental existence, and cannot be delivered over from hand to hand" (Blackstone 1766: bk. II, Chapter III). (Blackstone was obviously thinking of chattel money, not book money, which has a more complex ontology.) Blackstone lists 10 types of incorporeal hereditaments: he describes advowsons, tithes, commons of pasture, rights of way, offices, corodies, annuities, and rents as "rights"; commons of piscary, commons of estovers, franchises and dignities as "liberties". Evidently, we are dealing with a set of "reified rights", being an institutionalized social and political status with juridical incidents including prerogatives and immunities attached; incorporeal hereditaments are more closely akin to choses in action in this respect than either is to "data objects" (which, as I have already argued, are not reified rights). This is all long before the Hohfeldian (or any comparable) scheme of constrained vocabulary, so we cannot put too much on the terminology, but I think the point is clear that we are concerned with a broader set of jural incidents than Hohfeldian "claim rights".

Blackstone's reference to "the logicians' manner of speaking" and his claim that incorporeal hereditaments have "only a mental existence" are important. Intuitively, we all know and accept that this must be the case. Rights are obviously dependent on the intentionality of a community of human beings for their existence: they are obviously "ideational objects". But what about other things that we can "think up" that are not rights? The Bar Association consults cited above, for example, ask whether happiness is the right type of "thing" (which it obviously is not; with respect, the example is not even very helpful because happiness is a universal and an abstract concept rather than any kind of "object" or instantiation and can only be described as a "thing" in a much broader and therefore irrelevant sense). The Law Commission's criteria of objects' ontological independence from (i) persons and (ii) the legal system seems, in light of the foregoing discussion, to be pointing directly at this question. When is a something—albeit intangible and housed within a data architecture on a network of computers—sufficiently "thing-like" in a phenomenological sense to attract property rights *outside* the categories of reified rights? That is the question that Low's analysis, for all its learning, seeks to dispatch quietly and bury far from view. But it is the question that we really need to answer.

4 We Need to Talk About Things

> "The time has come", the Walrus said, "To talk of many things: Of shoes—and ships—and sealing-wax—Of cabbages—And kings...". (Carroll 1871: Chap. 4)

In the title of his chapter, Low pokes some gentle fun at the notion of "ideational objects" as presented by David Fox in an early contribution to the present debate.[35] Fox's argument is that a crypto-coin is an ideational construct:

> Its function and value as a medium of exchange or investment commodity exist only in the shared understanding of the users who make transactions on a cryptocurrency system. The coin itself has no intrinsic value. The source of its value is extrinsic to itself, imposed by the collective belief of the people who use it. (Fox 2019: para. 6.13)

The "coin" takes the form, he continues, as a chain of records in a database that forms part of a networked system in which these understandings operate. In a later explanation, Fox elaborates that to call something an "ideational construct" makes clear that it is not a spatio-temporal, tangible object, but that it means more than saying that all the participants who transact in it share a belief that it represents some specific *locus* of tradable value in a market. That is, there is something (or some thing) more than "value" at hand.

Fox continues that many objects recognized by the law are wholly or partly "ideational": "they have relevant attributes over and above their basic physical or technical properties" (Fox 2022).[36] He takes this fundamental premise from the branch of analytical metaphysics called social ontology—on which MacCormick, incidentally, built his "institutional" legal theory.[37] Money is, in fact, one of the standard go-to examples for debates in social ontology.[38] A physical coin is a composite object, too. "[T]he £1 coin struck by the Royal Mint is something more than a stamped metal disc", continues Fox; "[i]ts status as an asset in the law includes its capacity to discharge debts, and assumes a general body of rules on the performance of monetary

[35] He seems to miss the irony that choses in action are quintessentially ideational.

[36] I would use the terminology of "ability" rather than "power" to avoid confusion, but there is no substantive difference in our views here.

[37] The distinction between "institutional" and "brute" facts is drawn from Anscombe (1958). It was taken up by John Searle and operationalised in his explanation of how social objects—dependent on the states of mind of human beings—can exist within a broadly materialist metaphysics. See Searle (1995, 2010).

[38] The "Searle-Lawson debate" on the conceptual apparatus for doing social ontology—whether a matter of creating institutional facts through "X counts as Y in C" declarations or through "social positioning" within a "totality"—draws repeatedly on the nature of money. See, for example, Lawson (2016).

obligations" (Fox 2022). In the Searleian scheme, these are "deontic powers" that the coin—an *institutional* rather than a *brute* fact—emanates in virtue of the acceptance by a community that it "counts as" £1 of "money". Fox continues:

> The view proposed here is that a digital asset is an ideational thing containing different components. It is more complex than the £1 coin since it lacks any tangible basis and its most significant properties are matters of digital functionality rather than legal attribution. Like the coin, however, it comprises more than one component. It is grounded in, but not confined to, the technical features of its own digital design. Its outward manifestation is a string of data generated by transactions between participants on a distributed ledger system. But to see the asset as mere data would ignore its larger functionality, just as we would fail to appreciate the full economic or legal significance of a coin by treating it as a mere metal disc. (Fox 2022)

To understand cryptoassets, we need to see them as (i) a set of transactional functionalities within the relevant technical system coupled with (ii) a set of community expectations which the law can recognize through its own specialist categories of analysis, if it so chooses—such as ownership, title and transfer. (In the latter, the law may be "legalizing" extra-legal conventions as Low suggested *pace* MacCormick, but that fact must not eclipse (i), which is a technological artefact, completely.)[39] Fox concludes that the most important functionality is the "capacity" of the person who holds the private key to effect new transactions on the ledger. Perhaps it is useful to tease out four alterative cases:

- A £1 coin: an "ideational" pound is tied to a physical (metal) token; the operative rules are those governing chattels/choses in possession.
- A £1 cheque: an "ideational" pound is tied to a debt (a chose in action, ie, an intangible artefact of the legal system itself), which is recorded on a physical (paper) instrument; the operative rules are those governing the document as a chattel/chose in possession under the theory of documentary intangibles and the doctrine of merger. (A banknote could be treated in the same way for all intents and purposes; ontologically, cheques and banknotes are peas in a pod.)
- A £1 bank account balance: an "ideational" pound, implicitly bound up with a debt is declared to exist in a bank ledger book but, while ontologically dependent on the existence of the book, is not tied to the book in the same way as a documentary intangible; the operative rules are those governing choses in action. (It probably does not matter too much whether the "book" is physical or digital.)
- £1 worth of bitcoin: an "ideational" object (not denominated in, though perhaps measured by reference to, the pound *qua* unit of account) is not tied to any recognizable chose in action or chose in possession, but is ontologically dependent on

[39] Previously, I wrote: "Artefacts have a material dimension, but their material form does not capture the essence of the existence of artefacts on the social plane. In social reality, artefacts operate by virtue of being collectively recognized or accepted, by human beings, as having certain properties. *Law is one of the modes in which that recognition can take place, and the effects of recognition (or non-recognition) establish facts that are local to the legal system in question*" (Allen 2021c: 67). This relates to the dynamic between legal and extra-legal modes of social recognition and acceptance relied on by Low, above, and again speaks to the need for more careful theorizing when adopting such an approach.

the existence of the Bitcoin network, which stores the relevant data in the state of its database; the operative legal rules are yet to be determined.[40]

The "ideational pound" moves around when we pass the coin or negotiate the cheque, the "ideational pound" moves around when we create and delete bank account ledger entries with the stroke of a pen or the click of a mouse, and the "ideational bitcoin" moves around when the blockchain ledger is altered. The difference is that in the first and last cases, there is no readily identifiable chose in action, whereas in the case of conventional digital bank money there is. So we need to look for the *digital equivalent* of the coin—obviously, there is no *actual* coin—and craft a mechanics of property law that can structure these transactions in ways that are (broadly) functionally equivalent and conformable with first principles.

4.1 Things as Institutional (not Brute) Facts

Commercial lawyers may well ascribe "property status" too liberally to anything of value (ie, anything which is bought and sold).[41] Not everything that humans value is necessarily a fitting object of property rights (at least not *all* property rights). Yet the concept of value is important in a rigorously thing-based approach to property law, too. As Joshua Fairfield explains, we need not get bogged down in the philosophy or anthropology of the concept to see that value is, at base, a *socially-constituted phenomenon.* Further, "[s]ocial value has two components, a community that attaches value and a nexus to which community value attaches" (Fairfield 2022: 7). In the case of a non-fungible token ("NFT") linked to a GIF of a fun sporting moment, for example, "[t]ying the moment to an entry in a cryptoledger, and creating a community that recognizes the owner of the ledger entry as having some special relationship with the moment takes turning an experience into a thing" (Fairfield 2022: 7). This gets us closer to the *socio-technical* object of our enquiry—a complex object which is a phenomenon of *both* a technological artefact (such as a ledger entry in an information architecture held in a network of computers) *and* social conventions (including ultimately legally recognized social conventions) combined.

Understanding the distinction and the connection between these two aspects of legal "things" is crucial. "Much of what makes a thing a thing in property [law]", argues Fairfield, "is the conveyance of rights that are a function of a social agreement, not physics" (Fairfield 2022: 8). This is important: it is *through rights* that we *deal with objects*—even physical objects—and those rights are constitutive of the object as a "thing" in the legal sense. We cannot follow the approach, popular in the last century, of decomposing the concept of property completely into the proverbial "bundle of Hohfeldian sticks" with no core; doing so makes the objects of property rights informationally complex to the extent that property law per se cannot serve

[40] I am grateful to Johan David Michels for suggesting a clearer exposition of this point, in particular, in his comments on the draft.

[41] For example, see Goode (2023).

its functions.[42] A simple farm, for example, can have complex arrangements of owners, easements, and servitudes. Further, it needs to be clear whether houses and outbuildings, plant and equipment, livestock, or even standing crops comprise parts of the "farm" (*qua* thing)—at least as a matter of default rule. This fundamentally sound insight underlies the "informational turn" that property theorists such as Henry Smith and Fairfield himself have pursued in the past decades (Smith 2015). According to Fairfield:

> Thing-ness constrains the extravagances of Hohfeldian property: although we can split off the right to possess from the right to exclude, use, destroy, copy, manage, repair, and so on, there is a gravitational pull to tie these sticks back into a useful bundle centered on the asset, the thing. (Fairfield 2022: 1)

Tellingly, the attempted disintegration of the concept of property into a bundle of sticks has not been successful; as James Penner notes, over the decades of the ascendancy of this approach "[n]o-one has ever produced a general description of the incidents of property which transcends a reliance, either explicitly or implicitly, on an underlying relation between the property owner and the 'things' he owns" (Penner 1996: 733). In Fairfield's account, a "thing" in the law of property is thus what Bruno Latour calls a "quasi-object" (Fairfield 2022: 7):

> Like a brick (given its shape by [both] physics and culture), a thing is an amalgamation of understandings about the extent of the resources conveyed with the thing, the rights conveyed with the thing, a mixture of material affordance and social permission. (Fairfield 2022: 7)[43]

I have generally eschewed Latour's kind of scholarship for the more workaday idiom of analytic philosophy. John Searle, for example, explains how a physical object (like a brick) can have a socially-constructed, mind-dependent second life, as it were, as an "institutional fact" constructed through his "X counts as Y in C" formula.[44] As alerted to above, this broad scheme has been operationalized masterfully by legal theorists, most notably MacCormick, within a broadly Hartian framework. I have

---

[42] "Like contract law, property law is understood as an instrument of optimal resource allocation in states with a market-based economic order. Property law promotes this objective by guaranteeing rights of exclusion and rights of control over things. It does this, in turn, by furnishing property rights effective against third parties. This helps to define relationships between persons by reference to their entitlement to use things" (Bar 2023: [1.18]). See also at [10.1] on the informational function of "thingness".

[43] I agree in part; although the brick is in part formed by culture—a preference for an arbitrary size, for example, or ornamental shape—it is still often used as a brute object for its physical properties. In his own words, Latour makes the point: "Quasi-objects are in between and below the two poles [of nature and society], at the very place around which dualism and dialectics had turned endlessly without being able to come to terms with them. Quasi-objects are much more social, much more fabricated, much more collective than the "hard" parts of nature, but they are in no way the arbitrary receptacles of a full-fledged society." Bruno Latour (Catherine Porter trans.), *We Have Never Been Modern* (Harvard University Press 1993), cited in Fairfield (2022: 6).

[44] For a review of Searle's 1995 statement of the theory, and some background, see Turner (1999). There have been developments of Searle's theory since then: see Searle (2010) for the refined (and more concise) account.

returned repeatedly to a passage by Neil MacCormick and Ota Weinberger, which inspired the *Alice* theme of my title:

> If law exists at all, it exists not on the level of *brute creation* along with shoes and ships and sealing wax or for that matter cabbages, but rather along with kings and other paid officers of state on the plane of *institutional fact.* (MacCormick and Weinberger 1986: 49)[45]

It is worthwhile to briefly unpack what it means for something to "exist on the plane of institutional fact". It would be a grave mistake to assert that, because objects have a social dimension to their ontology, that they are not "real" (Allen 2020: Chap. 6). Quoting MacCormick again (in a passage that makes his debt to Hartian hermeneutic positivism clear), "institutional facts" are those facts that "depend not *only* on some physical events and occurrences which are supposed to have taken place, but *also* on an interpretation of these (and/or other) events or occurrences in terms of some stable set of norms" (MacCormick 2010: 65).[46]

Conceptually, objects of brute reality must pass through a kind of "veil" and be recognized as *legal objects* in order to be objects of dealings within the realm of law at all. Many objects that could straightforwardly be "chattels" are not objects of property rights at all, for example; most fundamentally, in modern legal systems, we treat animals as "things" but members of our own species categorically as "persons"—subjects, not objects, of the legal system. This is often so even after death. Even human body parts (and products) tend to remain outside the category of objects in which persons can hold property rights, although the boundary lines are characteristically blurry within (and widely variable between) legal systems. This is a legal-policy decision, not a legal-technical one, however; systems of chattel slavery have existed and, although they draw morally repugnant distinctions between some humans as subjects and other humans as objects, they are *technically* coherent. The point—which I will expand below—is that no brute object is straightforwardly and automatically an "object of property rights".

Taken to an extreme, the physical world melts away and *everything* becomes virtual; short of forgetting the material world entirely, in a certain sense *all of law's objects are ideational.* The institutional social practice we know as "law" *just is* a language-based system of norms and convention that depends on (because it exists in) the mental dispositions of a human community. In the case of chattels, a "thin" kind of ideational gloss is impressed on physical objects of external reality that are not, like a right or corporation, observer-dependent; however, at least in the decision to admit that an object is an entity of which the legal system will take cognizance (for example, by granting rights and duties in it), there is a bit of imagination all the way down. As F.H. Lawson observes (foreshadowing Fairfield, above), the intellectual constructs of property law move "in a world of pure ideas from which everything physical or material is entirely excluded" (Lawson 1951: 79).[47] This profound insight is a little like law's dirty laundry, but it is crucial. Importantly, human communities

---

[45] Emphasis mine.

[46] Emphasis mine.

[47] Cited—I think not with approval—by Gray and Gray (1998: 25).

use *record-keeping technologies* to stabilize their institutional normative order and the objects in it over time; the technologies we use expand the horizons of the possible as they evolve, rendering the ontology of law's objects more complex.[48] This insight frames the debate in which we are currently engaged.

4.2 Property Into, and Out Of, Thin Air

With this in mind, we can move towards substantiating my heretical claim that digital artefacts have more to do with "land" than with choses in action. In their seminal analysis of the different frames of analysis taken by the common law to the idea of property in land, Kevin Gray and Susan Gray illustrate the "property as right" framing as follows:

> All "property" relationships with land are, accordingly, analysed at one remove—through the intermediacy of an estate or interest in land. No citizen can claim that he or she owns the physical *solum*, merely that he or she owns some unitary jural right in or over that *solum*. One has "property" in an abstract right rather than "property" in a physical thing. (Gray and Gray 1998: 26)

With respect, I think this needs a certain degree of refinement—it is not just a "right in the land" that is the object of ownership, though the parcel of land *qua* object of property rights is a creature of the institutional normative order we call the law. It is not completely "decomposable" to a right (or set of rights), not least because it *does* have an external referent. Nonetheless, this passage introduces the reasons why I think common lawyers are better equipped than their Continental counterparts to develop a concept of "things" (and units of land in particular) despite their traditional antipathy for that approach and the potentially confounding idea of relative/radical title. That said, we do need to impose some kind of filter on our concept of what can be an object of property rights. Munich phenomenologist Adolf Reinach observed, about a decade and a half after the passage of the new German Civil Code, that we create incorporeal objects all the time through our intentional conduct in the world:

> The concept of a thing [*Sache*] in no way coincides with that of a bodily object, even if positive enactments [such as the German Civil Code] would restrict it to this. Everything which one can "deal" with, everything "usable" in the broadest sense of the word, is a thing: apples, houses, oxygen, but also a unit of electricity or warmth, but never ideas, feelings, or other experiences, number, concepts, etc. (Smith and Zaibert 2003: 52; Reinach 1983: 53)

(Reinach's robust exclusion of feelings and experiences, as well as numbers and universals like concepts, should allay the Bar Association consultees' concerns about happiness being a "thing".) This is true for a broader phenomenological account of "things" in the sense of "all that exists and is the case". For our *legal* phenomenology, we need to restrict the category in a manner that reflects the *purposes of property*

[48] On the concept of "document complexes" that enable more complex socio-economic relations (many of which are fundamentally mediated by law), see generally (Smith 2013).

law, namely: regulating persons' access to scarce resources of value to human life (in the broadest sense). Either way, the time has come to step through the looking glass and see what we find there.

4.3 Towards a Conception of Data in the Law of Things

Aligned with the "informational turn" and the approach to property as the law of things, James Grimmelman and Christina Mulligan have recently made the case that data can, under at least some circumstances, be a "thing". This raises the problem of explaining *how*: what is the "it" that we are talking about when we claim this or that right in data (Grimmelmann and Mulligan 2023: 839)? They correctly separate the question of "is there a cognizable thing?" from the question "which rights (if any) should a legal system grant, as a matter of legal policy, in a given thing?" (We will return to this question in due course, below—it is one of the other matters that gets all muddled up in Low's treatment). And they rightly note that data are quite different to chattels: recognizing chattels as "things" appears to be merely a question of finding pre-existing brute facts, such as physical boundaries that individuate one thing from another and make it an obviously socially valuable resource over which legally sanctioned power (Gray and Gray 1998: 1)[49] can be exercised by a person (Grimmelmann and Mulligan 2023: 840). Drawing on the "informational turn" literature, they continue:

> [D]espite appearances, the boundaries of things are social, not natural. A thing is a thing when people can and do recognize it as a thing. For physical objects, the boundaries of a thing often derive from physical properties, because it is easy for people to observe and agree on those properties. But the thinghood itself inheres in the recognition, because this is what makes it possible for people and social institutions (including the legal system) to talk and reason about discrete things. As long as data can be *recognized* as a discrete thing, that is enough. (Grimmelmann and Mulligan 2023: 841)

An earlier attempt to trace the boundaries of data was made by Michels and Millard, focused on digital files (Michels and Millard 2022: 323). Effectively, they argue that there are three distinct levels at which we could look for a fitting object of property rights in a digital file: the "physical layer" (ie, data stored as bits on a flash drive), the "logic layer" (ie, files presented as an icon with a file name and access path), and the "content layer" (ie, images, texts, sounds, etc.) (Michels and Millard 2022: 332). They argue that a "thing" capable of being protected by property rights could be found at the intermediate, logic layer, *provided* the data structure there possesses certain characteristics. Reasoning by analogy to the legal treatment of cryptoassets, they urge an approach based on *characteristics* rather than *categories*,[50] and derive a list of criteria from a mix of sources (including rehabilitated *Ainsworth* criteria, as well as criteria like separability, excludability and rivalrousness drawn from the broader

[49] They use the terminology of "socially permissible power".

[50] See Michels and Millard (2022: 345) for a discussion of their proposed categories.

literature). Currently, Michels is refining this argument, re-labelling the "content layer" as a "virtual layer" (I am tempted to say "phenomenological" or "institutional" layer) and introducing a nuanced discussion of the differences that can arise for the emerging law of "digital assets" when we choose to focus on the logical layer or the virtual layer, respectively.[51]

The technical details of their account have been criticized by Daniel Seng and Kelvin Low, chiefly that Michels and Millard have misunderstood the way that digital files work both as a matter of information systems and the way that they interact with the physical storage medium in both cloud and local storage scenarios. Seng and Low are critical of the notion that a property law relevant object might be found at the logic layer, and accuse Michels and Millard of misunderstanding the law of property fundamentally, to boot. Without endorsing that critique, I am less concerned presently with the technical details pertaining to digital files, as important as they are. I am not committed to this or that digital artefact (such as a digital file) being a "thing"; I am concerned with the question what kind of characteristics any given digital artefact would have to have to be a "thing". And in that respect, I find Michels and Millard more convincing than Seng and Low. In other words, while aspects of the *technical* critique may or may not land, it is bound up with Seng and Low's confused understanding of the *legal* aspect of the debate (Seng and Low 2025).[52]

The key to understanding the difference of opinion is in the taxonomy that Seng and Low "extrapolate" from Michels and Millard:

> The problem with [the Michels and Millard] classification is that it mixes up the two different conceptions of property, with the result that the classification is distorted or bent. *In personam* contractual rights appear twice in the classification, once as personal rights contradistinguished from property rights, but then again as a thing in action under property rights. The problem is that near the top of Michels and Millard's taxonomy, property is ownership but as one moves downwards, property metamorphosises into mere "asset", enabling a chose in action to be (property as asset) *and* not to be (property as ownership). (Seng and Low 2025: 5)

In fact, their taxonomy differs from the one *actually* set out by Michels and Millard. While there are problems with the framing of Michels and Millard's original argument, this appears to be a borderline case of strawmanning.[53] I am loathe to get

---

[51] This is my gloss on a draft chapter I have on file and is not necessarily representative of Michels' final argument.

[52] See in particular discussion under the heading "Human Perception is Not Reality" from 13. As we have seen immediately above, human perception *is* reality—a certain kind of reality, to which law belongs, is ontologically subjective, being dependent on human perception.

[53] The original Michels and Millard taxonomy of the "traditional view" starts with "Property Rights", hived off into "Real Property" and "Personal Property", which is in turn hived into "Things in Possession", "Things in Action" and "Patents". In other words, it is all really conventional stuff. The "extrapolated" taxonomy by Seng and Low starts with "Rights", which are divided into "Personal Rights" and "Property Rights", the latter being further divided into "Real Property" and "Personal Property", the latter being finally divided into "Things in Possession", "Things in Action", and "Patents". Seng and Low thus criticize Michels and Millard for including contractual rights both at the second-order level of "Personal Rights" and at the fourth-order level of "Things in Action", and claim that the taxonomy should itself be hived into two. However, post-cleavage, we actually have

bogged down on the point, however. As I will argue below, starting our taxonomic exercise with the category of "rights" will almost certainly get us lost. I would not start with the category of "property", either; although it is often unavoidable in English legal parlance, it can just as easily set us off on the wrong track. (Shortly, I will set out von Bar's tri-partite classification of property law's objects, which represents a radical departure from the various binaries traditionally used, including that between "real" and "personal" property.)

At this juncture, Seng and Low again deploy the "property syllogism" argument against the mixed taxonomy they impute to Michels and Millard (Seng and Low 2025: 5–9). They support this with some comparative property law observations. With respect, all this proves is that no legal system deals adequately with intangible objects of property rights (which is news to no-one). Zooming out, then, from the details, what the Seng and Low *contra* Michels and Millard debate does show is that we need to be careful in finding our point of departure and approach to the classification of the objects of property rights.

4.4 Von Bar's Tri-Partite Schema

To my great surprise, Seng and Low expressly endorse the strict Pandectist[54] view that only corporeal objects can be "things" that can be "owned", and make some passing arguments about categories—such as the German "object" (*Gegenstand*, which is used to fudge objects that should be protected by some kinds of property right but do not meet the corporeality requirement of § 90 German Civil Code). The problem with common lawyers, they suggest, is that we too easily slip between the register of talking about "property as things" and "property as assets" or wealth; not every asset is a "thing". That is no doubt true, but it does not preclude *some* "assets" being "things"—ie, that some rights can be reified. Precluding that would, indeed, need more argument. And conversely, all this says little about the object of our present enquiry, which is apparent *res* that are not reified rights.

In *Foundations of Property Law: Things as Objects of Property Rights*, von Bar presents an approach that radically departs from any of the 28 national approaches dealt with in the treatise. At the outset, von Bar rejects in the clearest terms the same Pandectist approach as "a step that today stands in the way of a common European understanding of property law no less than the concept of property in the modern common law" (Bar 2023: [5.43]). It is perfectly logical and legitimate to hold (i) that there is a categorical difference between *in personam* and *in rem* rights and (ii) that some *in personam* rights can be "reified" (in the original German *verdinglicht*,

something that looks more like Michels and Millard's original taxonomy. See Michels and Millard (2022: 338); Seng and Low (2025: 5, 8).

[54] The Pandectists were a group of nineteenth century German jurists who, among other things, formulated the narrow approach to "things" and the restriction of the right of ownership to things ultimately adopted in the German Civil Code: see Giglio (2012).

literally "thing-ified"); they can happily appear in the catalogue of "objects of *in rem* rights" once this has occurred. We just need to explain how the alchemy happens. For his part, von Bar approaches the province of property law as a matter of three questions:

- In which objects can property rights arise?
- Who can hold those rights?
- Which legal abilities do those rights give the person who holds them?

While common lawyers might identify easily with the third question, and to a lesser extent the second, the first is less intuitive.[55] The potency and relevance of von Bar's argument stem from the fact that, although he starts with the first question (and his answer is implicit in the very title of the book), he holds a nuanced view of the relationship between *rights* and *things* that speaks to *both* common lawyers and civilians. Holding a rather unflattering mirror to Seng and Low (the common lawyers turned Pandectists) von Bar manages to capture the virtues of both legal traditions while abandoning their idiosyncratic vices.

"Thing" is a legal term of art, and von Bar defines it axiomatically: "a 'thing' is anything in which a property right can arise" (Bar 2023: [1.2]).[56] Only such a broad definition, he argues, can free us from the particularities of individual jurisdictions and allow us to see the "reflexive relationship between property rights and their objects" (Bar 2023: [1.2]). This approach is saved from circular self-reference by the fact that property rights are limited in their types, and the logical correspondence between types of property rights and different types of object. This is, incidentally, what avoids the problem identified in McFarlane and Douglas' property syllogism. "[T]he right of ownership, for example, is not directed to the same purposes as rights such as usufruct, hypothec, or pledge [so the] number of possible property rights is limited". Thus, the *numerus clausus* of property rights is integral to understanding the concept of things and delineating *which things attract which rights* (Bar 2023: [1.2]). There is a legal-policy aspect to this question, but also a legal-technical one. The nature (ontology) of the object must inform the catalogue of rights that a person can hold in it; that catalogue should be appropriate and adapted to its nature. The policy debate can only start once the preliminary legal-technical issue has been resolved.

The first step towards a rational scheme of property law, then, is to abandon the traditional dichotomies that structure national traditions. For example, while the dichotomy between corporeal and incorporeal objects is found in many legal systems, it does not correspond to the distinction between moveable and immoveable things, not even in legal systems that stipulate the corporeality of *all* "things". Von Bar concludes that while the attribute of corporeality is given greater importance in some

---

[55] This point is made in Amy Held's forthcoming review of the book; manuscript on file with the author as at 25 June 2024. While the point is good, it is undoubtedly more true of the traditional approach and of historical common law accounts; I think it is also true of Low's approach, despite his comparative references and apparent concern with describing the *res* in question.

[56] Emphasis mine. See also the further discussion and refinement of this point in Ch 10.

legal systems than others, it is ultimately incapable of providing a *summa divisio* of all things: "it is at best suited (and on closer inspection not even that) to distinguish between the different manifestations of *moveable* things" (Bar 2023: [5.55]).

Von Bar's treatise demonstrates (exhaustively, and for his translator, exhaustingly) that, as a matter of empirical fact, "property rights" are granted to persons in a very broad class of objects. This is where von Bar's commitment to a "common European" conception of property law is crucial: from a *ius commune* perspective, the logical incoherence of *all* legal systems, even on their own terms, can reveal pathways toward coherence on a European (or more broadly comparative) level; each legal system as an artefact which can explored to create a coherent, overarching scheme of property law based on the reflexive relation between property rights and their objects. Taking this approach, no legal system can be taken at face value. He again uses the German Civil Code as an example, which names one of its books "The Law of Things" and stipulates that only "corporeal objects" can be things—but grants *some* property rights in incorporeal objects. If one measures it on its own terms, he says, the strict Pandectist approach has not even been followed in German law; "[s]uch an approach, therefore, would be totally impossible in respect of Europe as a whole" (Bar 2023: [4.1]). We should thus be extremely circumspect about Seng and Low's apparent endorsement of the approach for the common law. Von Bar explains:

> If one takes all the Member States together, one is compelled to accept that property rights in the European Union relate to a much broader class of objects, according to statute, judicial decisions, and scholarly opinion: property rights exist in corporeal and incorporeal objects, in living and non-living objects, in both real objects in the external world and mere credit card numbers, in electricity and heat, in aggregations of changing composition, in parts of land and buildings, and in integrated components of moveable goods. *Nearly everything that is not a subject (i.e. a person) can slip, for better or worse, into the role of an (apparently functional) object of property rights.* The challenge is to capture the nearly endless range of national variations on this theme in a single picture. The fact that almost everything that is an object of commerce is recognized as an object of property rights somewhere in Europe entails, conversely, that there are innumerable objects that are excluded from the catalogue of 'property' in some other part of the Union. Moreover, it is sometimes even the case that, in order to preserve flexibility and keep potential avenues of development open, some legal systems consciously avoid any systematic categorization of the possible objects of 'property rights'. (Bar 2023: [4.1])

In place of these flawed and idiosyncratic taxonomies, von Bar suggests a three-tiered, cumulative scheme of "objects", "objects of legal transaction", and "things" (in the original: *Gegenstände, Gegenstände des Rechtsverkehrs,* and *Sachen*).[57] We can take comfort that "happiness" appears nowhere in this schematic. "Objects" is the broadest category: it includes "anything of which a rule-set is willing and able to take notice of for private law purposes" (Bar 2023: [4.2]). It therefore includes "everything which (i) is not a person and (ii) is an entity that appears sufficiently ascertainable that it can be successfully incorporated into a legal system's complex of private law rules" (Bar 2023: [4.3]). In turn, "objects of legal transaction" are those objects that can

[57] My summary draws on Amy Held's forthcoming review of the book in the Oxford Journal of Legal Studies; manuscript on file with the author as at 25 June 2024.

be bought, sold, and gifted (for example). This category encompasses both "goods" in the English sense of chattels (corporeal objects) as well "goods" in the sense used in many jurisdictions of objects that "have utility and can be appropriated to a person" (Bar 2023: [5.11]–[5.13]).[58] "Objects of legal transaction" includes some phenomena, such as electricity or heat, that are the objects of legal verbs but are not necessarily suitable objects of property rights in the full sense. "Objects of property rights"—"things"—are a subclass of objects of legal transaction (Bar 2023: [5.15]) and the final category in von Bar's schema.

4.5 *Different Types of Things*

The category of "things" is, in turn, divided into three sub-categories in recognition of the fact that "not all things can be the object of all property rights in any given legal system" (Bar 2023: [4.2]). This is not just to provide the flexibility necessary to accommodate the idiosyncrasies of national law, although that is incidentally important to von Bar's *ius commune* inspired project; it is also based on a nuanced understanding of different things' different ontologies and the normative aims of property law itself.

The first and most intuitive category is "real things". It is important to remember that we are dealing with a novel terminology here, and that this category corresponds more closely to the common law concept of chattels than it does to land:

> Objects of legal transaction that are corporeal and controllable are particularly well suited to the creation of monopoly (or "property") rights. The most obvious form of control over an object is physical control: what one can "possess" in this sense is the ideal candidate for a fitting object of *erga omnes* property rights… We call such things "real"; one could also call them "natural" things. What is decisive is that their existence and possession depend only on the facts of the external world. A legal system finds such things *realiter*, one need not "make" them controllable (and therefore "things") in order for legal system to create subjective [ie, property] rights in them. (Bar 2023: [5.24])

Besides real things, all other objects of legal transaction require a rule of positive law to gain the status of "things": "they are creatures of law in their nature as things" (Bar 2023: [5.25]). To reflect the fact that they are legally-constituted, von Bar labels this category "normative" things:

> If the word did not have such a pejorative implication, one could also speak of "fictive" things. A claim, for example, is not a feature of the external world. The existence of a pledge over a claim does not only presuppose the decision, as a matter of positive law, that a claim can be pledged, but also (and more importantly) that there should exist such a thing as a "claim" in the first place. Consequently, claims are "normative" things in their role as the points of reference for security rights such as pledges. (Bar 2023: [5.25])

---

[58] The distinction between the two is made in many civilian jurisdictions with distinct terms, eg, *chose* and *biens* in Belgian and French law, but not in English law. *Biens* in French has obvious semantic connections to the English 'goods' but *chose* and its Romance equivalents are generally used in the sense of (merely) a corporeal object. This corresponds to German *Waren* which is a cognate of the English 'wares.'

From this, two fundamental insights emerge. The first (which should be obvious by now) is that we are concerned with more than the dichotomy between corporeal and incorporeal things. The second is that the nature of normative things will bear on the type of property rights that are (i) necessary and (ii) appropriate to protect them: a claim, for example, necessarily presupposes a bilateral relationship, and the right of "ownership" may or may not be appropriate to such an object. (We will return to this point shortly.)

This leads us to a more subtle, and important point. What many of us regard as the "realest" of real things—land—actually contains an essential normative element. (This echoes the point made by Gray and Gray, above.) In my view, this is of utmost importance to our understanding of cryptoassets and other digital artefacts as objects of property rights, too. The point is counter-intuitive and will need some explanation. Barry Smith and Leo Zaibert remind us that land is not as straightforward an object of property rights as it seems to us, intuitively, as the heirs of a landed-property society. Various words for possession and ownership (in various languages) hark back to the primate behaviour of "sitting" on territory the animal claims, but this says little about the actual extent and boundaries of what land the "besitter" claims.[59]

> The crucial importance for political affairs of landed property (or real estate, we shall use these two expressions interchangeably) has been eloquently summarized by Rousseau: "The first person who, having fenced a plot of ground, took it into his head to say *this is mine* and found people simple enough to believe him, was the true founder of civil society". (Smith and Zaibert 2003: 51)[60]

There are two salient aspects to Rousseau's quip, they say—one concerning geography, and the other concerning ontology (and the ontology of social reality in particular):

> First, the act of fencing off need not, in the context of this passage, be restricted to the case where some physical boundary is constructed. It can be seen as including also the establishment of fiat boundaries—for example, when you tell people where the borders of your property lie, or when you simply mark its corners. *To fence off a plot of land is to create something new.* The land itself, of course, exists before the parcel is plotted, *but the act of fencing it off nonetheless creates a new object.* Second, this act alone is not sufficient for object-creation. The latter requires also the existence of what John Searle calls collective intentionality; that is, it requires that other persons (simplemindedly or not) *believe* that the land is indeed the property of [him] who fenced it off. Only then can property be said to arise. (Smith and Zaibert 2003: 51, 52)[61]

A comprehensive study of landed property thus needs to embrace three interconnected dimensions: (i) a "geographic dimension", exploring how "real estate" is related to the *land itself*, being the surface of our planet (and thus also to institutional *boundaries*); (ii) a "cognitive dimension", exploring the interrelations between geospatial phenomena and our "culturally entrenched beliefs and convention"; and

---

[59] The word play is mine, not Smith and Zaibert's; it is a play on German *Besitzer*, from "sitzen" (to sit) which is mirrored in Latin *possedere* from *sedere* (to sit).

[60] Citations omitted.

[61] Citations omitted. Emphasis mine.

(iii) an "ontological dimension", exploring "what real estate is" (Smith and Zaibert 2003: 52).[62]

This helps to ground von Bar's conceptual schema, which is rooted in the culturally-entrenched beliefs and conventions of the legal systems of Europe, in particular, but does an admirable job of embracing all of these three dimensions such that its insights can be extrapolated more broadly. Returning to the details of that scheme, there are two types of "normative thing" in von Bar's account. The first, "purely normative things" are, for the most part, coterminous with common law choses in action and incorporeal hereditaments, and with civilian *res incorporales*. They are *purely* normative because they are pure creatures of the legal system. As we shall see, there is some bite to the "property syllogism" argument here, because the catalogue of property rights that a legal system can grant persons in purely normative things is logically limited by the nature of those "things": you don't need "ownership" of a right, and thinking about "owning rights" itself leads us into a conceptual conundrum even before we get to the policy questions.[63]

The other category is "normative objects with a physical substrate": effectively, on von Bar's empirical survey of European property laws, "land units". The terminology is not elegant—we can blame von Bar's translator—but it is accurate, and it follows closely the terminology (though not the concept) of German law's *Grundstück*. Land units are probably the most original feature of von Bar's scheme. Because the distinction between real and normative things does not correspond reliably to that between corporeal and incorporeal things, the familiar rights in land (such as servitudes/easements or hypothecs/mortgages) do not relate to the *land* itself. The object to which these rights relate is a *normative* one created by the law—not just a bald ape sitting on a patch of ground, but (as we have seen above) using words and maps to project a spatial boundary outwards, upwards, and downwards to create a "new object" with an implicitly social ontology in an implicitly social context:

> Land is, indeed, a corporeal object. As long as it has not been parceled up, however, it remains an integral part of the earth; it is not (yet) a thing because the planet earth is not even an object for the purposes of private law. The surface of the earth and the soil are, by nature, not subject to human control without more. The relevant part of the earth's surface, which we call a land unit, only becomes an ownable "thing" when it is, by means of legal rules, separated from other parts of the earth's surface. The law governing land units must, accordingly, always posit two distinct subject matters (which complement and complete each other, but which remain fundamentally distinguishable): one body of rules that determines which *erga omnes* rights are possible in land units, and another body of rules that determines what a land unit actually "is", how it is identified, and how it is delimited (vertically and horizontally) from its surroundings. (Bar 2023: [5.26])

Again, "Blackacre" only exists because of cadastral registers and legal rules that stipulate how far it extends *ad coelum et ad inferos*, or indeed (if the UK Supreme Court

[62] Citations omitted.

[63] See the discussion in G. L. Gretton, Ownership and its Objects' (2007) 71 Rabels Zeitung 802, 821, cited in Allen (2018a: 95 n. 109).

is correct) whether it includes some right against prying eyes.[64] The upshot of this is that, paradoxically, the common law conception of land—namely of *estates and interests in land*—is more aligned with von Bar's conception than most civilian conceptions of land, or indeed the folk conceptions of land as something quintessentially physical.

4.6 What Kind of "Things" Are Cryptoassets?

With the above framework in mind—(i) objects, (ii) objects of legal transaction, and (iii) things, which are in turn broken down into (a) real things, (b) normative things, and (c) normative things with a physical substrate—we can finally ask: what kind of things are cryptoassets?

On the one hand, von Bar classifies energy and information as "examples of phenomena which can be disposed of by sale or gift", making them objects of legal transaction, which "cannot be grasped conceptually as legal objects to which a legal system can apply the tool of *erga omnes* property rights" (Bar 2023: [5.17]). This is because they are not *controllable*:

> What cannot be controlled can be an "object" [*Gegenstand*] but not a "thing" in the sense of property law. Many objects belong to this category— not least the planet on which we live. All "things" are objects, but not all objects are "things"—not by a long way. The concept of an "object" provides a second useful service in our conceptual schema. It also excludes persons from the concept of "things". No-one "belongs" in the property law sense— either to himself or to any other person. Persons are definitionally beyond the purview of property rights. (Bar 2023: [10.6])

This is a correct expression of an idea that is present, but oddly inverted—and so muddled beyond utility—in Stevens' argument that "cryptoassets are not property":

> Some proponents of the view that crypto is "property" have focused not on its value, but on the factual ways in which it resembles physical things. In particular, it is rivalrous and in practice possible to exclude others from. This is the layperson's mistake with which we began. Tables, chairs, areas of land, mobile phones and pieces of paper are not property because they are things. *They are property because we have legal rights in relation to those things.* The moon and the fish in the sea are things, but they are not "property". Nobody has ever identified any right in relation to crypto nor how it would be vindicated. Therefore, it is not property. (Stevens 2023)

The sentence in italics (my emphasis) hits the nail on the head, if we disregard the surrounding text. Using von Bar's scheme (and terminology), the moon and the fish in the sea are *objects*, but they are not *things* (or even *objects of legal transaction*). They are not things axiomatically because the legal system does not grant *erga omnes* rights in them to any person. The legal system refuses do to this on a very sound

[64] See *Fearn and Ors v Board and Trusteees of the Tate Gallery* [2023] UKSC 4. The ruling has caused some excitement and requires tort lawyers to engage with the nature of the object that torts like nuisance protect.

basis—both legal-technical and legal-policy: that they are beyond human control, such that *erga omnes* monopoly rights in them would serve no purpose. The ultimate end of property law is regulating access, within a community of agents, to things of actual and potential value. The regulation of the moon and fish in the sea occurs, if at all, via other modes of legal ordering, not the law of (private) property. Stevens is tantalizingly close—tables and chairs are things because the law grants persons rights in them. Property law's objects—things—and the rights it grants in things are mutually, reflexively constitutive. But Stevens remains stuck in a frustrating "rights-and-remedies working backwards" mode of reasoning that, with respect, rather confuses than advances the debate.

Now we can answer our question. Cryptoassets are, it seems, digital artefacts that *can* be controlled within the relevant system. This is precisely why there has been such interest in their property law treatment in recent years. The "third category" proponents, to which I count myself, are neither shilling for crypto, nor fools blinded by some superficial and apparent, rather than real, possibility of the need for systemic development. As Fox observes, cryptoassets (and presumably other kinds of digital assets, if designed and instantiated properly) share some of the attributes that make chattels suitable objects of property rights:

> They can be specific, rivalrous, transferable, and capable of existing independently of the person who holds them for the time being. The same properties that make tangible things, like coins or bicycles, suitable subjects for [I would say "objects of"] ownership can be built into the design of digital assets. (Fox 2022)

We have arrived, then, at something very similar to the *tertium quid* question—but armed with a proper framework. How do we accommodate cryptoassets into our taxonomy of property law, and does that taxonomy require any modifications to serve a digital society? The starting point is that cryptoassets are not "mere" information. Secondly, they are obviously not "real things". Thirdly, they are not just "purely normative things" because there is some "there" there, which we might call some kind of instantiated "data object". The closest cognate is, actually, von Bar's land units—normative things with a physical substrate. Cryptoassets are, in my view, *normative things with a data substrate.* It is a testament to von Bar's scheme, in my view, that "data" fit rather well in it.[65] In a first step, it is necessary to create a "data object" and identify what it is and where it "lives". As with the land unit, the thing is neither (i) *just* the "ideational object" (mind-dependent, phenomenological impression) nor (ii) *just* the technical data structure (the mind-independent "fact" of brute reality).

For this approach to work—which I think it can—we need to identify the data substrate (the "string of digital signatures" in the case of Bitcoin) and then establish a set of legal rules to determine how those data compose an "object" rather than "mere information". One aspect of doing this will concern arguments about control,

---

[65] Von Bar has never been primarily concerned with explicating the position of data per se, but the description that follows does, I think, do justice to our conversations and emails on the topic without undue distortion. Still, the usual caveat applies.

reliability, rivalrousness, and all of that. Another aspect will be to describe the "normative" element, which I have suggested works even within a broadly materialist metaphysical worldview, as set out above.

4.7 *What Kind of Property Rights Are Fitting for Digital Things?*

The final question is what the catalogue of property rights in data objects should comprise. Recall von Bar's three questions. The first step is to identify the object of property rights. In the second step, it is necessary to define the possible rights in that object and finally, in the third step, it is necessary to decide who can hold those rights. Being a suitable object of *property rights in general* does not imply that something is a suitable object of *all* property rights. In particular, von Bar sees the right of ownership as being naturally limited to real things and normative things with a physical substrate; purely normative things, as creatures of the legal system, do not need the kind of third-party protection that property rights (definitionally) provide. Though it seems a very "German" thing to do, in fact it is consistent with his radical departure from German law (Bar 2023: [8.7]).

This debate is tangential to cryptoassets, assuming cryptoassets are "normative objects with a data substrate" as opposed to "purely normative objects". It is nonetheless interesting to walk through for the sake of completeness, and to allay the fears of "third category" detractors. Von Bar points to Franz von Zeiller as the major proponent of the "ownability" of incorporeal objects. In his 1812 commentary, von Zeiller wrote in apology for § 353 Austrian Civil Code, for whose drafting he was responsible.[66] This set the stage for debate in the nineteenth century, in which not just Austrian but virtually all civilian systems became preoccupied with this juristic

[66] "If I am owner of a corporeal thing, e.g. a clock, I can alienate, use, degrade, or destroy it. But in the case that I hold only a right in the clock such as a right of use, pledge, possession, or an obligational claim, the entitlements that flow to me directly over this corporeal thing are much less extensive than those that flow to the owner. The difference lies only, however, in the difference of the object. In the latter case, the clock does not belong to me, rather, the right of possession, or use, or pledge is my property. With these rights I can deal freely and exclusively to the extent that their nature allows, as can a creditor over his credit; I can use my right wholly or partially or not at all; I can transfer it to another, or disclaim it unconditionally; I can (in a possessory or petitory sense) enforce it. Here, too, we find the characteristic features of ownership; whether it is applied to things animate or inanimate, moveable or immoveable, the concept is not displaced. The concept of ownership is, accordingly, to be extended to incorporeal things, or rights." Franz von Zeiller, *Commentar über das allgemeine bürgerliche Gesetzbuch für die gesammten Deutschen. Erbländer der Österreichischen Monarchie*, vol. II/ 1, pp. 110–111, cited in Bar (2023: [8.7]).

problem, where some of them remain to this day (Bar 2023: [8.8]).[67] Through all this, however, the question has been framed incorrectly:

> A preliminary question must be answered before one can meaningfully engage with the question whether non-physical objects of legal transaction are fitting objects of the right of ownership. *Does a purely normative object even need to be owned, or be capable of ownership, in order for a legal system to ascribe it exclusively to a person?* This is certainly not the case for many immaterial assets. Thus, a sensible first step would be to determine which purely normative things can be ascribed to a person even without the right of ownership. The criterion that enables us to determine this class of objects emerges, in turn, from a simple test. Can the object conceivably exist without one knowing to whom it belongs? To put it the other way around, *is its ascription to a person an intrinsic criterion of its existence?* This is the case, for example, with claims. A claim only arises because there exist a creditor and a debtor; a creditor-less claim is not conceptually possible. A real thing or a land unit, on the other hand, must be ascribed to the exclusive use of a person; the right to its use is not immanent within its existence. Precisely for this reason, such things need the legal concept of ownership, and claims do not. Claims, in other words, are not unfitting objects of ownership because they are not "corporeal objects". It is true that they are not, but this feature only leads one accidentally to the true answer. Claims are not fitting objects of the right of absolute ownership because they cannot even be imagined without legal attribution to some person. (Bar 2023: [8.9])

In my view, this both contextualizes and partly mollifies the MacFarlane and Douglas "property syllogism". It also underscores the importance of the criterion of "independence from the legal system" posited by the Law Commission and supported by the majority of scholars. In short, it would seem that data objects should attract the full range of property rights—up to an including ownership. If this is the case, we common lawyers can be happy that we do not need to do any really heavy lifting to accommodate ownable data objects in our conceptual universe.

The final aspect to touch on is a *legal-policy* debate about whether we should grant persons all property rights in any given category of data objects. I think that critics such as Low and Stevens are *actually* concerned with the legal-policy debate, as they are outspoken crypto-sceptics, but have couched their opposition in legal-technical terms instead. For what it's worth, I think that most cryptoasset projects

67 "Not a few codifications became fixed on the idea that the right of ownership is only possible in 'corporeal objects'— more precisely, objects to which those codifications attribute corporeality; in the relevant national terminology, such objects are generally 'moveable' and 'immoveable' things. Germany (§ 903 German Civil Code), Greece (Art. 999 Greek Civil Code), 40 and Portugal (Art. 1302 Portuguese Civil Code) belong to this group, as do for example the Netherlands (Art. 5:1(1) Netherlands Civil Code), Hungary (§ 5:13 Hungarian Civil Code), and Poland (Art. 140 Polish Civil Code). The legal systems of the common law, on the other hand, distinguish between 'realty' and 'personalty', and distinguish in the latter category between choses in possession and choses in action (as set out above), *but do not connect this with the proposition that 'incorporeal things' are unfitting objects of ownership.* They rather approach the question as one of property rights; the abstract question, in which objects those rights can be held, is hardly ever posed independently. By way of contrast, § 353 Austrian Civil Code puts it very clearly: 'Everything that belongs to someone, all his corporeal and incorporeal things, are his property [*Eigentum*].' Finally, in a third group of legal systems, the question of ownership in 'immaterial' goods continues to be debated intensely. Contemporary debates within French jurisprudence, for example, are barely distinguishable from those in Austrian jurisprudence of 150 years ago."

are nonsense and will prove to have a net negative impact on society, the economy, and the environment. I think that regulators should have outlawed Bitcoin before it got to any kind of scale. But that's a policy debate, not a debate about legal theory or even legal doctrine. And in our ever-more digital society, it does no-one a service to confuse those two domains, whichever side one is on.

5 Conclusion

This chapter has presented a vigorous defence of the "third category" approach to accommodating cryptoassets, and other types of digital artefact, in the law of property. Using Low's position as a foil, I have attempted to identify what the real questions are, as well as how I think they ought to be answered. I hope that this exercise is useful to direct future iterations of the "*tertium quid* debate" in a (more) fruitful direction, as recent contributions have not, in my view, necessarily advanced our understanding. In particular, the main proponents of the camp against a third category approach have failed, or refused, to engage with the real questions in a productive way, and the debate has become more complicated as a result. Zooming out from the common law systems, I hope that my exploration might be of explanatory value to those from other legal traditions and for a comparative understanding of the set of problems currently facing every legal system (Hung 2024).

The task is a generational, perhaps even epochal, burden. While I have focussed on the common law, no national law system has been very adept at accommodating intangible objects within their conceptual framework. Despite decades of opportunity since the advent of the networked digital era, we are still some distance from a property law really well-adapted to a data-driven digital economy. Cryptoassets, whatever their substantive merits or demerits, have forced a conversation in recent years that is of much wider significance.

In particular, the account presented in this chapter has attempted to shore up the position suggested by the Law Commission of England and Wales (and endorsed by a number of first instance courts) by providing a thorough conceptual account of property law that builds on the foundations of social ontology, conventional property theory, and von Bar's recent contribution to "common European property law". These resources, I hope, will provide something of use and interest to all those interested in the question of cryptoassets treatment in private law, and perhaps help to move toward a more stable and rational consensus position in the maturing literature.

References

AA v persons unknown, Re Bitcoin (2019) EWHC 3556
Allen JG (2018a) Property in digital coins. Eur Prop Law J 8(1):64

Allen JG (2018b) The office of the crown. Cambr Law J 77(2):298–320. https://doi.org/10.1017/S0008197318000338
Allen JG (2020) Imagining money. In: Fischer J, Stedmann G (eds) Imagined economies—Real fictions: new perspectives on economic thinking in Great Britain. Columbia University Press.
Allen JG (2021a) Cryptoassets in private law. In: Chiu I, G Deipenbrock (eds) Routledge Handbook of Financial Technology and Law, Routledge.
Allen JG (2021b) Law's virtual empires: game analogies and the concept of law. In: Fabra-Zamora JL, Villa Rosas G (eds) Conceptual jurisprudence, law and philosophy library, Springer International Publishing, Cham, https://doi.org/10.1007/978-3-030-78803-2_15
Allen JG (2021c) Bodies without organs: law, economics, and decentralised governance. Stanford J Blockchain Law Policy 4(1):53–78
Allen JG (2022) Non-statutory executive powers and judicial review, 1st edn. Cambridge University Press. https://doi.org/10.1017/9781009039321
Allen JG (2024) Public offices in processes of constitutional development In: Daly TG, Samaratne D (eds) Democratic consolidation and constitutional endurance in Asia and Africa. Oxford University Press, Oxford, https://doi.org/10.1093/oso/9780192899347.003.0002
Anscombe GEM (1958) On brute facts. Analysis 18(3):69–72
Bar C von (2023) Foundations of property law: things as objects of property rights, Allen JG (trans), Oxford University Press, Oxford, https://doi.org/10.1093/oso/9780198885337.001.0001
Blackstone W (1766) Commentaries on the laws of England, Clarendon
Bridge MG, Gullifer L, Low KFK, McMeel G (2022) The law of personal property, 3rd edn. Thomson Reuters/Sweet & Maxwell, London
Carroll L (1865) Alice's adventures in Wonderland. Macmillan
Carroll L (1871) Through the looking-glass, and what alice found there. Macmillan
Chan T (2023) The nature of property in cryptoassets. Leg Stud 43(3):480–498. https://doi.org/10.1017/lst.2022.53
Dubai International Financial Centre (DIFC) (2024) DIFC announces enactment of new digital assets law, New law of security and related amendments to select legislation, DIFC, https://www.difc.ae/whats-on/news/difc-announces-enactment-of-new-digital-assets-law---new-law-of-security-and-related-amendments, accessed 11 November 2024.
Fairfield J (2022) Property as the law of virtual things. Front Res Metr Analyt 7:981964. https://doi.org/10.3389/frma.2022.981964
Finn P (2017) Fiduciary obligations: 40th anniversary republication with additional essays, 1st edn. Federation Press, Sydney
Fox D (2019) Cryptocurrencies in the common law of property. In: Fox D, Green S (eds) Cryptocurrencies in public and private law. Oxford University Press, https://doi.org/10.1093/law/9780198826385.003.0006.
Fox D (2022) Digital assets as transactional power, https://blogs.ed.ac.uk/private-law/2022/01/20/digital-assets-as-transactional-power, accessed 12 June 2024.
Giglio F (2012) Pandectism and the Gaian classification of things. Univ Toronto Law J 62(1):1–28. https://doi.org/10.3138/utlj.62.1.1
Goode SR (2023) What is property? Law Quart Rev 139:1–4
Gray K, Gray SF (1998) The idea of property in land. In: Bright S, Dewar JK (eds) Land law: themes and perspectives. Oxford University Press, Oxford
Gray KJ, Gray SF (2009) Elements of land law, 5th edn. Oxford University Press, Oxford
Grimmelmann J, Mulligan C (2023) Data property. Am Univ Law Rev 72:829–883
Honoré T (1977) Real laws. In: Hacker PMS, Raz J (eds) Law, morality, and society. Clarendon Press
Hung AH-C (2024) Evolution of intangible property to crypto assets: legal pragmatism in Anglo-American Common Law and Chinese Civil Law. Chinese J Compar Law 12:cxae011, https://doi.org/10.1093/cjcl/cxae011
International Institute for the Unification of Private Law (2023) UNIDROIT principles on digital assets and private law, International Institute for the Unification of Private Law

(UNIDROIT), Rome, https://www.unidroit.org/wp-content/uploads/2024/01/Principles-on-Digital-Assets-and-Private-Law-linked-1.pdf
Kershaw D (2020) Corporate law's fiduciary personas. Law Quart Rev 136:454–480
Koepsell D (2022) Beyond human: smart-contracts, smart-machines, and documentality. Oxford University Press. https://doi.org/10.1093/oso/9780192858467.003.0015
Kumhof M, Allen JG, Bateman W, Lastra RM, Gleeson S, Omarova ST (2020) Central bank money: liability, asset, or equity of the nation? SSRN Electron J. https://doi.org/10.2139/ssrn.3730608
Kurtz A, Seltmann S, Bairoch A, Bittner M-S, Bruce K, Capes-Davis A, Clarke L, Crook JM, Daheron L, Dewender J, Faulconbridge A, Fujibuchi W, Gutteridge A, Hei DJ, Kim Y-O, Kim J-H, Kokocinski AK, Lekschas F, Lomax GP, Loring JF, Ludwig T, Mah N, Matsui T, Müller R, Parkinson H, Sheldon M, Smith K, Stachelscheid H, Stacey G, Streeter I, Veiga A, Xu R-H (2018) A standard nomenclature for referencing and authentication of pluripotent stem cells. Stem Cell Rep 10(1):1–6. https://doi.org/10.1016/j.stemcr.2017.12.002
Lastra R, Allen JG (2023) Lex cryptographia financiera In: Blair W, Zilioli C, Gortsos C (eds) International monetary and banking law post COVID-19. Oxford University Press
Law Commission of England and Wales (2024) Digital assets as personal property: Supplemental report and draft bill, https://lawcom.gov.uk/project/digital-assets
Law Commission UK (2024) Digital Assets, Law Commission, https://lawcom.gov.uk/project/digital-assets/, accessed 11 November 2024
Lawson FH (1951) The rational strength of the English Law. Oxford University Press, Oxford
Lawson T (2016) Social positioning and the nature of money. Camb J Econ 40(4):961–996. https://doi.org/10.1093/cje/bew006
Low KFK (2016) The user principle: Rashomon effect or much ado about nothing? Singapore Acad Law J 28:984
Low KFK (2020a) Quoines in cryptopia: When (if ever) are cryptoasset exchanges trustees? The Conveyancer and Property Lawyer 1:70–81
Low KFK (2020b) Bitcoins as property: Welcome clarity? Law Quart Rev 136:345–349
Low KFK (2024) Cryptoassets and the renaissance of the tertium quid? In: Bevan C (ed) Edward Elgar Handbook on property law and theory. Edward Elgar, https://www.ssrn.com/abstract=4382599, accessed 11 November 2024
Low KFK (2025) Third thing or sixth sense? I see ideational objects? In: Babie P, Giancaspro M (eds) Private law and digital assets, Springer
Low KFK, Hara M (2024) Cryptoassets and property. In: van Erp S, Zimmermann K (eds) Research handbook on European Property Law. Edward Elgar Publishing, https://ideas.repec.org/h/elg/eechap/19702_13.html
Low KFK, Lin J (2015) Carbon credits as EU like it: property, immunity, TragiCO_2 medy? J Environ Law 377–404, https://doi.org/10.1093/jel/eqv020
Low KFK, Teo EG (2017) Bitcoins and other cryptocurrencies as property? Law Innov Technol 9(2):235–268. https://doi.org/10.1080/17579961.2017.1377915
MacCormick N (2008) Institutions of law: an essay in legal theory. Oxford University Press, Oxford
MacCormick N (2010) Rhetoric and the rule of law: a theory of legal reasoning, Reprint, Oxford University Press, Oxford
MacCormick N, Weinberger O (1986) An institutional theory of law: new approaches to legal positivism, Springer Netherlands, Dordrecht, https://doi.org/10.1007/978-94-015-7727-4
Mäki U (1996) Scientific realism and some peculiarities of economics In: Cohen RS, Hilpinen R, Renzong Q (eds) Realism and anti-realism in the philosophy of science, Boston Studies in the Philosophy of Science, Springer Netherlands, Dordrecht, https://doi.org/10.1007/978-94-015-8638-2_32
Mäki U (2011) Scientific realism as a challenge to economics (and vice versa). J Econ Methodol 18(01):1–12. https://doi.org/10.1080/1350178X.2011.553372
McFarlane B, Douglas S (2022) Property, analogy and variety. Oxf J Leg Stud 42(1):161–186. https://doi.org/10.1093/ojls/gqaa043

Michels JD, Millard C (2022) The new things: property rights in digital files? Camb Law J 81(2):323–355. https://doi.org/10.1017/S0008197322000228
Moses LB (2008) The applicability of property law in new contexts: from cells to cyberspace. Sydney Law Rev 648
Palka P (2017) Virtual property: towards a general theory [PhD], European University Institute, IT, https://doi.org/10.2870/700083, accessed 11 November 2024
Penner JE (1996) The "bundle of rights" picture of property. UCLA Law Rev 43(3):711–820
Penner JE (2020) Property rights: a re-examination. Oxford University Press, Oxford
Reed C, Murray AD (2018) Rethinking the jurisprudence of cyberspace, Edward Elgar Publishing, Cheltenham, UK Northampton, MA, USA, https://doi.org/10.4337/9781785364297
Reinach A (1983) The a priori foundations of the civil law. Aletheia 3:1–142
Searle J (1995) The construction of social reality. Free Press
Searle JR (2010) Making the social world: the structure of human civilization, Oxford University Press, New York, Oxford, https://doi.org/10.1093/acprof:osobl/9780195396171.001.0001
Seng DKB, Low KFK (2025) Data objects: New things or no-thing more than ignis fatuus, https://doi.org/10.2139/ssrn.4308631
Smith B (2013) Document acts. In: Konzelmann Ziv A, Schmid HB (eds) Institutions, emotions, and group agents. Springer
Smith B, Zaibert L (2003) Real estate: foundations of the ontology of property. In: Stuckenschmidt H, Stubjkaer E, Schlieder C (eds) The ontology and modelling of real estate transactions. Ashgate
Smith H (2015) The persistence of system in property law. Univ Pennsylv Law Rev 2055
Smith HE (2012) Property as the law of things. Harv Law Rev 125(7):1691–1726
Sokol M (1994) Bentham and Blackstone on incorporeal hereditaments. J Legal Hist 15(3):287–305. https://doi.org/10.1080/01440369408531110
Solinas M (2019) Bitcoiners in Wonderland: lessons from the Cheshire Cat. Lloyd's Marit Commer Law Quart 3:433–456
Stein G (1937) Everybody's autobiography. Random House
Stevens R (2023) Crypto is not property. Law Quart Rev 139:615. https://doi.org/10.2139/ssrn.4416200
Turner SP (1999) Review: Searle's social reality. Hist Theor 38(2):211–231
UK Jurisdiction Taskforce, Lawtech Delivery Panel (2019) Legal statement on cryptoassets and smart contracts
Watts P, Low KF (2024) The case for cryptoassets as property. In Agnew S, Smith M (eds) Law at the cutting edge: essays in honour of Sarah Worthington, Hart Publishing, https://doi.org/10.5040/9781509965182
Wendehorst C (2023a) Proprietary rights in digital assets and the conflict of laws. In: Bonomi A, Lehmann, M, Lalani S (eds) Blockchain and private international law, international and comparative business law and public policy, International and Comparative Business Law and Public Policy, Brill
Wendehorst C (2023b) Proprietary rights in digital assets and the conflict of laws. In Bonomi A, Lehmann M, Lalani S (eds) Blockchain and Private International Law, Brill, Nijhoff, https://doi.org/10.1163/9789004514850_007

Private Law Remedies for Cryptocurrency Fraud

Aaron M. Lane

Abstract This chapter provides an analysis of legal mechanisms for addressing fraud and scams involving cryptocurrency, drawing on both practical legal experience and the new comparative economics. Although illicit transactions account for a small portion of total cryptocurrency transaction volumes, individuals incur significant private losses and there are unique enforcement challenges in the Web3 ecosystem. The prevalent legal approach to addressing cryptocurrency-based fraud is through public enforcement mechanisms. This chapter argues that in some circumstances private law and civil litigation mechanisms can offer a more efficient mechanism for addressing cryptocurrency-based fraud with tools to identify perpetrators, tailored legal claims, and secure assets. The chapter concludes by making recommendations to enhance these private law remedies.

Keywords Cryptocurrency · Civil procedure · Dispute resolution · Private law

1 Introduction

Fraud, scams, and financial crimes occur in any economy. The Web3 economy is no different. Illicit transactions account for less than half of 1% of all cryptocurrency transactions in a given year (Chainalysis 2024). But as cryptocurrency adoption—and its market valuation—continue to rapidly expand and rise, so too does the need for robust legal measures to navigate these digitally native, global environments. For at least a decade, policymakers have been grappling with the issue of how to regulate cryptocurrencies (e.g., Brito & Castillo 2013; de Filippi 2014). This chapter highlights the overlooked private law remedies for addressing harms in the Web3 economy.

A. M. Lane (✉)
School of Law, RMIT University, Melbourne, Australia
e-mail: aaron.lane@rmit.edu.au

GW Competition & Innovation Lab, The George Washington University, Washington, DC, USA

P. Babie and M. Giancaspro (eds.), *Private Law, Digital Assets, and Infrastructure*,
https://doi.org/10.1007/978-981-96-7121-2_10

Cryptocurrencies are the payment rails for the emerging Web3 ecosystem. This chapter takes the term "Web3" to describe the next phase of the internet, built on decentralised blockchain networks. While Web1 infrastructure allowed users to read (e.g., email, websites) and Web2 infrastructure allowed users to write (e.g., social media networks), Web3 allows users to own (Dixon 2024). Web3 payments infrastructure promises to democratise financial services—providing users with greater accessibility, direct control over their own financial assets, and the ability to acquire an ownership stake in the network itself. By removing layers of corporate intermediaries such as banks, credit card providers, and payment gateways, decentralised payment networks drive down transaction costs that enable innovative products not previously possible in traditional finance (Davidson et al. 2018; Berg et al. 2019). But while the reduction in transaction cost "friction" introduces novel opportunities, it also introduces new practical and legal challenges.

In 2008, the proposed launch of Bitcoin was shared amongst an obscure email list (Nakamoto 2008). The first Bitcoin to be transferred on the nascent network was—at the time—essentially worthless. Today, according to industry price analytics website CoinMaketCap, over 8,000 cryptocurrencies are traded daily with a combined market cap exceeding US$2.5 trillion. Value is heavily concentrated, with the top two cryptocurrencies in Bitcoin and Ethereum accounting for around 70% of the market. Millions of users around the globe now have valuable cryptocurrency holdings and many have direct control over these assets through hardware and software wallets.

While self-custody is exciting for proponents of financial freedom, Bitcoin and Ethereum do not have a head office. There is no bank branch to visit. There is no telephone call centre to dial into. There is no executive management team that can be summoned to appear in Court or before a Parliamentary inquiry. What happens if something goes wrong with a transaction? What happens if I mistakenly send cryptocurrency to the wrong address? What happens if someone obtains my private keys? What happens if I lose my recovery information? What happens if someone steals my cryptocurrency?

One introductory example suffices. In 2023, James Howells made global headlines for a simple decade-old mistake. Howells had thrown out his computer hard drive in the weekly rubbish collection. What he did not realise at the time was that the hard drive contained the private keys to access his Bitcoin. A decade later—and with the Bitcoin reportedly now worth £275 million—he was on a mission to recruit Newport City Council to search through its landfill to find the hard drive, in exchange for a share in the bounty (Middleton 2023).

Howells was not the first person to lose cryptocurrency and will not be the last. It was reported that Howells has retained a legal team for a reasonably straightforward matter. What then for those that have more complex factual scenarios—not knowing where the cryptocurrency went or who has control of it? This chapter will grapple with those hard problems.

Given the growth in both value and usage, it is not surprising that there have been frequent calls to regulate cryptocurrency activities and introduce more friction into the frictionless system. By "regulate" proponents almost exclusively mean *ex ante* public regulation of one form or another. What is overlooked is the availability to *ex post* private causes of action that provide legal remedies. Private legal action includes not only the ability for potential plaintiffs to bring litigation but also powerful civil procedure orders that enable potential plaintiffs to compel information from and restrain property of third parties.

Accordingly, this chapter seeks to understand how private law remedies can address the unique challenges presented by the Web3 economy and proceeds as follows. Section 2 will discuss the key characteristics of cryptocurrency in Web3 ecosystem and positions cryptocurrency-based fraud within the wider context of cryptocurrency crime, illustrated with a worked hypothetical example. Section 3 will introduce the trade-offs between public and private enforcement in addressing this problem, drawing on the new comparative economics (Djankov et al. 2003a) to evaluate the public law and private law mechanisms. This section analyses the application of corporate regulation, taking the example of regulating digital currency exchanges. Section 4 will consider the application of private law remedies from the common law tradition, and the tools of civil procedure to help secure those remedies. Section 5 will consider future directions to enhance those private law remedies. Section 6 will conclude.

2 The Problem of Cryptocurrency Fraud

Fraud and scams are not new phenomena but deeply rooted in the exploitation of information asymmetry. One of the earliest documented attempts from ancient Greece (360 BC) was Hegestratos, the owner of a ship. Knowing that the ship was empty, Hegestratos exploited the purchaser of corn by receiving an advance payment for the non-existent shipment (Johnstone 1998). In modern times, Bernie Madoff's infamous Ponzi scheme defrauded thousands of investors of billions of dollars through the elaborate appearance of a legitimate investment fund (Henrique 2011). For fraudulent activity to remain undetected, perpetrators will go to great lengths to obscure the true nature of a transaction (e.g., produce high-quality fraudulent artwork), obscure their true identity (e.g., using shell companies), or obscure their tracks to escape the jurisdiction (e.g., physically relocating). Similarly, in today's digital environment, professional fraudsters employ sophisticated methods to conceal their activities and identities, complicating detection and legal recourse. This section aims to outline the characteristics of Web3 and define the problem of fraud using cryptocurrency.

2.1 Web3 Characteristics

The Web3 ecosystem is a technology stack of blockchain technology plus decentralised applications, with more-direct digital ownership. While there is rapid change and innovation that will continue to develop, we can nevertheless identify six core characteristics of the Web3 ecosystem that present both challenges and opportunities for pursuing cases of fraud.

Decentralisation: there is no central authority with oversight of the foundational blockchain network. Instead, a distributed network of computers interacts (through consensus algorithms such as proof of work or proof of stake) to update the shared ledger of transactions. For cryptocurrency applications this is its key feature not a bug—it avoids the problems of centralisation (such as business model pivots, insolvency, and censorship) that had plagued digital currency projects in the 1990s and early 2000s. But in a fraud context, no central authority means fraudulent transactions cannot be stopped at a network infrastructure level.

Immutability: decentralised blockchains are immutable, meaning that once transactions are confirmed, they cannot be altered or reversed—although they can only be added to. This immutable characteristic ensures the integrity and trustworthiness of the transaction history, which is fundamental for transaction security. Similarly, though, immutability is double-edged. If fraudulent transactions are made, victims have no recourse to reverse these transactions.

Sovereignty: individuals have unprecedented control over their digital assets, allowing users to directly hold and manage cryptocurrencies, non-fungible tokens (NFTs), and other digital assets without the need for traditional banking or financial intermediaries. There is great economic promise in this new dynamic. But this also requires a higher degree of vigilance, education, and security awareness. Most users are accustomed to the protective layers offered by institutional safeguards.

Programmability: Blockchain-enabled digital assets are programmable through the use of smart contracts, which automate transactions and agreements based on set conditions. In this way, the blockchain network operates like a virtual computer. This has amazing potential for innovation—enabling intricate decentralised applications that were never before possible. But it also presents new vulnerabilities. The smart contract code may contain unintended loopholes that fraudsters *use* to carry out scams, manipulate transactions, or siphon off assets. The programmable nature of these assets allows scammers to automate money laundering (such as by using mixing and tumbling applications) to obscure the destination of scammed funds.

Interoperability: the Web3 ecosystem enhances connectivity between different blockchain networks, enabling users to transfer assets and utilise new and innovative applications without being locked into a single platform (in contrast to the social media platforms of Web2). While interoperability fosters a more connected and functional digital environment, it also introduces complexities in tracking and securing transactions across multiple platforms. In the context of fraud, interoperability can be exploited by malicious actors who find weaknesses between systems. Furthermore, scams may become more sophisticated as by spanning multiple networks and services, efforts to trace illicit activities and identify the perpetrators become increasingly complex.

Transparency: most blockchain networks are public and open source, meaning that transaction details are radically transparent. It is an enduring myth that cryptocurrency transactions are anonymous. Rather, cryptocurrency is pseudonymous with each transaction tied to a unique and identifiable wallet address. To be sure, that wallet address is a string of numbers and letters that do not necessarily match to somebody's real-world identity—what is termed the "identity attribution challenge". But transactions can be traced across blockchain networks. As will be discussed in further detail below, new software analytics leverages transparent transaction information to provide new opportunities for analysing and uncovering the origin and destination of fraudulently obtained funds.

2.2 *Cryptocurrency Fraud in Context*

The Web3 environment is radically different compared to previous eras, providing fraudsters with new products and markets to take advantage of. In other joint work, the author has developed a taxonomy of cryptocurrency crime based across two vectors—the *actus reus* and the *modus operandi*—illustrated in Table 1 (Allen & Lane 2024).

On the *actus reus*, we appropriate the criminal law term to distinguish between categories of unlawful acts. There are two main ways malicious actors illegitimately obtain cryptocurrency from others. First, they can steal it—taking assets without permission and without any pretence of a legitimate transaction. In this method, technical and forensic knowledge is required to commit the theft and avoid detection. Second, alternatively, they can use deceptive practices where the perpetrator misleads the victim into voluntarily handing over money, assets, or information.

On the *modus operandi,* there is also a spectrum of contexts that malicious actors choose to operate. These choices will be informed by a combination of technical abilities and opportunities—feeding into the fraudster's economic calculation (Allen & Lane 2024). "Decentralised" contexts involve and exploit technologies unique to Web3's decentralised environment (e.g., smart contracts, decentralised autonomous organisations, decentralised finance). They are likely to require the highest degree of technical knowledge for execution. Similarly, the victims tend also to the most technologically sophisticated and know that they are operating in Web3. "Intermediary-enabled" contexts involve exploiting centralised intermediaries (e.g., digital currency exchanges, social media platforms) that necessarily require many victims. "Conventional" contexts involve a classic theft and fraud techniques with cryptocurrency as the asset being stolen or used for payment. While the techniques may appear indiscriminate (e.g., breaking into multiple premises, contacting multiple persons), the

Table 1 Taxonomy of cryptocurrency crime (Adapted from Allen & Lane 2024)

	Conventional	Intermediary-enabled	Decentralised
Theft	Physical Theft of Hardware Wallets, Paper Keys or Recovery Phrases	Stealing from a Digital Currency Exchange	Smart Contract Exploits
Fraud	Investment or Romance Scam with Cryptocurrency as Payment Method	Fake Initial Coin Offerings/ Pump and Dump Schemes	Decentralised Finance Rug Pulls

perpetrators are ultimately seeking to steal or defraud a single victim. While more is known about the psychology of fraud victims than about perpetrators (Norris et al. 2019), it is clear that an intuitive understanding of psychology is more important than technical knowledge in convincing others to hand over significant assets under deception.

2.3 Fraud Scenarios

This chapter is principally focused on the problem of conventual fraud. However, to illustrate the various types of deception that individuals can fall victim to, let us consider the following scenarios—which are fictional but informed by the author's legal experience (Posner 2017).

Jane is a recently divorced investor approaching retirement. She decides to invest a portion of her divorce settlement—say $100,000—to generate higher returns than a bank. If Jane invested in traditional securities—say buying shares in a company publicly traded on the Australian Stock Exchange—there are several points of "friction". Jane withdraws $100,000 from her fund's bank (who pays her interest but also charges a monthly account fee for keeping her funds secure) and deposits it with a popular brokerage platform (who takes a commission on the trade). Settlement occurs two business days after executing the trade. The shares are held not by Jane or the brokerage platform but are in the custody of a share registry (typically paid for by the listed company). If there was an instance of fraud in this scenario—such as unauthorised redirection of funds along the way—detection and correction of fraud benefits from the friction of transaction time delays, the various middlemen, as well as the physical, onshore presence of the institutions involved. While legal action may need to be brought for recovery, there are various onshore targets to pursue investigation—and local banking transactions to trace.

Now consider that Jane falls the victim to a "Conventional Fraud" investment scam. Jane begins an online relationship with a Jerry on a dating website. After weeks of talking online and over the phone, Jerry mentions that he is investing in a new opportunity that is not available on the popular share trading platforms. He has special access to a platform called "WealthStream360" and gives Jane an access code to set up a profile on the website. Jerry claims that due to international regulations and the need for rapid transaction clearance, the platform requires payments in cryptocurrency for its supposed tax advantages and efficiency. Trusting his advice, Jane converts her $100,000 into the Tether (USDT) cryptocurrency (a stablecoin pegged to the US dollar) through a popular digital currency exchange. WealthStream360 provides Jane with a public address to send Tether and instructs her to send an email to confirm the deposit. A few hours later, her WealthStream360 account shows the deposit. She makes what she thinks are trades on the platform. Weeks later, Jerry stops talking to her after she tells him she has no more money to invest. She requests a withdrawal of profits on her WealthStream360 account. After being told she needed to pay additional fees, taxes, and other charges, Jane discovers that the investment platform is a fake.

In this "Conventional Fraud" setting, the use of cryptocurrency as a method of payment provides Jane with additional challenges over an investment scam using fiat currency. To be sure, there are centralised entities in this story—a bank and a digital currency exchange—that provide enforcement targets. But once transferred, cryptocurrency is instantaneous and irreversible—the digital currency exchange has no technological ability to recover the funds once it is sent. Additionally, the pseudonymous nature of blockchain transactions obscures tracing the identity and location of the ultimate recipient of the funds (who may be Jerry, the persons behind the WealthStream360 website, or another third party that had no direct contact with Jane).

If Jane was in a "Intermediary-enabled Fraud" setting she might be influenced on social media to use her existing cryptocurrency portfolio to buy into an initial coin offering (ICO) "pump and dump" scheme—a fraud where perpetrators buy up (or create) an alternative cryptocurrency and inflate the price by driving demand through social media hype (i.e., the pump). Then, after the price reaches a desired level, the perpetrators sell off their holdings causing the price to fall (i.e., the dump). Jane is ultimately left with worthless or significantly devalued digital assets. Unlike the conventional context, the purchases can be, but are not necessarily, filtered through centralised digital currency exchanges. Furthermore, the nature of crypto pump and dump schemes means that they are faster in both rate and speed as compared to traditional market manipulation (Kamps & Kleinberg 2018).

Another challenge in the "Intermediary-enabled Fraud" category is that fraudulent schemes often rely on a network of operators—creating separation between the masterminds and others assisting (knowingly or not). Those driving social media hype in the above pump and dump example is illustrative of this point. The schemes rely heavily on promoters or influencers on various social media channels (Momtaz 2021). These promoters aren't the masterminds of the fraudulent scheme, but rather pump the scheme in the promise of receiving incentives such as offer of bonus tokens. Ironically, often these incentives are not paid either (Sapkota et al. 2020). What it means, though, is that the person shilling the bogus crypto token to Jane is not typically the recipient of the scheme's proceeds.

Lastly, let's consider "Decentralised Fraud". Jane invests $100,000 worth of Ethereum by sending tokens from her cryptocurrency wallet into an address for "PunkArtDAO"—a Decentralised Autonomous Organization advertised as a collective investment vehicle for acquiring the popular non-fungible token collection "Crypto Punks". Jane receives governance tokens, representing her supposed proportional stake in the fund. However, Jane and the other investors do not realise that the smart contract code allowed the founders to drain the funds from the PunkArtDAO's treasury without authorisation. Before updates could be made, PunkArtDAO lost three quarters of its cryptocurrency holdings—meaning Jane's investment was now worth $25,000. This tactic is called a "rug pull". But there is some controversy as to whether this crypto-native decentralised fraud is deception in the true sense. Unlike conventional or intermediary-enabled investment frauds, the smart contract code governing DAOs is public and runs on the top of an open source blockchain network. Technically, investors in Jane's circumstances could have audited the smart contract code (or engaged somebody on her behalf). The smart contract code will operate as it has been programmed to do and so there is an argument that the "code is law" (De Filippi & Wright 2018).

This section has shown that Web3 characteristics inherently present unique challenges and opportunities for fraud involving cryptocurrency and has drawn on other work to show how this type of fraud exists within a wider taxonomy of cryptocurrency crime (including theft) and across a spectrum (including conventional, intermediary-enabled or decentralised fraud).

The perpetrators of fraudulent schemes impose significant social costs on unsuspecting users. Between 2019–2023, an estimated US$36.7 billion was lost to cryptocurrency-based scams (Chainalysis 2024). Over two-thirds of this amount were from "conventional" scams, i.e., romance, investment, giveaway, charity, or impersonation. Accordingly, the remaining focus of this chapter narrows its focus to conventional fraud. The next section will examine institutional possibilities for addressing the problem of cryptocurrency-based fraud.

3 The Rise of Regulators

How can we understand the range of institutional possibilities available to address the problem of cryptocurrency fraud? In this section, we draw on the new comparative economics (Djankov et al. 2003a; Shleifer 2005, 2012) and introduce the Dispute Resolution Possibilities Frontier (Allen et al. 2019) to provide a basic framework for analysing the trade-offs between different institutional dispute resolution choices. This section will then discuss three examples that illustrate the prevalent legal approach to addressing cryptocurrency-based fraud.

3.1 The Dispute Resolution Possibilities Frontier

The assessment of how to best address the problem of cryptocurrency fraud is a governance question because of the existence of social costs (actions by one person or entity that imposes economic costs on another) and the economic reality that the action to address social costs will itself impose costs on others (Coase 1960). For our purposes, in broad terms, it requires balancing the apparent need for regulatory oversight or legal intervention to limit the social costs of fraud (identified in the previous section) without unduly inhibiting the innovative potential of Web3 technologies.

Harvard economics professor Andrei Shleifer and colleagues developed the new comparative economics framework (Djankov et al. 2003a; Shleifer 2005, 2012), which recognised that there was no single way to address this type of governance

Chart 1 Dispute resolution possibility Frontier (Adapted from Djankov et al. 2003a; Allen et al. 2019)

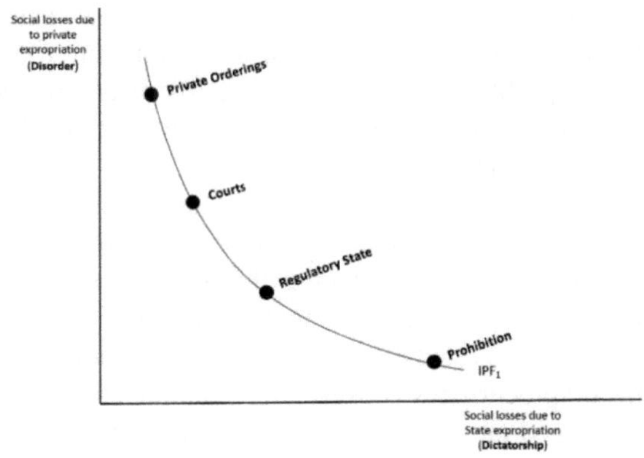

question. Rather, there are a range of institutional possibilities arrayed on a spectrum—each with a different combination of social costs. Those social costs can be separated as "disorder" (the risk of social costs from private individuals) or "dictatorship" (the risk of social costs from governments or regulators exercising the power of the state). No institution is perfect and so institutional efficiency will be achieved if one institutional possibility lowers the cost of "disorder" without increasing "dictatorship" and vice versa. Initially developed as a tool to study regulation, the new comparative economics framework can also be applied to understanding dispute resolution (Allen et al. 2019).

For the purposes of this chapter, let us consider four key dispute resolution possibilities for addressing cryptocurrency fraud, illustrated in Chart 1.

First, Private Orderings. This encompasses *ex post* mechanisms of non-binding alternative dispute resolution well known to lawyers—such as negotiation and mediation. These systems can be effective where mutual incentives align to cooperate and reach an agreement. There is a high degree of disorder costs associated with these options owing to their lack of enforceability through technical or legal means. In the context of cryptocurrency fraud, the risks of disorder are high because fraudsters inherently do not engage in good faith negotiations. Unlike theft scenarios (such as ransomware) where there's the possibility of a negotiation between hacker and victim (such as encryption code for ransom payment), deception-based fraud scenarios typically leave the victim without anything to negotiate with. It is possible that in deception-based scenarios, victims may resort to illicit vigilante action to take against fraudsters that we can observe in other circumstances, such as revenge hacking (Chng et al. 2022) or revenge violence (Duran-Martinez 2015)—obviously characterised by high disorder costs.

Second, Courts. This encompasses *ex post* private litigation through courts with powers to enforce judgements. The enforceability of judgements in a court's jurisdiction (reducing dictatorship costs) is the exercise of state judicial power to expropriate property (increasing dictatorship costs). Mechanisms like rules of evidence, civil procedure and judicial tenure (all increasing dictatorship costs) limit the ability of litigants to subvert the litigation process. Disorder costs remain. The private funding of litigation is a persistent limitation to access to justice, while collective action problems exist where the costs of enforcement exceed an individual's loss. In cryptocurrency fraud, courts face limitations due to inherent pseudonymity and cross-jurisdictional challenges.

Third, Public Regulation. This encompasses the *ex post* regulatory enforcement of ex ante legislation and regulation (including the criminal law). This institutional possibility aims at reducing the number of cryptocurrency-based fraud disputes through corporate regulation that must be followed (reducing disorder costs). At the same time, if regulations are restrictive or not well-calibrated to the unique aspects of the cryptocurrency ecosystem, regulation could stifle innovation, discourage investment, and move activity to less regulated jurisdictions (all symptoms of increasing dictatorship costs). There is also the risk that regulators are captured by their political masters or the industry they are seeking to regulate (Stigler 1971).

Fourth, Prohibition. This encompasses the extreme approach of banning specific or all activity that uses cryptocurrency in a particular jurisdiction or type of users (such as retail or non-commercial users) in order to remove the threat of cryptocurrency fraud from this place or cohort—preventing disputes from arising in the first place. While this reduces the cost of disorder, it is non-zero as outright bans will drive cryptocurrency usage underground. Meanwhile, the costs of dictatorship are significant because those that are the subject of the prohibition are deprived of the benefit of this technology. So, while cryptocurrency bans may be officially justified on the basis of financial crime, it may also be an attempt to prevent capital flight (Shin 2022).

The perception of disorder and dictatorship—and deciding on how best to economise these costs—is largely subjective (Allen & Berg 2017). This means that different jurisdictions will end up deciding on a different balance of dispute resolution strategies. Realistically, though, the extreme ends of the dispute resolution possibility frontier—complete prohibition and total absence of government action—are unlikely to be politically palatable in most jurisdictions where cryptocurrency fraud is a significant problem but where cryptocurrency and other Web3 technologies are seen as positive innovations. Accordingly, this leaves private litigation through courts and regulatory enforcement of public regulations to two competing strategies. While these possibilities are not mutually exclusive (jurisdictions can and do have both options), there has tended to be a focus on public regulation to tackle cryptocurrency-based fraud and therefore a "rise of regulators" (Shleifer 2012).

3.2 Three Examples of Public Regulation

To illustrate the public regulation possibility, let us explore three examples—anti-money laundering and counter-terror financing (AML/CTF), the licensing of digital currency exchanges for retail consumers trading and custody provision, and the imposition of securities laws through regulation by enforcement. All of these examples involve the application of corporate regulation that imposes obligations on digital currency exchanges. Accordingly, the regulatory enforcement target tends to be these exchanges or related businesses. As these efforts are jurisdiction-specific, we will focus on regulatory efforts in particular jurisdictions to provide some colour—but the basic points can be generalised to almost any jurisdiction.

Example 1: Anti-money Laundering and Counter-Terror Financing

Money laundering has long been a concern associated with fraudulent activities, well before the advent of digital currencies, as fraudsters seek to wash the criminal stains from the funds through legitimate financial channels. For instance, in the 1990s, there were concerns that new "instantaneous" payment technologies that included credit cards, ATMs and electronic wire transfers, could be used for money laundering purposes (Zagaris & MacDonald 1992). Cryptocurrency is the next generation of technology to facilitate borderless instantaneous payments. And where cryptocurrency is obtained by deception, it makes sense that fraudsters will attempt to launder those proceeds and convert at least some of the funds into fiat currency. AML/CTF regulations have emerged as public regulatory efforts aimed at mitigating the risks associated with payment platforms—effectively conscripting financial services companies to do the law enforcement work of disrupting criminal networks.

In Australia, the major piece of legislation is the *Anti-Money Laundering and Counter-Terrorism Financing Act 2006* (Cth) ("the Act"). The Act, amongst other things, requires providers of "designated services" to register with the regulator, the Australian Transaction Reports and Analysis Centre (AUSTRAC). These providers operate across financial services (including banks, non-bank lenders and deposit-taking institutions, insurers, investments and securities businesses, foreign currency exchanges), trading precious metals, and gambling services. Registered entities must have an AML/CTF program (including Know Your Customer (KYC) obligations to verify the identity of customers), monitor and report suspicious transactions, and keep detailed records of all transactions.

Following amendments to the Act that came into effect in 2018, exchanging digital currency for money or exchanging money for digital currency, in the course of carrying on a digital currency exchange business is now a "designated service" requiring registration. "Digital currency" is defined broadly under the Act to include cryptocurrency (but excludes government-issued stablecoins).

Accordingly, the AML/CTF regime now captures the on-ramps and off-ramps to the crypto economy. Through digital currency exchanges, regulators and law enforcement agencies can track cryptocurrency payments from bank accounts, through exchanges, and onto the blockchain. This reduces the risk of harm principally from conventional fraud by disrupting criminal networks and assisting in the identity attribution challenge—i.e., helping law enforcement to trace and potentially recover illicit funds.

However, disorder costs remain. Significantly, the perpetrators of cryptocurrency-based fraud can use fraudulent or stolen identity documents to bypass KYC checks.

They may use remote access technology to assist victims into registering for these exchanges themselves.

Furthermore, regulation imposes measurable dictatorship costs. First, perpetrators do not pay the compliance costs—these are borne by digital currency exchanges and financial institutions and, in turn, their customers. Research has shown that these compliance costs are substantial, with a 2007 study estimating the annual cost to the Australian banking industry alone at $1.02 billion (Sathye 2008). Meanwhile, taxpayers cover the costs of compliance on the government side. Second, the obligations of designated services are publicly enforced under the threat of civil or criminal penalties, depending on the breach. This means that if a person has suffered loss or damage as a result of a lack of compliance with the AML/CTF program, for example, the person is not able to bring action for recovery or mandate compliance under the Act.

Example 2—Regulation by Enforcement

In 2017, around 800 Initial Coin Offerings (ICO) were launched, raising an estimated total of $US20 billion according to Forbes (Kauflin 2018). ICOs were a novel method for blockchain startups to raise capital. Firms could issue their own tokens in exchange for cryptocurrency from investors, seemingly without the regulatory trappings of traditional capital finance. But not all of those ICOs were legitimate.

Centra Tech Inc. launched the "Centra Token", an ERC20 token on the Ethereum blockchain. The company marketed the token to investors on the basis of the business model and products. Central to the pitch was that the company had partnerships and agreements with Visa and Mastercard, along with a major bank, allowing users to conveniently spend their cryptocurrency though a physical card. Centra drafted champion boxer Floyd Mayweather and the Grammy award-winning DJ Khaled to promote the launch. These marketing efforts were obviously persuasive, with Centra pocketing $25 million in a number of months. As it happened, though, the agreements with Visa and Mastercard did not exist. Executive biographies in the marketing materials were bogus too. In the United States, the SEC successfully brought proceedings against the founders of Centra for securities fraud (SEC 2024). In March 2021, the co-founder and primary perpetrator was sentenced to eight years imprisonment, while another co-founder was sentenced to one year and one day (DOJ 2021). Mayweather and Khaled settled proceedings for failing to disclose commissions in promoting the ICO (SEC 2024).

At the time, there were no crypto-specific laws, regulations or rules in the United States (and indeed this remains the case at the time of writing). As such, it was not clear as to whether the Centra Token—and other tokens like it—were properly "securities" for the purposes of securities laws, which would require licensing and impose disclosure obligations on the issuers. Or were the tokens commodities? In which case a distinct regulatory regime would apply (and competition from other regulators for regulatory turf). Are all crypto asset tokens the same?

Regulators are in something of a bind in answering this question. The SEC had the option of sitting back until the legislature provide the regulator with a clear and updated mandate. But charged with enforcing securities laws, a sit-on-your-hands approach would be open to criticism of not acting to curtail fraudulent conduct. Instead, the SEC sought to enforce its own understanding of the application of settled corporate law and principles to address the disorder costs associated with these new fundraising activities. This approach is known as "regulation by enforcement". This approach opens itself up to criticism that it lacks the transparency and predictability of *ex ante* rules (Park 2007; Goforth 2022). Additionally, the tactics of regulators of issuing cease and desist notices exemplify the relatively high dictatorship costs associated with public enforcement—as the law is unclear and yet businesses are deterred because of the significant costs of defending threatened legal action.

Example 3—Licensing of Exchanges

Legislatures around the world are grappling with how best to regulate crypto assets—not just to address the problem of fraud but also to address other consumer protection issues like custody management, cyber security and solvency. While most jurisdictions have been slow to act, there appears to be a consensus around imposing publicly enforced corporate law frameworks on centralised crypto asset exchanges by requiring a license—which is issued and monitored by existing corporate regulators.

Singapore was one of the first jurisdictions to impose licensing requirements on crypto asset businesses through the *Payment Service Act 2019* (SG). Under this legislation, the Monetary Authority of Singapore (the country's central bank and financial regulator) issues licenses to and regulates "Virtual Asset Service Providers" (VASP).

To obtain and maintain a license to operate, the Act provides three key requirements that go directly to perceive costs of disorder. First, the VASP must have a permanent place of business or a registered office in Singapore, and its executive director must be either a citizen or permanent resident of Singapore. This physically anchors the VASP to the jurisdiction. While there may be other economic reasons for these requirements, for our purposes it makes it easier for the MAS to monitor compliance and to enforce orders against the VASP's assets and responsible personnel. Second, the VASP must meet a "fit and proper person" test which has character (reducing the risk of consumer harm from fraudulent or illicit activities) and competence components (reducing the risk of consumer harm from negligence). Third, the MAS must be satisfied of the financial condition of the VASP (reducing the risk of consumer harm from insolvency)—base capital of SG$100,000 for a standard license and SG$250,000 for a major institution license (MAS 2024).

Other examples of this include Hong Kong's regime for "Virtual Asset Trading Platforms" regulated by the Hong Kong Securities and Futures Commission (commenced in 2023), Dubai's regulations for "Virtual Asset Service Providers" (commenced in 2023), and the European Union's Markets in Crypto Assets regulation (commencing in 2024). Although similar, jurisdictional competition may emerge. It is likely that the jurisdictions that implement "crypto-friendly" regulations will reap economic rewards (Novak & Pochesneva 2019).

On the other hand, the entire point of licensing is to increase the barriers to entry and capture rents (e.g., Stigler 1971). The other potential dictatorship costs of these approaches mirror the other examples in this section. Namely, the real costs of complying with regulatory frameworks and that aggrieved consumers do not typically have legally standing in the courts to prevent a license being granted or to bring enforcement action for breach of the licensing conditions.

The contribution of this section has been to illustrate the role of public regulation in addressing cryptocurrency fraud—introducing the DRPF as a framework for understanding how public regulation is placed amongst to other institutional possibilities. Through a discussion of AML/CTF regulations, regulation by enforcement, and licensing of exchanges, this section has demonstrated how the public enforcement of corporate law frameworks can mitigate the risks of fraud associated with crypto assets—such as improving transparency and traceability, deterring bad actors and imposing ex ante consumer protection measures. The next section will explore ex post private law remedies as an alternative institutional possibility for addressing cryptocurrency fraud.

4 The Private Enforcement Alternative

There are more lawyers than law enforcement officers. In Australia, there are 99,400 barristers and solicitors compared to 62,300 police officers across the country (Australian Government 2024). Other jurisdictions are no doubt similarly blessed with the abundance of legal professionals projected to reach a global market of US$1.4 trillion by 2030 (Straights Research 2023). The purpose of the rise of public regulations and regulators is to gain intelligence, disrupt, and prevent future crime and hold proven offenders publicly accountable. The purpose of civil litigation is more targeted—seeking compensation for legal wrongs. As such, legal professionals are an underappreciated resource in combatting cryptocurrency-based fraud. In this section, we will identify the circumstances in which civil litigation through courts is a more institutionally efficient dispute resolution mechanism compared to public enforcement.

Let us return to Jane—our victim of cryptocurrency fraud. In conducting a preliminary review of Jane's file there are three challenges or vectors that a civil litigator will be considering. First, the identity attribution challenge—who has committed the fraud? Second, the cause of action challenge—what is the legal wrong that has been committed and can this be proven? Third, the assets challenge—can the assets be frozen or recovered, or does the perpetrator have assets within the reach of the jurisdiction? Let's now consider these in turn and the private law mechanisms that assist in addressing these challenges.

4.1 The Identity Attribution Challenge

In order to bring legal proceedings, Jane needs to establish, with a reasonable degree of certainty, the identity and location of those behind the fraudulent scheme. For a conventional fraud, the task is difficult as the real identity *is* likely to be deliberately concealed. The more productive place to start, therefore, is identifying the recipient of the funds. The transparency of blockchain networks, discussed in the section of this chapter, means that cryptocurrency transactions can be traced. That's not to say that it is easy or costless—but blockchain analytics firms have emerged in recent years (e.g., Chainalysis, TRM Labs and QLue) offering proprietary software for tracking, analysis and visualisation that runs on the top of the open source blockchain transaction records. It is possible, therefore, to trace the funds from Jane's bank account, to Jane's cryptocurrency exchange, to the wallet address on the blockchain, to the recipient's cryptocurrency exchange, to the recipient's bank account.

There are civil litigation tools to assist in obtaining the identity of a prospective defendant. Chief among these are preliminary discovery orders (also variously known as pre-action or pre-suit discovery across the United States and Norwich Pharmacal orders in the United Kingdom) that can be sought against intermediaries that are inadvertently caught up in the fraudulent conduct. Generally, the applicant needs to show: (a) a cause of action against a prospective defendant; (b) that they have made reasonable inquiries and is unable to sufficiently ascertain the identity of the prospective defendant; and (c) a third party has in its position a document or other information that would assist in ascertaining their identity (see e.g., Order 32 *Supreme Court (General Civil Procedure) Rules 2015* (Vic)) In Jane's case, preliminary discovery application could be made against cryptocurrency exchanges or banks who are likely to hold identity information about the owner of a relevant account (including personal information but also IP address logs providing a launchpad for further investigation). Without a court order, privacy laws mean that these intermediaries will not otherwise provide Jane with their customer information.

Another tool is the civil search order (also known as Anton Piller order), which permits the applicant to enter the respondent's premises for the purpose of securing evidence relevant to a proceeding or prospective proceeding. There are stronger requirements in addition to a preliminary discovery order, in that there must be evidence that potential or actual loss or damage to the applicant will be serious if the search order is not made, there is a risk that the respondent might destroy important evidentiary material in its possession (see e.g., Order 37B *Supreme Court (General Civil Procedure) Rules 2015* (Vic)). In Jane's case, these will be most useful where one person has been identified and there is evidence to suggest that they are part of a larger fraudulent operation. Accordingly, evidence obtained may be useful not only in proving the case against that respondent but may identify other respondents.

What happens if Jane cannot identify or locate the direct perpetrator? Then the attribution challenge shifts to others that can be identified. There may be those that will have secondary liability (i.e., they knowingly assisted or knowingly received fraudulent funds). Alternatively, intermediaries (e.g., banks and cryptocurrency exchanges, social media platforms) and advisors (e.g., financial advisors, smart contract auditors) may owe contractual or equitable obligations or have tortious liability.

4.2 *The Cause of Action Challenge*

Once Jane has ascertained the identity of the perpetrator, or a third party potentially liable in her case of cryptocurrency fraud, the next hurdle is pleading a cause of action. A cause of action is the set of facts or legal reasons that have been provided by the Parliament (in the case of a statutory cause of action) or identified by common law or equitable courts as entitling a party to be granted a remedy against another party. This involves identifying the specific legal wrongs committed—and a party may plead multiple and alternative causes of action. Accordingly, causes of action are more tailored than blanket regulatory rules. Let's examine three categories of typical common law and equitable actions.

Money had and received: Jane is required to show that another person received her funds under a mistake (e.g., Jane invests in what she believes is a legitimate digital asset, but the project turns out to be non-existent) or a complete failure of consideration (e.g., where it appears Jane has executed purported contracts with the fraudsters).

Fraudulent misrepresentation or deceit: Jane is required to show that the respondent made a false representation (e.g., the creators of a DeFi project falsely represented the security features of their smart contract), that the respondent knew or was reckless as to its falsity, had an intention to deceive (only required for deceit), that Jane relied on the representation and that Jane suffered loss and damage. Similar statutory causes of action also exist.

Contract, negligence (common law) or fiduciary (equity): Jane is required to show that the respondent had a contractual relationship, that a duty of care existed, or that a fiduciary relationship existed because of the trust and confidence between the parties (noting that statutory law often modifies or supplements these duties). Next, as a result of the breach of the contract, duty of care, or fiduciary duty, Jane suffered loss and damage. Unlike the other actions above, this will often be the grounds that Jane will rely on against her advisors (e.g., Jane receives investment advice from a financial advisor who recommends a high-risk crypto investment that he has an interest in, without disclosing the associated risks or their conflict).

Accordingly, Jane must marshal the evidence required to substantiate each element of claims. This will invariably involve gathering transaction records, communications, expert tracing reports, and other material. Generally, Jane has the burden of proof on the balance of probabilities. Although the more serious the allegation made (for allegations of fraud and illegal conduct) the more serious evidence that will be required to prove the case (*Briginshaw v Briginshaw* (1938) 60 CLR 336, 360–363 per Dixon J).

4.3 The Assets Challenge

The final challenge is the most practical. Civil litigation is expensive. Jane needs to ensure that prospective respondents have assets that are worth pursuing otherwise Jane's legal efforts may result in a pyrrhic victory. As such, private law enforcement involves consideration of whether the fraudster has assets that can be identified and secured.

As previously mentioned, identifying assets involves tracing the flow of funds from the initial transaction through various exchanges and wallets. Once potential assets are identified, civil litigation mechanisms can be deployed to freeze or seize those assets.

One civil litigation tool is a freezing order (also known as a Mareva injunction). The purpose of a freezing order is to prevent the fraudster from dissipating assets pending the outcome of the matter (see e.g., Order 37A *Supreme Court (General Civil Procedure) Rules 2015* (Vic)). Typically, Jane would apply to the court on an ex parte basis (i.e., without notice to the respondent). The respondent could be the fraudster—but it could be a third party such as an intermediary that has custody of the assets. In making ancillary orders, Jane can compel the respondent to provide information about what assets are held and how to access them, as examples.

Freezing orders have been successfully obtained in cases involving cryptocurrency. In September 2018, the Chancellery Division in the High Court of England and Wales in the case of *Vorotyntseva v Money-4 Ltd* [2018] EWHC 2596 (Ch) granted a freezing order after the applicant transferred £1.5 million worth of Bitcoin and Ethereum from wallets held with a cryptocurrency exchange to a wallet in custody of the respondents who purportedly operated a trading platform—and later neglected to confirm that they still held the cryptocurrency. In February 2024, the Supreme Court of Victoria in the case of *Rhino Trading Pty Ltd v Lotte Enterprise Pty Ltd* [2024] VSC 52 granted a freezing order after cryptocurrency exchange mistakenly credited a customer's trading account with $995,000 instead of $99,500 and allowing the customer to ultimately withdraw $491,934.76. The Court granted orders in circumstances where the customer had not responded to the exchange's request for repayment and "must have been aware of the overpayment" (at [42]). The Court also made orders preventing the customer from leaving Australia. As both *Vorotyntseva and Rhino Trading* demonstrate, freezing orders are designed to be sought quickly and at a preliminary stage of the proceeding.

A similar civil litigation tool is the property preservation order. While freezing orders are general orders restraining a person from dissipating any assets, property preservation orders are sought in relation to specific property. Applied to Jane's case, if Jane's cryptocurrency has been converted to cash, then a freezing order is appropriate to take foothold over the proceeds of her cryptocurrency. If Jane can identify the fraudster, and can prove that the fraudster is holding the cryptocurrency, Jan could then seek an order preserving that cryptocurrency itself.

Such a circumstance was considered in the Supreme Court of Victoria in the case of *Chen v Blockchain Global Ltd* [2022] VSC 92. The circumstances of the case are complex, but simply put Chen and Guo were directors of an insolvent cryptocurrency exchange and the liquidator was seeking to claw back assets from the directors. In separate proceedings, the court had previously granted a freezing order over assets that included 117 Bitcoin held in a "2 of 2" wallet (i.e., requiring both Chen and Guo's private key to sign a transaction). The central issue for the Court was that if one of the private keys were lost or forgotten, then the Bitcoin would be stuck in the wallet forever (potentially breaching the freezing order and/or further frustrating the court's processes)—a problem stemming from blockchain's immutability. Guo gave evidence that his "seed phrase" (i.e., a backup to generate the private key) was written down on a piece of paper and stored in a location in China. Chen brought an application for property preservation orders which would (a) require Guo to record his seed phrase in a sealed envelope (b) provide the envelope to the Court pending the hearing and determination of the dispute or further order (c) and for the seed phrase to be verified by a member of the Court or by a sworn statement from Guo's solicitor. The Court, in granting the order, was satisfied that "the Bitcoins may be, in effect, destroyed" (at [38]).

This section has highlighted the tools of private law in addressing cryptocurrency fraud. By dissecting three main challenges—the identity attribution challenge, the cause of action challenge, and the assets challenge—we have shown that civil litigation tools can reduce disorder costs associated with cryptocurrency fraud disputes with tools to identify perpetrators and others involved in the fraud, tailor legal claims to the facts and evidence on hand and get a handle on the assets of respondents prior to the conclusion of the dispute. Comparatively, at least for jurisdictions with strong and independent courts (Djankov et al. 2003a), private enforcement also lowers dictatorship costs as victims are empowered to take control of the litigation process, providing direct paths to recovery, without being held up by or beholden to law enforcement or regulators—and without political influence. Accordingly, where the three challenges can be met, private law provides an efficient dispute resolution possibility compared to corporate regulation.

5 The Future Agenda for Private Law

Private law mechanisms can be effectively marshalled to address cryptocurrency fraud, as detailed in the previous section. That section—and indeed the premise of this chapter—is optimistic for the role of private law. However, this is not to say that private litigation is free from disorder costs. As Andrei Shleifer and colleagues identified, "some mechanisms for influencing courts, such as hiring good lawyers, delaying proceedings, and seeking political help, are entirely legal" Djankov et al. (2003a, 602), "legal procedure is itself heavily regulated, burdensome, and expensive" (Shleifer 2010, 33)—a view that is supported by empirical evidence (Djankov et al. 2003b). As applied to the problem of cryptocurrency fraud, there are comparatively higher disorder costs associated with enforcing jurisdictional court orders in a Web3 ecosystem that is global, decentralised and immutable. With this in mind, this section offers four areas of future research that may enhance the efficacy of private law mechanisms and remedies for civil litigants.

5.1 Class Actions

One obvious problem with civil litigation is that the prospective costs are disproportionate to the loss, or that results are not guaranteed, and victims do not want to throw good money after bad. The silver lining is that victims of fraudulent schemes are rarely alone but are typically operated to entrap a significant number of victims (whereas theft-based misappropriation is targeted opportunistically at individuals with known assets or systematically targeted at high-net-worth "whales"). Class actions, or representative proceedings, are private law mechanisms for aggregating many smaller claims into a single lawsuit, allowing individuals who have suffered relatively minor losses to pool their resources and take collective legal action. One obvious collective action problem is that victims do not know each other. While plaintiff law firms and litigation funders have economic incentives for finding victims, there is a role for future research in evaluating the effectiveness of these measures.

5.2 Information Sharing and International Cooperation

Another collective action problem exists in civil procedure where documents obtained in one proceeding may not necessarily be able to use that document for another litigation without leave of the Court (known as the Harman obligation following the English decision in *Harman v Secretary of State for Home Department* [1983] 1 AC 280). Future research should consider to what extent the friction of civil procedure rules such as this adds unnecessary duplication.

The public sector also has a role in alleviating the collective action problem through information sharing. If information is collected in the course of a regulatory or criminal investigation, that could be passed to victims to obtain private relief without incurring the expense of pre-litigation mechanisms such as preliminary discovery. Consideration needs to be given to whether public law procedures such as Freedom of Information are fit for this purpose. Likewise, public sector agencies such as the Financial Crimes Enforcement Network (FinCEN) in the US and AUSTRAC in Australia have databases of fraudulent activities and actors, which could be used to help identify potential defendants across borders.

Another role for the public sector is to set the frameworks for civil recovery across borders. Cross-border enforcement of civil orders is a significant challenge in the context of cryptocurrency fraud, given its global nature, but not impossible. International cooperation can extend beyond criminal law enforcement to include civil remedies too. Future research is needed on mutual recognition agreements between courts, bilateral treaties, legal standards and the like to improve cross-border enforcement, allowing victims to recover losses even when fraudsters operate in different jurisdictions.

5.3 *Streamlined Civil Procedure*

The discovery tools canvassed in this chapter can be lengthy and limited. For instance, if pursuant to a discover order, a cryptocurrency exchange provided accounts which then showed funds being withdrawn to a bank account, the applicant would need to obtain a further discovery order from the bank. In the case of a freezing order, how can crypto assets be secured without the court demanding up seed phrases? Future research will consider efforts in different courts and jurisdictions to streamline and expedite the identification of fraudsters and their assets to reduce litigation costs.

5.4 *Alternative Forums*

Finally, decentralised dispute resolution mechanisms offer an innovative approach to adjudicating disputes in the cryptocurrency sector. Platforms like Kleros utilise blockchain technology to create decentralised, peer-to-peer courts, where jurors are randomly selected from a pool of verified participants. These are dispute resolution possibilities that are particularly suited for resolving disputes particularly those that arise directly within the Web3 ecosystem (Allen et al. 2019). While such mechanisms are still in their infancy, future research might consider the role that these new dispute resolution possibilities have in resolving "crypto-native" fraudulent conduct.

6 Conclusion

Web3 creates opportunities and challenges when it comes to pursuing recovery for victims of cryptocurrency-based fraud—while there are new fraud risks there are also new opportunities for investigations that flow from the use of public blockchains. There is no single type of cryptocurrency-based fraud (Allen & Lane 2024), and this chapter has focused principally on conventional schemes such as romance or investment scams. Similarly, there is no single legal mechanism to address the problem of cryptocurrency fraud but a variety of dispute resolution possibilities that exist across the spectrum from private orderings through to prohibition. While much of the academic, legal industry, and policy discourse to date has focused on the role and need for public regulatory response, the key contribution of this chapter has been to demonstrate private legal actions are capable of directly addressing the harms experienced by individuals—and may indeed provide a more efficient dispute resolution possibility compared to public regulation. Private remedies are far from perfect but, unlike public regulation, can deliver tailored results and obtain individual recovery of assets. As the Web3 ecosystem continues to grow, a renewed focus on strengthening private enforcement rights will be essential in combatting cryptocurrency-based fraud.

Acknowledgements The author thanks Andrew Tragardh and the team at Duxton Hill, where the author was previously Special Counsel and practised in matters involving cryptocurrency fraud. An earlier version of this chapter was presented to the 2024 Conference of the Society of Corporate Law Academics and the author acknowledges helpful comments from Professor Ross Buckley, Associate Professor Akshaya Kamalnath, and Dr Darcy Allen.

References

Allen DWE, Berg C (2017) Subjective political economy. New Perspect Polit Econ 13(1–2):19–40
Allen DWE, Lane AM (2024) Crypto crime as criminal entrepreneurship. Available on SSRN
Allen DWE, Lane AM, Poblet M (2019) The governance of blockchain dispute resolution. Harvard Negotiation Law Review 25:75–101
Australian Government (2024) Labour market insights. Web page. https://labourmarketinsights.gov.au/
Berg C, Davidson S, Potts J (2019) Understanding the blockchain economy: an introduction to institutional cryptoeconomics. Edward Elgar
Brito J, Castillo A (2013) Bitcoin: a primer for policymakers. mercatus center at George Mason University
Chainalysis (2024) The 2024 crypto crime report. Chainalysis
Chng S, Lu HY, Kumar A, Yau D (2022) Hacker types, motivations and strategies: a comprehensive framework. Comput Human Behav Rep 5:100167
Coase RH (1960) The problem of social cost. J Law Econ 3:1–44
Davidson S, Potts J, de Filippi P (2018) Blockchains and the economic institutions of capitalism. J Inst Econ 14(4):639–658
De Filippi P, Wright A (2018) Blockchain and the law: the rule of code. Harvard University Press
De Filippi P (2014) Bitcoin: a regulatory nightmare to a libertarian dream. Internet Policy Review 3(2):1–11
Department of Justice (2021) Leading co-founder of cryptocurrency company sentenced to 8 years in prison for ICO Fraud Scheme. Media Release, 4 March. https://www.justice.gov/usao-sdny/pr/leading-co-founder-cryptocurrency-company-sentenced-8-years-prison-ico-fraud-scheme
Dixon C (2024) Read write own: building the next era of the Internet. Cornerstone Press
Djankov S, Glaeser E, La Porta R, Lopez-de-Silanes F, Shleifer A (2003a) The new comparative economics. J Comp Econ 31:595–619
Djankov S, La Porta R, Lopez-de-Silanes F, Shleifer A (2003b) Courts. Quart J Econ 118(2):453–517
Duran-Martinez A (2015) To kill and tell? State power, criminal competition, and drug violence. J Conflict Resolut 59(8):1377–1402
Goforth CR (2022) Regulation by enforcement: problems with the SEC's approach to cryptoasset regulation. Maryland Law Review 82(1):107–159
Henrique DB (2011) The wizard of lies: Bernie Madoff and the death of trust. Henry Holt & Company
Johnstone P (1998) Serious white collar fraud: historical and contemporary perspectives. Crime Law Soc Chang 30:107–130
Kamps J, Kleinberg B (2018) To the moon: defining and detecting cryptocurrency pump-and-dumps. Crime Sci 7:1–18

Kauflin J (2018) Where did the money go? Inside the big crypto ICOs of 2017. Forbes, 29 October. https://www.forbes.com/sites/jeffkauflin/2018/10/29/where-did-the-money-go-inside-the-big-crypto-icos-of-2017/

Middleton J (2023) Robot dogs, AI and the plan to retrieve £165m crypto fortune lost in rubbish dump. The Independent, 7 November. https://www.independent.co.uk/news/uk/home-news/lost-bitcoin-crypto-james-howells-b2406517.html

Momtaz P (2021) Entrepreneurial finance and moral hazard: evidence from token offerings. J Bus Ventur 36(5):106001

Monetary Authority of Singapore (2024) Licensing for payment service providers. Web page. https://www.mas.gov.sg/regulation/payments/licensing-for-payment-service-providers

Nakamoto S (2008) Bitcoin: a peer-to-peer electronic cash system. White Paper

Norris G, Brookes A, Dowell D (2019) The psychology of internet fraud victimisation: a systematic review. J Police Crim Psychol 34:231–245

Novak M, Pochesneva A (2019) Toward a crypto-friendly index for the APEC region. J British Blockchain Assoc 2(1):1–7

Park JJ (2007) The competing paradigms of securities regulation. Duke Law J 57(3):625–690

Posner RA (2017) Legal research and practical experience. Univ Chicago Law Rev 84:239–248

Sapkota N, Grobys K, Dufitinema J (2020) How much are we willing to lose in cyberspace? On the tail risk of scam in the market for initial coin offerings. Available at SSRN: https://doi.org/10.2139/ssrn.3732747

Sathye M (2008) Estimating the cost of compliance of AMLCTF for financial institutions in Australia. Journal of Financial Crime 15(4):347–363

Securities and Exchange Commission (2024) Crypto assets and cyber enforcement actions. Web Page. https://www.sec.gov/spotlight/cybersecurity-enforcement-actions

Shin F (2022) What's behind China's cryptocurrency ban? World Economic Forum. https://www.weforum.org/agenda/2022/01/what-s-behind-china-s-cryptocurrency-ban/

Shleifer A (2005) Understanding regulation. Eur Financ Manag 11(4):439–451

Shleifer A (2012) The failure of judges and the rise of regulators. MIT Press

Shleifer A (2010) Efficient regulation. In: Kessler DP (ed), Regulation vs. litigation: perspectives from economics and law. University of Chicago Press

Stigler GJ (1971) The theory of economic regulation. Bell J Econ Manage Sci 2(1):3–21

Straights Research (2023) Global legal services market size is estimated to reach USD 1,429.22 billion by 2030, Growing at a CAGR of 5.25%: Straits Research. Global News Wire. https://www.globenewswire.com/news-release/2023/12/13/2795596/0/en/Global-Legal-Services-Market-Size-is-Estimated-to-Reach-USD-1-429-22-billion-by-2030-Growing-at-a-CAGR-of-5-25-Straits-Research.html

Zagaris B, MacDonald SB (1992) Money laundering, financial fraud, and technology: the perils of an instantaneous economy. George Washington J Int Law Econ 26(1):61–107

AI, Digital Assets, and the Environment

The Future of Crypto-Asset Mining: The Inflation Reduction Act and the Need for Uniform Federal Regulation

Liz S. Guinan

Abstract Crypto-asset mining is energy-intensive and environmentally harmful, presenting challenges and opportunities for federal, state and local governments, regulators, and society as a whole. As a result, effective regulatory frameworks are necessary to address the explosion of energy and environmental issues caused by crypto-asset miners, who are under pressure to maximize earnings by using less expensive carbon-emitting energy. To date, crypto-asset mining has not been governed by a federal regulatory framework, but instead by a patchwork of state-by-state responses that vary from highly restrictive, such as the moratoria proposed in New York. This chapter examines existing federal, state, and local regulatory schemes that directly or indirectly address the negative effects of crypto-asset mining. Although different state and local regulations attempt to strike a balance between reducing crypto-asset mining's negative environmental and energy consumption impact and retaining crypto's economic benefits, the country will continue to suffer from crypto-asset mining's severe energy and environmental consequences until there is a unified response.

1 Introduction

Since their inception in 2009 (Kaur 2024), crypto-assets, also known as digital or virtual currencies, have sparked considerable debate. These digital currencies are traded among users and generated through the use of complex algorithms and significant computational power underpinned by blockchain technology. This decentralized digital ledger facilitates secure asset ownership and transaction agreements among parties who might otherwise lack mutual trust.

This chapter includes material originally published in the Sustainable Development Law and Policy Brief [Vol.23/Issue 2, Spring 2023], republished with permission.

L. S. Guinan (✉)
Cole, Scott & Kissane, P.A., Miami, FL, USA
e-mail: liz.guinan@gmail.com

P. Babie and M. Giancaspro (eds.), *Private Law, Digital Assets, and Infrastructure*,
https://doi.org/10.1007/978-981-96-7121-2_11

Central to the debate around these digital currencies is the process of crypto-asset mining, a computationally intensive task essential for validating and creating new digital currency units. This process is underpinned by blockchain technology, a decentralized ledger that ensures transaction integrity across a network of users.

The environmental footprint of crypto-asset mining has come under scrutiny due to its substantial energy consumption, primarily driven by the Proof-of-Work (PoW) consensus mechanism (Nakamoto 2008). This has led to concerns over the sustainability of mining practices, particularly as operations often seek out the cheapest energy sources, which can include carbon-intensive fossil fuels. The result is a significant environmental impact characterized by high greenhouse gas emissions, electronic waste, and excessive water usage, raising public health and ecological concerns.

In response to these challenges, the United States has seen a piecemeal regulatory approach, with state and local governments implementing various measures to mitigate the environmental impact. However, the federal response has been more indirect, with initiatives like the Inflation Reduction Act of 2022 (Russo 2022) and Executive Order 14,067 (The White House 2022) focusing on broader energy and environmental standards rather than directly addressing crypto-asset mining. This fragmented regulatory landscape underscores the need for a unified approach that balances the economic benefits of crypto-assets with their environmental and energy implications.

This chapter explores the environmental and regulatory challenges surrounding crypto-asset mining, with a focus on the U.S. context. It contains four main parts. Section 1 introduces the rise of crypto-assets and the environmental consequences of their energy-intensive mining processes. Section 2 delves into the specific environmental impacts, such as greenhouse gas emissions, e-waste, and water consumption, associated with crypto-asset mining. Section 3 examines current regulatory responses, highlighting both state-level initiatives like New York's moratorium and federal efforts through the Inflation Reduction Act. Finally, Sect. 4 proposes a unified regulatory framework that addresses these environmental concerns, combining federal leadership with local solutions to promote sustainable crypto-asset mining practices.

2 Crypto-Asset's Energy and Environmental Impact

2.1 Overview of Crypto-Asset Mining

Bitcoin, created by Satoshi Nakamoto,[1] is considered the pioneer of digital currencies, building on ideas like "B-money" (Brito and Castillo 2016)[2] and "Bit Gold" from the 1990s (Sharma 2024). Ethereum (2024), with its Ether cryptocurrency, is another leading name, showcasing the capabilities of blockchain technology—a decentralized ledger that differs significantly from centralized databases by distributing information across all network nodes (Madhok 2022). There are three main ways to obtain crypto-assets: (1) directly by exchanging conventional currency and paying an exchange fee, (2) in exchange for a product or service, or (3) by mining crypto-assets (Garnett 2024).

The concept of mining crypto-assets gained traction after Nakamoto published the Bitcoin white paper in 2008, initiating mining operations in 2009 (Garnett 2024). Mining involves creating new crypto units and validating transactions on the blockchain, with miners motivated by rewards such as money, reputation, and stake in the network. The goal is to ensure transaction verification and network reliability.

Bitcoin and several other cryptocurrencies rely on the "proof-of-work" (PoW) consensus mechanism, where miners solve complex problems to earn the right to add the next block to the blockchain, receiving a block reward if successful (Napoletano 2023). However, PoW is criticized for its high energy consumption, which, despite its role in securing transactions and expanding the blockchain, raises concerns about its efficiency and environmental impact (Greenley and Clark 2019).

The origin of crypto-assets, particularly Bitcoin, marked the beginning of a new digital currency era, leveraging blockchain to facilitate secure and anonymous transactions. However, the energy-intensive nature of mining these assets, particularly through PoW, has raised significant concerns. Studies, including those from the University of Cambridge (2024) and the White House Office of Science and Technology Policy (2022), highlight the vast energy consumption and carbon emissions associated with crypto-asset mining, comparable to the energy usage of entire countries. The global Bitcoin hash rate has dramatically risen, doubling from the end of 2021 to July 2023 (Jenkinson 2024), indicating a significant increase in mining activity worldwide.

The infrastructure required for mining has evolved, with specialized hardware and cooling systems significantly increasing the energy demand. This has contributed to a substantial carbon footprint, leading to electronic waste, water use, and land degradation issues. The environmental and public health impacts necessitate reevaluating crypto-mining practices, emphasizing the importance of transitioning towards more sustainable and energy-efficient technologies.

[1] Satoshi Nakamoto is still unknown, and their exact identity and intentions for establishing Bitcoin are unclear.

[2] See also Nakamoto (2008).

2.2 Energy Use and Infrastructure Impacts

Crypto-asset mining, similar to traditional commodity mining, poses significant risks to energy consumption and the environment, challenging U.S. goals to mitigate greenhouse gas emissions and keep global warming under 1.5 degrees Celsius (Narayanan 2016). The energy demands of crypto-asset mining include the electricity used, timing, potential grid stress, energy sources, and the number and location of mining operations, all of which contribute to environmental concerns.

As of 2023, the annual global electricity consumption for Bitcoin mining was estimated at about 95.58 terawatt-hours (TWh) (Lepcha 2023). Bitcoin is projected to account for 60–77% of the global crypto-asset electricity usage (Gate Learn 2024), indicating a significant share of the crypto-mining industry's energy consumption. This represents an increase in energy consumption for crypto-asset mining, highlighting the industry's growing energy demands and its potential environmental impact.

Crypto-asset mining infrastructure primarily requires energy for operating blockchain validation devices and cooling systems to manage the heat generated. The energy demand escalates as the blockchain grows, with studies by Digiconomist and the Cambridge Bitcoin Energy Consumption Index (CBECI) (University of Cambridge 2024; Kohli et al. 2023)[3] in July 2021 estimating Bitcoin's energy consumption to be on par with countries like Sweden or Thailand, equivalent to the annual electricity usage of nearly 11 million U.S. households. This underscores the pressing need for more sustainable mining practices.

Initially, Bitcoin mining was possible with simple computer equipment. However, today's mining operations utilize advanced hardware like ASICs (KryptykHex 2020)[4] for higher efficiency, albeit with greater energy requirements and significant heat production, necessitating sophisticated cooling systems (Greenley and Clark 2019). This evolution has led to increased competition among miners and heightened concerns over the environmental toll of crypto-asset mining, highlighting the industry's substantial energy consumption and carbon footprint.

2.3 The Environmental and Public Health Effects

The environmental and public health consequences of crypto-asset mining can be divided into four categories; this section considers each in turn.

[3] See Digiconomist and the Cambridge Bitcoin Energy Consumption Index (CBECI) said that Bitcoin would use between 29.96 TWh and 135.12 TWh and between 26.41 TWh and 176.98 TWh of energy, which is the same amount of energy that Sweden and Thailand use.

[4] ASICs are built to perform the complex calculations required by the Proof of Work ("PoW") consensus algorithm, which is used by many cryptocurrencies including Bitcoin. These specialized chips are far more efficient than traditional computer hardware, allowing miners to mine cryptocurrencies at a much faster rate.

2.3.1 Greenhouse Gas Emissions

The environmental impacts of crypto-asset mining have continued to evolve, with a significant focus on greenhouse gas emissions (White House Office of Science and Technology Policy 2022: 25).[5] Recent analysis highlights the potential of using flared natural gas for Bitcoin mining as a way to reduce emissions. Currently, gas flaring contributes to approximately 406 million tons of CO_2 emissions annually (CoinShares 2024). However, utilizing this otherwise wasted flared gas for Bitcoin mining could potentially reduce these emissions to about 152 million tons of CO_2, indicating a significant opportunity for emission reduction in the sector (White House Office of Science and Technology Policy 2022: 25).[6]

2.3.2 Electronic Waste and Water Use

The issue of electronic waste (e-waste) remains critical, with mining hardware becoming obsolete every 1.5 years, leading to significant e-waste challenges (Courtillat–Piazza et al. 2024). The Bitcoin network alone generates an estimated 30.7 kilotons of e-waste annually (Jain 2022), contributing to the global e-waste problem. Furthermore, the use of water for cooling in some mining operations, such as those by power plants like Greenidge (Gopalakrishnan 2022), poses risks to local ecosystems, with large amounts of water drawn from natural sources and discharged at higher temperatures, endangering wildlife and ecology (Gopalakrishnan 2022).

2.3.3 Land Use

The land-use impact of crypto-asset mining operations has been a concern, particularly in regions like upstate New York, where converting power plants to mining operations could impede state efforts to eliminate greenhouse gas emissions. Europe, accounting for about 10% of world crypto mining (Smith-Meyer 2022), is seeing increased activity, particularly in Germany, Ireland, and Sweden, leading to potential policy actions to mitigate environmental impacts.

2.3.4 Noise Pollution

Noise pollution from mining operations continues to be a concern for both human health and wildlife, with the constant operation of high-velocity fans in air-cooled

[5] Citing World Business Council for Sustainable Development (2004).

[6] Citing Digiconomist (2024).

mining computers (Williams 2022).[7] This aspect of mining operations can lead to sleep disturbances, stress, reduced quality of life for humans (Williams 2022; Winotoatmojo et al. 2024), and potential negative effects on wildlife behavior and ecosystems.

2.3.5 Regulatory Actions and Sustainability Efforts

Efforts to address the environmental and public health impacts of crypto-asset mining are increasingly becoming a focus of regulatory actions and sustainability initiatives. The White House has called for crypto-mining standards to minimize environmental impact (De and Gkritsi 2022), urging for standards to reduce energy usage and promote transparency and sustainability in the sector. Furthermore, federal agencies are encouraged to gather data to monitor and mitigate crypto-assets' impacts, including setting energy conservation standards for mining equipment and operations.

Europe is also moving towards regulatory action to manage the environmental impact and energy use of crypto mining. The REPowerEU Plan (European Commission 2022) emphasizes controlling the ICT sector's energy consumption, including crypto mining, as part of the European Green Deal to fast-forward the clean transition in response to energy supply challenges.

These developments indicate a growing recognition of the environmental and public health challenges posed by crypto-asset mining and a concerted effort towards more sustainable practices and regulatory oversight to mitigate these impacts.

3 Existing Regulatory Responses to Crypto-Asset Mining

While state and local governments have taken steps to address the environmental impact of crypto-asset mining (Brown 2023), a cohesive federal strategy remains elusive. The Inflation Reduction Act and Executive Order 14067 (The White House 2022) represent initial steps towards understanding and potentially regulating the energy use of crypto-assets (*Inflation Reduction Act of 2022* 2022).

Over the past decade, the surge in cryptocurrency mining has garnered widespread attention and increasingly rigorous regulatory scrutiny. Notably, China once hosted around 75% of the global cryptocurrency mining operations, driven by an abundance of affordable, renewable energy, and government incentives designed to attract miners, predominantly those mining Bitcoin. However, by late 2021, China imposed stringent restrictions (Campbell 2021) on cryptocurrency mining and trading, virtually eradicating these activities within its borders.

As a result of China's stringent stance, the United States has emerged as the new epicenter for cryptocurrency mining, now contributing to over a third of Bitcoin's

[7] For a detailed discussion of the environmental impacts of crypto-asset mining, see Allen (2022).

total computational effort (Kearney 2024), known as the "hashrate." Texas, particularly, has seen a significant influx of cryptocurrency mining operations (Wilser 2023), attributed to its cost-effective energy solutions and a regulatory environment that favors cryptocurrency advancements. The state's proactive approach includes the early incorporation of cryptocurrency and blockchain technology into its commercial legislation, with leadership figures such as Governor Greg Abbott expressing ambitions for Texas to lead in the global cryptocurrency domain (Pollard 2021).

The expansion of cryptocurrency mining in the United States, especially through energy-intensive "proof-of-work" mining processes, has elicited criticism from various quarters. Critics argue that these operations place undue stress on electrical grids, elevate energy costs for local communities, and potentially increase reliance on non-renewable energy sources, counteracting efforts to reduce fossil fuel dependency.

In reaction to these concerns, legislators at the state and federal levels have been advocating for further research into the environmental impacts of cryptocurrency mining. They have proposed legislation to curb greenhouse gas emissions and overall energy consumption by mining operations, focusing on transitioning away from the "proof-of-work" mining model. This legislative focus (Parker 2021) underscores the growing call for a more sustainable approach to cryptocurrency mining in the United States.

The Biden Administration also released a report entitled "Climate and Energy Implications of Crypto-Assets in the United States" (White House Office of Science and Technology Policy 2022). The findings from the "Climate and Energy Implications of Crypto-Assets in the United States" report suggest a comprehensive approach towards mitigating the environmental impact of cryptocurrency mining. The report highlights the importance of establishing environmental and social standards through collaboration between federal entities such as the Environmental Protection Agency (EPA), the Department of Energy (DOE), state governments, local communities, and the cryptocurrency sector (The White House 2022).

These collaborations aim to develop environmental performance criteria that focus on reducing energy and water consumption, minimizing noise pollution, and encouraging the use of clean and zero-emission energy sources to mitigate the environmental footprint of crypto-assets. Additionally, the report emphasizes the need to ensure energy reliability by evaluating the impact of cryptocurrency mining on the electricity system's reliability and adequacy. It suggests that the DOE, in coordination with relevant commissions and corporations, should conduct reliability assessments and, if necessary, develop and enforce updated standards and emergency procedures.

The report also recommends collecting and analyzing data from cryptocurrency mining operations to inform policy decisions. This involves assessing mining energy usage, the fuel mix, and the environmental justice implications, among other factors, to understand crypto-assets' energy and climate implications more meaningfully.

Promoting energy efficiency through legislative and regulatory means is another key finding. The report calls for the administration to collaborate with Congress to enable the DOE and other regulatory bodies to introduce and regularly update energy efficiency regulations for mining hardware and blockchain operations.

Furthermore, the report advocates for transparency and enhancing environmental performance within the crypto-asset industry. It suggests that industry associations should publicly report mining locations, electricity usage, greenhouse gas emissions, and e-waste recycling efforts according to established protocols.

Finally, the report identifies the need for further research and innovation to improve the environmental sustainability of digital assets. It encourages federal research agencies to support the development of new methodologies for crypto-asset impact modeling, assessing environmental justice impacts, and exploring beneficial uses for grid management and environmental mitigation.

Yet, concrete actions, such as the Crypto-Asset Environmental Transparency Act (Markey 2023), face opposition, reflecting the complex balance between fostering innovation and ensuring environmental sustainability. The evolving regulatory discourse highlights the urgent need for comprehensive policies that address the unique challenges posed by crypto-asset mining while supporting the transition to greener energy sources.

The regulatory landscape for crypto-asset mining in the United States is complex and varied, reflecting a mix of state-level enthusiasm and concern over the industry's rapid growth, energy consumption, and environmental impact. In the absence of comprehensive federal regulations specifically targeting the energy use and emissions of crypto-asset mining, several states have stepped forward with their own approaches, each attempting to balance the economic opportunities the emerging industry presents with environmental and energy sustainability goals. The remainder of this part examines legislative actions and debates in specific states.

3.1 New York

New York has emerged as a pivotal battleground for crypto-asset mining regulation, particularly due to concerns over the environmental impact of using carbon-based energy sources for such energy-intensive operations. In November 2022, Governor Kathy Hochul signed a groundbreaking bill (Ferré-Sadurní and Ashford 2022: 2)[8] that prohibits the use of carbon-based power sources by some crypto-asset mining companies (Sigalos 2022b). This legislation, the first of its kind in the United States, imposes a two-year moratorium on granting permits for expansions or renewals to existing proof-of-work (PoW) crypto-asset mining operations that do not use renewable energy (Sigalos 2022b).

The bill was largely a response to public and environmentalist concerns over the operations of companies like Greenidge Generation, which had repurposed a dormant fossil fuel plant in the Finger Lakes region for crypto-asset mining (French 2022). Critics argue that such operations not only significantly increase carbon emissions

[8] Senate Bill S. 6486-D was passed by the New York State Senate in June 2022 and passed by the New York State Assembly in April 2022: (Parker 2021).

but also have adverse effects on local ecosystems, such as raising the temperature of nearby bodies of water, which can be detrimental to aquatic life (Sigalos 2022b).

3.2 *Texas*

In Texas, a significant portion of the United States' Bitcoin computational efforts, over 28% (Niiler 2023), is concentrated, showcasing the state's dominant role in the cryptocurrency mining industry. This information, highlighted by Foundry USA's Hashrate Map (Foundry 2023), positions Texas at the forefront, with other states like Georgia, New York, and New Hampshire also contributing, but to a lesser extent.

The landscape of Bitcoin mining across the United States has seen considerable shifts since December 2021, with Texas experiencing a substantial increase in its share of the national hash rate, a measure of the computational power used in mining and processing Bitcoin transactions. This change reflects a broader diversification across the United States, with more states participating in Bitcoin mining by 2023.

The global Bitcoin hash rate itself has seen a dramatic rise, doubling from the end of 2021 to July 2023, indicating a significant increase in mining activity worldwide. During a period in July 2023, Texas's reported hash rate was captured during a power curtailment phase (Pereira 2023: 30), suggesting that the actual figures might be higher than recorded. Power curtailment involves reducing mining activity to help balance the energy grid during peak demand times, demonstrating the mining community's adaptive strategies to energy consumption challenges.

3.3 *Wyoming*

In contrast to New York's regulatory stance, Wyoming has positioned itself as a haven for crypto-asset mining operations through a series of legislative efforts aimed at creating a favorable economic and regulatory environment (Dewey 2024).[9] The state has not required crypto-asset mining operations to register as Money Services Businesses, distinguishing these operations from traditional financial transaction intermediaries and thus subjecting them to fewer regulatory hurdles (Justia Law 2020). Although Wyoming considered establishing "industrial power zones" for deregulated energy consumption by large power consumers like crypto miners, this proposal did not pass (Bleizeffer 2022). Nevertheless, Wyoming's friendly stance towards crypto-assets extends beyond mining, with laws that exempt crypto-assets from property taxation, aiming to lower operational costs for miners and attract more such businesses to the state. Overall, the case in Wyoming may be the beginning of a "race to the bottom" among state regulators because of these regulatory exemptions and special deregulation zones (Reiners 2022).

[9] Explaining mining's legality depends on where one lives.

3.4 Montana

Montana has taken a nuanced approach (Morigeau 2019) to regulating crypto-asset mining, with a focus on promoting renewable energy. Missoula County, in particular, enacted zoning regulations requiring crypto-asset mining operations to develop or purchase renewable energy to offset their electricity consumption fully (Kidston 2021). This initiative aimed to mitigate the environmental impact of crypto mining and align with broader community goals for clean energy. However, the state legislature later passed a bill that effectively repealed these local zoning laws (Zolnikov 2023), reflecting the ongoing debate over the best ways to regulate the environmental impact of crypto mining while supporting economic development.

3.5 Washington

Washington State has been another significant hub for crypto-asset mining, thanks to its abundant and cheap hydroelectric power. The state and its Public Utility Districts (PUDs) have taken steps to manage the increased energy demand from mining operations (Denkmann and Cowan 2023) through revised electricity rate-design measures and the introduction of clean energy standards. These efforts aim to ensure that the crypto-mining industry contributes its fair share to the state's energy infrastructure and environmental goals. For example, the Chelan County PUD adjusted its rate structure (Rachel Hansen 2023) to impose higher fees on crypto miners, reflecting the industry's intensive energy use.

3.6 Overall Implications

The contrasting approaches of states like New York, Wyoming, Montana, and Washington illustrate the broader challenges and debates surrounding crypto-asset mining regulation in the United States. As states navigate the trade-offs between fostering innovation and economic growth and addressing environmental and energy concerns, the evolving regulatory landscape underscores the need for informed, balanced policies that can accommodate the unique aspects of the crypto-asset mining industry.

Notably, Texas has become a hub for cryptocurrency mining operations, attributed to its relatively low energy costs and a regulatory environment conducive to mining activities. The state's electricity prices are notably below the national average, offering significant cost savings for energy-intensive operations like cryptocurrency mining. This competitive advantage has attracted numerous large mining operations to Texas, especially following regulatory crackdowns in other parts of the world, such as China.

Texas's approach to managing the energy demands of Bitcoin mining includes incentive programs for major energy consumers, including miners, to modulate their energy usage. Companies participating in these programs, like Riot Platforms, have benefited financially through power credits (Gkritsi 2023a, 2023b) for reducing their energy consumption during critical periods, further integrating the cryptocurrency mining industry into the state's energy ecosystem.

Whether through direct regulation of energy sources, incentives for renewable energy use, or adjustments to tax and zoning laws, state legislatures and regulators are at the forefront of shaping the future of crypto-asset mining in the United States. However, is this fragmented approach sufficient? The following section explores the need for a comprehensive, unified regulatory framework.

4 Proposal for a Unified Regulatory Scheme

The lack of standardized U.S. laws on crypto-asset mining's energy and environmental impacts has led to disparate state regulations. A unified federal regulatory scheme is necessary to address these concerns. This section considers a proposal, divided into two parts: a federal response in the form of the Inflation Reduction Act (IRA) and state and local government tools in the absence of federal leadership.

4.1 The IRA and Federal Regulatory Tools

Federal strategies to mitigate crypto-asset mining's negative impacts include: tax credits (Deloitte 2022) and incentives, carbon-based energy source taxation (Deloitte 2022),[10] energy conservation (Department of Energy 2014),[11] efficiency standards (Scott 2016),[12] performance standards (Environmental Protection Agency 2024),[13] and waste and water limits.[14] The IRA, signed by President Biden, is a significant climate initiative offering incentives for clean energy, potentially benefiting crypto

[10] Considering the role of excise tax credits provided by the Inflation Reduction Act.

[11] Noting that in response to stakeholder comments, DOE clarified that the proposed scope of coverage for computer and battery backup systems would only apply to consumer products (and not commercial products).

[12] The Federal Data Center Consolidation Initiative ("FDCCI") succeeded the Data Center Cost Initiative ("DCOI") in 2016. According to the FDCCI and the DCOI, government agencies must develop and report on strategies "to consolidate inefficient infrastructure, optimize existing facilities, improve security posture, realize cost savings, and transition to more efficient infrastructure."

[13] Describing that a "standard of performance" is defined as the "degree of emission limitation achievable through the application of the best system of emission reduction which... the Administrator determines has been 'adequately demonstrated.'"

[14] The Resource Conservation and Recovery Act ("RCRA") is a federal law in the United States that was enacted in 1976. The purpose of the law is to protect public health and the environment from the potential hazards of waste disposal by regulating the generation, transportation, treatment,

mining by promoting renewable energy use. Federal actions, like excise taxes on carbon-based energy, aim to make renewable sources more attractive for mining operations.

4.1.1 Federal Energy and Environmental Standards

Attention has focused on DOE and EPA measures, like energy conservation and efficiency standards, to curb crypto mining's energy use. Voluntary programs like ENERGY STAR and mandatory standards could reduce mining's energy consumption (*Energy Policy and Conservation Act of 1975* 1975: §6294(a)(2)(I)).[15] The Clean Air Act's new source performance standards could enforce emissions limits on mining operations, promoting cleaner energy sources.

4.1.2 Federal Waste and Water Regulations

No specific federal waste disposal rules for crypto mining exist, but operations must comply with existing hazardous waste regulations. Water usage is similarly unregulated, but mining discharges are subject to the Clean Water Act, ensuring they meet quality standards.

4.2 State and Local Regulatory Options

States and localities have developed various approaches to mitigate mining's impacts, including bans, rate designs, zoning, demand response programs, and permitting requirements. Moratoria could push miners towards renewable energy or out of state, impacting local economies. Encouraging renewable energy use in mining aligns with broader climate change mitigation efforts, though transitioning poses challenges like higher costs and infrastructure needs.

4.2.1 Ban or Moratoria on Crypto-Asset Mining

A moratorium on crypto-asset mining could lead to diverse outcomes: some miners might adopt renewable energy, others might relocate, while the rest could halt operations (Sigalos 2022a, 2022b). Given the industry's preference for predictability,

storage, and disposal of hazardous waste. See (*Resource Conservation and Recovery Act* 1976: §6901). Also, the Safe Drinking Water Act ("SDWA") is a federal law enacted in 1974 to protect public health by ensuring the safety of public drinking water supplies throughout the United States. The EPA is in charge of enforcing the law. See (Safe Drinking Water Act 1974: §300 g-1).

[15] Describing the labeling requirements for computers and computer monitors.

such a moratorium could significantly disrupt mining activities, especially at this early stage (Sigalos 2022a, 2022b). This disruption extends beyond the immediate operations to impact investment in sustainable energy sources and the economic well-being of communities reliant on mining for employment opportunities in fields like engineering and construction.

Crypto-asset miner migration, spurred by bans or moratoria, risks job losses and reduced tax revenue, particularly in regions like New York, which has seen its share of the crypto-mining network halve following legislative actions (Sigalos 2022a, 2022b). This exodus to more mining-friendly states, such as Texas and Georgia, underscores the potential economic fallout for areas imposing strict regulations. Critics, including industry insiders and politicians, warn of the adverse economic effects and the perception of hostility towards the blockchain industry, which could stifle its growth and innovation within affected regions.

Conversely, restrictions on crypto mining using carbon-based fuels could drive a transition towards renewable energy sources, aligning with broader environmental goals. This shift not only addresses the significant energy demands and carbon emissions associated with mining but also presents an opportunity to bolster the renewable energy sector through increased demand, innovation, and investment. However, transitioning to renewable energy is complex, potentially costly, and fraught with challenges, including reliability issues and the need for new infrastructure to support widespread renewable energy adoption.

4.2.2 Electricity Rate-Design Measures

Local governments, like Chelan County, Washington, have started implementing special electricity rate increases targeted at crypto-asset miners to reflect the actual cost of power consumption and mitigate environmental impacts. Chelan County introduced a new rate (Rate 36) on June 1, 2022, increasing costs by twenty-nine percent specifically for crypto miners, transitioning from a previously lower rate designed for high-density loads (Elliott 2022). This move aims to cover the true costs associated with crypto mining's energy demands and generate additional revenue while encouraging environmental sustainability. The county also offers transition plans allowing existing mining operations to gradually adjust to the new rates, balancing economic development with environmental and infrastructure concerns.

Despite these efforts, there are concerns within the crypto industry about the feasibility and complexity of transitioning, including potential requirements for new investments in equipment and training. Malachi Salcido, a crypto-mining CEO, mentioned that the new rates would compel a shift from crypto mining to data processing operations in some of his facilities, indicating a possible trend towards diversification and innovation in the tech sector beyond just crypto mining (Roberts 2022). This approach by Chelan County could serve as a model for other regions seeking to regulate crypto mining's energy use while fostering technological advancement and environmental stewardship.

4.2.3 Zoning and Land-Use Measures

States and local governments are increasingly exploring innovative zoning and land-use regulations to manage crypto-asset mining operations. These efforts aim to address the unique challenges posed by crypto mining, such as energy consumption, noise pollution, and safety concerns in residential areas.

Missoula County, Montana, and Wyoming provide contrasting approaches to crypto-mining regulation through zoning laws.[16] Missoula County attempted to mitigate the environmental impact of crypto mining by enforcing conditional use zoning laws that required miners to offset 100% of their electricity consumption with renewable energy. However, this stringent requirement, aimed at combating climate change, was later overturned by the state of Montana (Gkritsi 2023a, 2023b). This illustrates the difficulty of enforcing local environmental standards on crypto-mining operations, especially when juxtaposed with states like Texas, which incentivizes crypto mining with lower costs and fewer regulations.

On the other hand, Wyoming considered the creation of "innovation zones" or "economic development zones" specifically designed for high-energy-consuming industries, including crypto mining. These zones aim to attract high-tech industries by offering lower energy costs and simplified regulatory processes, leveraging Wyoming's abundant wind power to fuel economic growth and job creation. While supporters argue that these deregulated zones could spur innovation and technological advancement, critics raise concerns about the environmental impacts of large-scale crypto-mining operations, especially in states grappling with climate change. While some lawmakers supported these zones, they ultimately were not established.

These examples highlight the ongoing debate among policymakers, industry leaders, and environmental advocates on how to balance economic development with environmental sustainability in the rapidly evolving field of crypto-asset mining. The success of these regulatory experiments remains to be seen, but they represent important discussions on the future of crypto mining and its place within local and state economies.

4.2.4 Demand Response and Large Flexible Load Registration Programs

Demand Response Programs (DRP) and Large Flexible Load Registration (LFLR) programs are initiatives aimed at optimizing the electricity grid's functionality but differ in their approach, scope, and target participants (Trabish 2023). DRPs incentivize consumers, including crypto miners, to reduce electricity usage during peak demand periods through financial rewards (Chernis 2022). These programs aim to mitigate the environmental impact of activities like crypto mining by easing

[16] For Montana, see Missoula County (2011); Missoula County Community and Planning Services (2021).

grid strain during high-demand times, offering lower rates for off-peak usage as a motivator.

Conversely, LFLR programs target large energy consumers, such as factories, data centers, and crypto miners, offering incentives to adjust their energy consumption in response to grid needs, which helps in preventing grid instability. In regions like Texas, legislation like Senate Bill 1751 (Kolkhorst et al. 2023) could require crypto miners to register as "flexible load" operators, suggesting a more formal regulatory move towards integrating large energy consumers into grid management strategies. However, the bill was stopped in a House committee in 2023 (Gkritsi 2023a, 2023b).

While both programs share the goal of enhancing grid efficiency and stability, DRPs focus on broad consumer participation in energy savings, whereas LFLR programs are tailored towards large-scale consumers with the capacity for significant load adjustments. The success of integrating crypto-mining operations into these programs hinges on overcoming challenges such as the difficulty in reducing energy use due to the continuous and intensive nature of mining activities and the decentralized, anonymous structure of the Bitcoin network.

4.2.5 Permitting and Licensing Requirements

State and local governments may require crypto-asset mining operations to obtain permits and licenses in order to ensure compliance with state and local regulations, as well as to monitor and mitigate any potential negative effects. Assessing the environmental impact, energy usage, safety measures, and adherence to building codes may all be part of the permitting process. Several states and local governments have enacted regulations requiring crypto-asset mining operations to obtain permits and licenses, ensuring regulatory compliance and mitigating potential negative effects.

For instance, the New York State Department of Environmental Conservation requires an environmental impact assessment and proof of compliance with air quality standards (Clean Air Act Title V air permit) for crypto-asset mining operations in the state (New York State Department of Environmental Conservation 2024a, 2024b). Another example is Washington State Department of Ecology oversees environmental permitting and may require crypto-asset mining operations to obtain permits related to water use, wastewater discharge, and stormwater management (Washington State Department of Ecology 2024). These examples demonstrate how state and local governments can regulate crypto-asset mining operations and ensure compliance with environmental, energy, safety, and building code regulations through permitting and licensing processes.

4.2.6 Waste Disposal Requirements and Water Usage Limits

Overall, waste disposal requirements for crypto-asset mining operations can vary depending on the jurisdiction but many jurisdictions have waste disposal requirements in place to ensure that crypto-asset mining operations are properly disposing of their waste. Several state and local governments in the United States currently have waste disposal requirements for crypto-asset mining. These requirements can include regulations around the disposal of e-waste, such as requiring crypto-asset mining companies to recycle or properly dispose of their old mining equipment.

However, there are no specific state-level regulations in the United States concerning the disposal of heat waste generated by crypto-asset mining operations; although, some states, such as New York (Parker 2021) or Wyoming, are taking steps to encourage the use of excess heat for other purposes. As a result, some crypto-asset mining companies have developed innovative ways to use the heat generated by their operations to heat neighboring buildings or greenhouses (Lyon 2023).

In addition to waste disposal requirements, regulations regarding water usage in crypto-asset mining operations are not yet widespread; however, some jurisdictions are beginning to address the issue of water conservation and management in relation to these operations. In particular, New York (New York State Department of Environmental Conservation 2024a, 2024b)[17] and Montana (Zolnikov 2023) have implemented regulations limiting the amount of water that can be used for crypto-asset mining operations, particularly in areas where water resources are scarce, or water conservation is a concern (Collins 2023).[18]

As the energy and environmental impacts of crypto-asset mining become more widely recognized, more jurisdictions may begin to implement more innovative regulations that balance the economic benefits of crypto-asset mining with the energy and environmental implications. As a result, ongoing debates are required to determine which regulatory approach—federal, state, or local—will produce the best results in terms of balancing all interests.

4.2.7 State Tax Incentives and Exemptions

The taxation of crypto-asset mining at the state and local levels varies depending on the jurisdiction, but in general, it is similar to the taxation of any other business activity. As a result, the Multistate Tax Commission (MTC) launched an investigation into crypto-asset issues in 2021 (Hamilton 2021) as part of its review of state taxation of digital products and services from both an income and a sales/use tax standpoint (Hamilton 2021). Presently, in the United States, for example, earning crypto-assets through mining, receiving them as a promotion, or receiving them as payment for goods or services is considered regular taxable income (Rodeck 2022). The entire fair market value of the coins you received that day will be taxed at a regular income tax rate (Rodeck 2022). Furthermore, if you own the mining equipment, you may be

[17] Imposing regulations pertaining to water usage and requiring an environmental impact statement for new permits and developments in the crypto-asset mining industry.

[18] Noting that "while policymakers and cryptocurrency companies recognize mining's impact on energy systems and carbon emissions, there has been little to no reflection regarding its impact on water resources."

subject to property taxes; however, in some cases, the cost of your mining equipment can be written off as a deduction in the year of purchase (Brooks 2024).

Texas, for example, has taken a pro-business stance by rewarding cryptocurrency miners who use carbon-based or low-carbon energy sources (including renewable) (Green and Kazi 2022). However, due to the low cost of carbon-based energy, crypto-asset miners continue to rely on it (Green and Kazi 2022). Moreover, here are a few examples of Texas' crypto-asset mining tax initiatives include: (1) sales tax exemption,[19] (2) competitive electricity rates (Green and Kazi 2022),[20] (3) property tax exemptions (Green and Kazi 2022),[21] and (4) job creation incentives. Other states, such as Kentucky, are catching up with tax incentives and offering even more than Texas, including (1) sales tax exemption,[22] (2) competitive electricity rates (Lawrence 2021),[23] (3) business investment tax credits (Lawrence 2021),[24] (4) job creation incentives,[25] and (5) workforce development programs (Team Kentucky Cabinet for Economic Development 2022). Even though the state of Kentucky is transitioning to renewable sources of energy, most crypto-asset mining operations in the state still rely on the state's carbon-intensive electrical grid (Team Kentucky Cabinet for Economic Development 2022).

5 Conclusion

The United States is still in a phase of evolving and contentious debate regarding the regulation of cryptocurrency and crypto-asset mining, with significant developments expected beyond 2024. The U.S. Congress is grappling with crypto regulation (Yaffe-Bellany 2023), indicating that a comprehensive regulatory framework is unlikely to be established before 2025. This situation allows for continued emergence of court rulings and agency policies that will shape the landscape in the interim.

---

[19] Texas offers a sales tax exemption for equipment used in the mining of cryptocurrencies. This means that crypto-asset mining companies in Texas can save on the cost of purchasing mining equipment. See Grant II (2023).

[20] Recognizing Texas' historically low costs of electricity, making it an attractive destination for energy-intensive industries like crypto-asset mining.

[21] Recommending property tax abatements to crypto-asset mining facilities to spur the growth of the Texas market.

[22] See Rudy et al. (2021): Providing for sales and use tax exemptions for commercial mining of cryptocurrency; (Smith 2021): Providing tax exemptions for purchase of equipment to construct, retrofit, or upgrade commercial crypto-asset mining equipment; Glickman (2021): Recognizing enactment of two bills above.

[23] Claiming Kentucky can provide electricity at lower rates than most other states.

[24] Recognizing the importance of treating cryptocurrency like traditional manufacturing and industrial facilities to support continued development.

[25] See Smith (2021): Declaring it in the best interest of Kentucky to offer job creation incentives to bring crypto-asset mining companies to the state.

Efforts to harmonize securities laws with blockchain technology have seen the SEC proposing amendments to redefine terms such as "exchange" and "dealer," which could have profound implications for decentralized finance (DeFi) (Dewey 2024). These changes suggest an attempt to integrate traditional securities laws with the realities of peer-to-peer networks and could significantly impact how crypto and DeFi operations are conducted, potentially requiring many to register as dealers and become members of regulatory bodies like FINRA.

In the realm of environmental regulation, the Crypto-Asset Environmental Transparency Act (Markey 2023), reintroduced by Senator Edward J. Markey and Representative Jared Huffman,.aims to crack down on the environmental impacts of crypto mining. This legislation requires large crypto-mining operations to disclose their emissions and calls for a comprehensive investigation by the EPA into the industry's environmental effects. This act highlights the growing concern over the substantial energy consumption and greenhouse gas emissions associated with crypto mining.

At the state and local levels, some governments have already begun to take action against the environmental impacts of crypto mining. The fact that New York has temporarily banned new crypto-mining operations that do not use renewable energy reflects a proactive approach to mitigating environmental concerns.

These developments indicate a complex and fragmented regulatory environment for crypto-assets in the United States, spanning both financial and environmental domains. The need for a unified federal regulatory framework remains a critical discussion point. However, ongoing legal, environmental, and policy considerations at the national and state levels will likely influence the pace and direction of regulatory evolution.

References

Allen J (2022) Is Bitcoin the new gold? the two may be more similar than you think, including their value, uses, and deleterious effects on the environment. Barry l Env't & Earth LJ 12:65

Bleizeffer D (2022) Deregulated power zones lose legislative energy, WyoFile, http://wyofile.com/deregulated-power-zones-lose-legislative-energy/, accessed 12 November 2024

Brito J, Castillo A (2016) Bitcoin: a primer for policymakers. Mercatus Center, George Mason University, Arlington, Arlington, Virginia

Brooks M (2024) Crypto mining taxes: Beginner's guide 2024, CoinLedger, https://coinledger.io/blog/how-to-handle-cryptocurrency-mining-on-your-taxes, accessed 12 November 2024

Brown A (2023) States debate whether to restrict—Or invite—Crypto mining • stateline, Stateline, https://stateline.org/2023/03/21/states-debate-whether-to-restrict-or-invite-crypto-mining/, accessed 12 November 2024

Campbell C (2021) Why China is cracking down on Bitcoin mining and what it could mean for other countries, TIME, https://time.com/6051991/why-china-is-cracking-down-on-bitcoin-mining-and-what-it-could-mean-for-other-countries/, accessed 12 November 2024

Chernis D (2022) Demand response provides a competitive edge through optimal crypto mining energy consumption, CPower Energy, https://cpowerenergy.com/demand-response-provides-a-competitive-edge-through-optimal-crypto-mining-energy-consumption/, accessed 12 November 2024

CoinShares (2024) CoinShares 2024 mining report, CoinShares, https://coinshares.com/resources/research/2024-mining-report/, accessed 12 November 2024

Collins C (2023) Where cryptocurrency, water and conflict collide, United States Institute of Peace, https://www.usip.org/publications/2023/03/where-cryptocurrency-water-and-conflict-collide, accessed 12 November 2024

Courtillat-Piazza L, Pirson T, Golard L, Bol D (2024) A cradle-to-gate life cycle analysis of bitcoin mining equipment using sphera LCA and ecoinvent databases. https://doi.org/10.48550/ARXIV.2401.17512

De N, Gkritsi E (2022) White House calls for crypto mining standards to minimize environmental impact, CoinDesk, https://www.coindesk.com/policy/2022/09/08/crypto-mining-energy-implications-need-further-study-white-house-report-says/, accessed 12 November 2024

Deloitte (2022) Inflation Reduction Act reinstates excise tax credits and Superfund excise tax, https://www2.deloitte.com/content/dam/Deloitte/us/Documents/Tax/us-tax-inflation-reduction-act-reinstates-excise-tax-credits-and-superfund-excise-tax.pdf

Denkmann L, Cowan A (2023) When power is cheap, crypto moves in. The fallout in rural WA is complex, KUOW, https://www.kuow.org/stories/small-town-surge-rural-washington, accessed 12 November 2024

Department of Energy (2014) Energy conservation program: proposed determination of computer and battery backup systems as a covered consumer product, https://www.federalregister.gov/documents/2014/02/28/2014-04423/energy-conservation-program-proposed-determination-of-computer-and-battery-backup-systems-as-a

Dewey JN (2024) Blockchain & cryptocurrency laws and regulations 2025, GLI, https://www.globallegalinsights.com/practice-areas/blockchain-cryptocurrency-laws-and-regulations/, accessed 12 November 2024

Digiconomist (2024) Bitcoin Energy Consumption Index, Digiconomist, https://digiconomist.net/bitcoin-energy-consumption/, accessed 12 November 2024

Elliott S (2022) Bitcoin miners will see 29% rate hike on hydroelectric power in Washington, Decrypt, https://decrypt.co/102420/bitcoin-miners-will-see-29-rate-hike-hydroelectric-power-washington, accessed 12 November 2024

Energy Policy and Conservation Act of 1975, 42 U.S.C. (1975)

Environmental Protection Agency (2024) Standards of performance for new, reconstructed, and modified sources and emissions guidelines for existing sources: oil and natural gas sector climate review: correction, https://www.federalregister.gov/documents/2024/08/01/2024-13206/standards-of-performance-for-new-reconstructed-and-modified-sources-and-emissions-guidelines-for

Ethereum (2024) Ethereum Whitepaper, Ethereum, https://ethereum.org/en/whitepaper/, accessed 12 November 2024

European Commission (2022) REPowerEU, European Commission, https://commission.europa.eu/strategy-and-policy/priorities-2019-2024/european-green-deal/repowereu-affordable-secure-and-sustainable-energy-europe_en, accessed 12 November 2024

Ferré-Sadurní L and Ashford G (2022) New York enacts 2-year ban on some crypto-mining operations, The New York Times, https://www.nytimes.com/2022/11/22/nyregion/crypto-mining-ban-hochul.html, accessed 12 November 2024

Foundry (2023) Foundry USA pool hashrate by state. Foundry, https://medium.com/foundry-digital/foundry-usa-pool-hashrate-by-state-f9dc92e7bc3b, accessed 12 November 2024

French MJ (2022) Hochul administration moves to shut gas powered cryptocurrency plant, POLITICO, https://www.politico.com/news/2022/06/30/hochul-administration-moves-to-shut-gas-powered-cryptocurrency-plant-00043497, accessed 12 November 2024

Garnett AG (2024) How to invest in cryptocurrency, Investopedia, https://www.investopedia.com/investing-in-cryptocurrency-5215269, accessed 12 November 2024

Gate Learn (2024) 60+ Bitcoin mining and energy consumption statistics for 2023 you need to know, Gate Learn, https://www.gate.io/learn/articles/60-bitcoin-mining-and-energy-consumption-statistics-for-2023-you-need-to-know/1265, accessed 12 November 2024

Gkritsi E (2023a) Montana Senate passes bill protecting crypto miners, CoinDesk, https://www.coindesk.com/policy/2023/02/23/montana-senate-passes-bill-protecting-crypto-miners/, accessed 12 November 2024
Gkritsi E (2023b) Texas bill that would limit miners' participation in cost-saving grid programs stopped in house committee, CoinDesk, https://www.coindesk.com/policy/2023/05/30/texas-bill-that-would-limit-miners-participation-in-cost-saving-grid-programs-stopped-in-house-committee/, accessed 12 November 2024
Gkritsi E (2023c) Riot platforms at the heart of Texas' debate over Bitcoin mining's effect on the grid, CoinDesk, https://www.coindesk.com/consensus-magazine/2023/07/25/riot-platforms-at-the-heart-of-a-texas-debate-over-bitcoin-minings-effect-on-the-grid/, accessed 12 November 2024
Glickman J (2021) Cryptocurrency miners are now eligible for Kentucky tax incentives, Aprio, https://www.aprio.com/cryptocurrency-miners-are-now-eligible-for-kentucky-tax-incentives/, accessed 12 November 2024
Gopalakrishnan S (2022) In the Finger Lakes, a cryptocurrency mining plant billed as 'green' has a dirty coal ash problem, Energy News Network, http://energynews.us/2022/08/25/in-the-finger-lakes-a-bitcoin-mining-plant-billed-as-green-has-a-dirty-coal-ash-problem/, accessed 12 November 2024
Grant II GA (2023) No tax on crypto purchases—Texas proposals go big on digital assets, Forbes, https://www.forbes.com/sites/digital-assets/2023/02/14/no-tax-on-crypto-purchases---texas-goes-big-on-digital-assets/, accessed 12 November 2024
Green D, Kazi S (2022) Cryptocurrency in Texas, Comptroller.Texas.Gov, https://comptroller.texas.gov/economy/fiscal-notes/archive/2022/aug/crypto-tx.php, accessed 12 November 2024
Greenley HL, Clark CE (2019) Bitcoin, blockchain, and the energy sector, Congressional Research Service
Hamilton A (2021) MTC to begin exploring cryptocurrency issues. Tax Notes Federal, 171(Doc. 2021-20849):1486
Inflation Reduction Act of 2022, Pub. L. No. 117-169, 136 Stat. 1818 (2022)
Jain R (2022) Bitcoin mining generates 30.7 kilotons e-waste annually—enough to cover Luxembourg's e-waste five times | Business Insider India, Business Insider, https://www.businessinsider.in/cryptocurrency/news/bitcoin-mining-generates-30-7-kilotons-e-waste-annually-enough-to-cover-luxembourgs-e-waste-five-times/articleshow/91764218.cms, accessed 12 November 2024
Jenkinson G (2024) Bitcoin mining battles 2023—Surging hash rates test industry limits, Cointelegraph, https://cointelegraph.com/news/2023-bitcoin-mining-review-miners-battle-record-hash-rates-difficulty, accessed 12 November 2024
Justia Law (2020) Wyoming statutes annotated § 40-22-104, Justia Law, https://law.justia.com/codes/wyoming/title-40/chapter-22/section-40-22-104/, accessed 12 November 2024
Kaur G (2024) How and when did Bitcoin start? The complete Bitcoin history, Cointelegraph, https://cointelegraph.com/learn/the-history-of-bitcoin-when-did-bitcoin-start, accessed 12 November 2024
Kearney L (2024) Crypto miner lawsuit sets back US effort to track booming power use, Reuters, https://www.reuters.com/legal/crypto-miner-lawsuit-sets-back-us-effort-track-booming-power-use-2024-02-28/, accessed 12 November 2024
Kidston M (2021) Missoula County clamps down on crypto mining; requires 100% new renewable power, KPAX News, https://www.kpax.com/news/missoula-county/missoula-county-clamps-down-on-crypto-mining-requires-100-new-renewable-power, accessed 12 November 2024
Kohli V, Chakravarty S, Chamola V, Sangwan KS, Zeadally S (2023) An analysis of energy consumption and carbon footprints of cryptocurrencies and possible solutions. Digital Communications and Networks 9(1):79–89. https://doi.org/10.1016/j.dcan.2022.06.017
Kolkhorst L, Campbell D, Nichols R (2023) A bill to be entitled, https://capitol.texas.gov/tlodocs/88R/billtext/pdf/SB01751I.pdf

KryptykHex (2020) The astonishing speed increase of Bitcoin ASIC miners, D-Central, https://d-central.tech/the-astonishing-speed-increase-of-bitcoin-asic-miners/, accessed 12 November 2024
Lawrence K (2021) Kentucky Bill offers incentives for cryptocurrency mining, GovTech, https://www.govtech.com/policy/Kentucky-Bill-Offers-Incentives-for-Cryptocurrency-Mining.html, accessed 12 November 2024
Lepcha M (2023) 60+ Bitcoin mining and energy consumption statistics for 2024. Techopedia, https://www.techopedia.com/bitcoin-mining-and-energy-statistics, accessed 12 November 2024
Lyon J (2023) Brooklyn Bitcoin spa leaves crypto watchers hot and bothered, Protos, http://protos.com/brooklyn-bitcoin-spa-leaves-crypto-watchers-hot-and-bothered/, accessed 12 November 2024
Madhok D (2022) The world's second biggest cryptocurrency just got a lot greener | CNN Business, CNN, https://www.cnn.com/2022/09/15/tech/ethereum-merge-crytocurrency-energy-consumption-hnk-intl/index.html, accessed 12 November 2024
Markey EJ (2023) Crypto-Asset Environmental Transparency Act of 2023, https://www.markey.senate.gov/imo/media/doc/crypto-asset_environmental_transparency_act_-_march_2023pdf.pdf
Missoula County (2011) Cryptocurrency mining, Missoula County, https://www.missoulacounty.us/government/community-development/community-planning-services/planning-projects/cryptocurrency
Missoula County Community and Planning Services (2021) Crypto-asset mining zoning regulations. https://www.missoulacounty.us/home/showpublisheddocument/75210/637666330170030000
Morigeau S (2019) An act relating to cryptocurrency; Amending EXEMPT4 transactions from certain securities law; Allowing certain digital transactions; 5 Amending Section 30-10-105, MCA; and providing an effective date, https://archive.legmt.gov/bills/2019/billpdf/HB0584.pdf
Nakamoto S (2008) Bitcoin: a peer-to-peer electronic cash system.
Napoletano E (2023) Proof of work explained, Forbes Advisor, https://www.forbes.com/advisor/investing/cryptocurrency/proof-of-work/, accessed 12 November 2024
Narayanan A (2016) Bitcoin and cryptocurrency technologies: a comprehensive introduction. Princeton University Press, Princeton
New York State Department of Environmental Conservation (2024a) Air permits and registrations, New York State Department of Environmental Conservation, https://dec.ny.gov/regulatory/permits-licenses/air, accessed 12 November 2024
New York State Department of Environmental Conservation (2024b) Recycling consumer electronic waste, New York State Department of Environmental Conservation, https://dec.ny.gov/environmental-protection/recycling-composting/electronic-waste-recycling/recycling-consumer-electronic-waste, accessed 12 November 2024
Niiler E (2023) Bitcoin mining used more water than New York City last year, Wall Street Journal, https://www.wsj.com/science/environment/bitcoin-water-cryptocurrency-transactions-mining-607f46e9, accessed 12 November 2024
Parker KS (2021) Senate Bill S6486D, https://www.nysenate.gov/legislation/bills/2021/S6486
Pereira AP (2023) Texas is home to nearly 30% of all Bitcoin hash rate—Foundry, Cointelegraph, https://cointelegraph.com/news/texas-home-nearly-30-percent-bitcoin-hash-rate-foundry, accessed 12 November 2024
Pollard J (2021) Texas Republicans want to make the state the center of the cryptocurrency universe, The Texas Tribune, https://www.texastribune.org/2021/10/28/texas-republicans-blockchain-bitcoin/, accessed 12 November 2024
Rachel Hansen (2023) 'A fair shake': Chelan PUD commissioners update crypto, data center rates, Chelan County PUD, https://www.chelanpud.org/about-us/our-commissioners/commission-meeting-news/2023/08/21/a-fair-shake-chelan-pud-commissioners-update-crypto-data-center-rates, accessed 12 November 2024
Reiners L (2022) More crypto craziness in Wyoming. The FinReg Blog, https://sites.duke.edu/thefinregblog/2022/02/11/more-crypto-craziness-in-wyoming/, accessed 12 November 2024
Resource Conservation and Recovery Act, 42 U.S.C. (1976)

Roberts P (2022) Thrill is gone for Central WA's once-hot crypto industry, The Seattle Times, https://www.seattletimes.com/business/bloom-is-off-eastern-washingtons-once-hot-crypto-industry/, accessed 12 November 2024
Rodeck D (2022) Cryptocurrency taxes of November 2024, Forbes Advisor, https://www.forbes.com/advisor/taxes/cryptocurrency-taxes/, accessed 12 November 2024
Rudy S, Freeland C, Flannery P (2021) An act relating to the taxation of the commercial mining of cryptocurrency, https://apps.legislature.ky.gov/record/21rs/hb230.html
Russo A (2022) The Inflation Reduction Act and its $10 billion impact on crypto. Crypto Council for Innovation, https://cryptoforinnovation.org/the-inflation-reduction-act-and-its-10-billion-impact-on-crypto/, accessed 12 November 2024
Safe Drinking Water Act, 42 U.S.C. (1974)
Scott T (2016) Memorandum from the Federal Chief Information Officer, Tony Scott, on Data center optimization initiative to the heads of executive departments and agencies, https://obamawhitehouse.archives.gov/sites/default/files/omb/memoranda/2016/m_16_19_1.pdf
Sharma R (2024) Bit gold: Meaning, overview, and differences from Bitcoin, Investopedia, https://www.investopedia.com/terms/b/bit-gold.asp, accessed 12 November 2024
Sigalos M (2022a) Lawmaker who wrote New York crypto mining bill explains: 'It's not a ban', CNBC, https://www.cnbc.com/2022/06/04/new-york-crypto-mining-bill-senator-anna-kelles-interview.html, accessed 12 November 2024
Sigalos M (2022b) New York governor signs first-of-its-kind law cracking down on Bitcoin mining—here's everything that's in it, CNBC, https://www.cnbc.com/2022/11/23/new-york-governor-signs-law-cracking-down-on-bitcoin-mining.html, accessed 12 November 2024
Smith B (2021) An Act relating to commercial mining of cryptocurrency, https://apps.legislature.ky.gov/record/21RS/sb255.html
Smith-Meyer B (2022) Bitcoin in crosshairs as EU goes after non-green crypto, POLITICO, https://www.politico.eu/article/bitcoin-in-crosshairs-as-eu-goes-after-non-green-crypto/, accessed 12 November 2024
Team Kentucky Cabinet for Economic Development (2022) Just the facts: Incentives for Energy-related Business Act (IEBA)
The White House (2022) Executive order on ensuring responsible development of digital assets, The White House, https://www.whitehouse.gov/briefing-room/presidential-actions/2022/03/09/executive-order-on-ensuring-responsible-development-of-digital-assets/, accessed 12 November 2024
Trabish HK (2023) As states differ on the benefits of Bitcoin, is there a solution to its climate and power-system impacts? | Utility Dive, Utility Drive, https://www.utilitydive.com/news/bitcoin-ethereum-cryptocurrency-emissions-clean-energy-reliability-demand-response-climate-impacts/650231/, accessed 12 November 2024
University of Cambridge (2024) Cambridge Blockchain Network Sustainability Index, Cambridge Centre for Alternative Finance, https://ccaf.io/cbnsi/cbeci, accessed 12 November 2024
Washington State Department of Ecology (2024) Overview of permitting, Washington State Department of Ecology, https://ecology.wa.gov/Regulations-Permits/Permits-certifications/Overview-of-permitting, accessed 12 November 2024
White House Office of Science and Technology Policy (2022) Climate and energy implications of crypto-assets in the United States
Williams K (2022) An Appalachian town was told a bitcoin mine would bring an economic boom. It got noise pollution and an eyesore., Washington Post, https://www.washingtonpost.com/business/2022/03/18/bitcoin-mining-noise-pollution-appalachia/, accessed 12 November 2024
Wilser J (2023) How Texas became a global Mecca for Bitcoin mining, CoinDesk, https://www.coindesk.com/consensus-magazine/2023/07/24/how-texas-became-a-global-mecca-for-bitcoin-mining/, accessed 12 November 2024
Winotoatmojo HP, Lazuardy SY, Arland F, Setyawan AA (2024) Environmental impact of cryptocurrency mining: a case study of Bitcoin. J Scientech Res Dev 6(1):118–128. https://doi.org/10.56670/jsrd.v6i1.312

World Business Council for Sustainable Development (2004) A corporate accounting and reporting standard: revised edition

Yaffe-Bellany D (2023) Crypto firms start looking abroad as U.S. cracks down, The New York Times, https://www.nytimes.com/2023/06/07/technology/crypto-firms-start-looking-abroad-as-us-cracks-down.html, accessed 12 November 2024

Zolnikov D (2023) An act generally revising cryptocurrency laws, https://leg.mt.gov/bills/2023/billpdf/SB0178.pdf

Author Index

P. Babie and M. Giancaspro (eds.), *Private Law, Digital Assets, and Infrastructure*,
https://doi.org/10.1007/978-981-96-7121-2

Subject Index

P. Babie and M. Giancaspro (eds.), *Private Law, Digital Assets, and Infrastructure*,
https://doi.org/10.1007/978-981-96-7121-2

D

E

MIX
Papier aus verantwortungsvollen Quellen
Paper from responsible sources
FSC® C105338

If you have any concerns about our products,
you can contact us on
ProductSafety@springernature.com

In case Publisher is established outside the EU,
the EU authorized representative is:
Springer Nature Customer Service Center GmbH
Europaplatz 3, 69115 Heidelberg, Germany

Printed by Libri Plureos GmbH
in Hamburg, Germany